A FIELD GUIDE TO THE

WADERS

OF BRITAIN AND EUROPE

with North Africa and the
Middle East

A FIELD GUIDE TO THE

WADERS

OF BRITAIN AND EUROPE

with North Africa and the Middle East

Peter Colston   ·   Philip Burton

Hodder & Stoughton

SYDNEY LONDON AUCKLAND TORONTO

First published by Hodder & Stoughton in 1988

A **Domino Books** production

© in the text Peter Colston, 1988
© in the illustrations, Philip Burton, 1988
© in this edition Domino Books Ltd., 1988

ISBN 0 340 39936 8

Colour reproduction by Adroit Photo-Litho, Birmingham
Filmset by V & M Graphics, Aylesbury, and Wordsmiths, London
Printed and bound in Spain by Heraclio Fournier, Vitoria

Contents

Foreword

This is an unusual field guide in that it concentrates on a single bird group in a single area. The standard bird guides cannot stop to give special treatment to a group which, though difficult, comprises less than 15% of our avifauna. The magisterial world survey of *Shore Birds* by Marchant, Prater and Hayman, on the other hand – an exemplary reference book which we cannot recommend too highly to every birdwatcher – is necessarily concerned largely with other species never seen in Europe. And the relevant volume of the comprehensive *Birds of the Western Palearctic* (with some wader paintings also by Philip Burton), is not a book for use out-of-doors.

We therefore offer this guide to the birdwatcher in the hope that it may solve some problems in the field and at the same time perhaps stimulate further research. It describes and illustrates all breeding waders in Britain, Europe, North Africa and the Middle East, all regular visitors, and the odd rarity. Short accounts of the birds' life-histories have also been included. There has been a new impetus in wader field studies during the last decade, but there is still a great deal to discover even about the more common species and the enormous journeys they undertake annually between breeding grounds in arctic tundra or mountain-fells and overwintering areas on estuaries, shingly shores and mud-flats.

Many people in many countries have helped us, both in birdwatching expeditions and directly in preparing this book. We are extremely grateful to them all, but must single out for special thanks: K.D. Bishop, F. Buckle, M.J. Carter, Dr. N.J. Collar, Mrs. F.M. Colston, S.G.D. Cook, G.S. Cowles, K.D. Edwards, R.E. Emmett, I.C.J. Galbraith, P.J. Grant, Dr. C.J.O. Harrison, K. Harrison, P.J. Hayman, J. Izzard, R.J. Johns, Dr. A. Kemp, N. Kent, A. Livett, K.K. Malmström, J.H. Marchant, H.P. Medhurst, B.E. Newport, A.J. Prater, A. Quinn, Mrs. P. Ryan, T. Salinger, Dr. J.T.R. Sharrock, H. Shirihai, I. Sinclair, F.T.H. Smith, Dr. D.W. Snow, P.B. Taylor, Dr. P.S. Tomkovich, Mrs A. Vale, J.E. Walford, C.A. Walker, D.I.M. Wallace and P.A. Whittington. We are also most grateful to the Sub-Department of Ornithology at the British Museum (Natural History), Tring, Herts., for giving us the opportunity to study their very comprehensive collection of wader skins and library facilities.

We intend to keep this book up-to-date. On publication it takes account of developments we have heard of up to late summer 1987. We will always be most grateful for criticism, corrections or updatings from any source, and will answer them all. Please write to either of us at: British Museum (Natural History), Sub-Department of Ornithology, Tring, Herts.

Peter Colston
Philip Burton

Introduction

Waders are surely one of the most attractive and fascinating groups of the world's birds. The majority of the species comprise two large cosmopolitan families: Charadriidae (plovers) and Scolopacidae (sandpipers, snipes etc.) This book deals with 87 out of the world's 214 species, and covers an area west of the Urals, south to the Caspian and round the western border of Iran down to Kuwait, then westwards to include the eastern Mediterranean and northern coast of Africa, south to the Banc d'Arguin, Mauritania.

They range from small (stint-size) to large (curlew-size), mainly wading birds, frequenting marshes, freshwater and marine habitats and open fields, grasslands and mudflats. Most are noticeably gregarious except when breeding, and many species migrate long distances. Their bills show a great variety of specialised forms, reflecting their different feeding habits, a long bill often being correlated with long legs.

Most are diurnal but some are crepuscular or nocturnal. They nest on the ground, although the Crab Plover nests in burrows and the Green Sandpiper utilises old tree-nests of other birds. Usually both parents incubate, although in some species only one adult does so. Most are monogamous, but some are polygamous or polyandrous. The downy young are precocial, most of them either nidifugous or seminidifugous.

FEEDING

For all their immense travels, the world of waders is essentially a flat one, at the boundary of earth and sky. Virtually all their food is gleaned from the surface of water, mud or land, or just below it. Though not all the waders regularly feed while wading, the majority live in wet places or near water. Some, such as coursers, or some plovers and stone curlews, have learned to exploit more arid ground, but only one group – the pratincoles – have adopted an entirely different lifestyle, with their specialisations for aerial feeding. Despite the apparent simplicity of their habits, however, waders have evolved a fascinating variety of feeding adaptations, both behavioural and structural. With some knowledge of their prey it becomes easier to understand how this has come about, so it is worth spending a little time looking at the various types of animal which make up their diets.

Marshes and estuaries look deceptively barren places compared with, say, an oak wood or a meadow but teeming life is concealed just below the surface. On mudflats, where plants are few or absent, we can get some clue from the various trails, holes and other patterns created by concealed animals; for many waders, in fact, these tracks and signs are important aids in food finding.

Annelids or segmented worms, one of the largest groups of simple invertebrates, are an important part of the diet for many species. In land habitats these are represented by the familiar earthworms, but their marine counterparts, the polychaetes, are more varied, and fall into two main types. Errant polychaetes move freely, by swimming or crawling, though they are usually just below the surface when this is left dry by the tide. Sedentary polychaetes live permanently in tubes or burrows, their location often indicated by a pit, a tube tip or a casting.

Vastly the largest major group in the animal kingdom is the Arthropoda, or jointed-limbed animals, of which the principal representatives are the insects on land and freshwater, and the crustaceans in the sea and shore. Where insects are concerned, immature stages (larvae or nymphs) provide some important prey, but occur in quite different places to their adults. Examples of insect larvae taken by waders are the maggots of various flies (e.g. robber flies, some hoverflies) found in the mud bottoms of pools or lake edges, and among grass roots leatherjackets – the larvae of crane-flies ("daddy-long-legs") – and the caterpillars of some moths, such as Swift Moths. Most adult insects fly, and so are usually unavailable to waders, though a few, e.g. crane-flies and grasshoppers, sometimes emerge in such numbers that grassland waders may for a time catch them in quantities. However, most adult insects in wader diets are either flightless, like ground beetles, or aquatic, like water beetles and various water bugs (water boatmen, pond skaters etc.)

Crustacean larvae are mainly found as plankton in the upper waters of the sea, and are unlikely to be taken by waders, except perhaps phalaropes. These are even recorded taking whale lice (parasitic crustaceans) from the backs of whales, but for most waders, the principal crustacean prey are likely to be small crabs, shrimps or amphipods. The first two are familiar, but amphipods are easily recognised too by the side-to-side flattening of their small crescent-shaped bodies. They include sand-hoppers, little jumping animals often abundant under jetsam and driftweed on the upper shore; Turnstones know this, and turn it over to reveal them. Even more abundant, and more important as a staple food for many waders, is a tiny amphipod called *Corophium*, which lives in tunnels just below the surface of tidal mudflats; Dunlin and Redshank in particular take them in huge quantities. A few swimming crustaceans live in fresh or brackish water. Most are very tiny, but some, such as ostracods, are taken by a few fine-billed specialists like the Green and Marsh Sand-pipers.

Molluscs are the third great source of food for shore feeding waders, and are of two main types. Gastropods, or snails, have single, spirally-coiled shells, and are mostly found on the surface; periwinkles are a familiar example. They include a tiny, but extremely abundant species, *Hydrobia ulvae*, found in tidal mudflats. Though individually no more than 4mm long, they may be so numerous as to make the mud look granular, and are taken in great quantities by many waders. Bivalves, the other group, have two shells connected by a hinge, and are generally found below the surface of mud or sand. When water lies over the mud, they extend tubes or syphons to the surface for feeding and breathing; even after the mud is exposed, these may leave tracks or depressions, giving a clue to their location. Molluscs are also abundant on rocky shores, and species such as dog whelks and periwinkles are a major source of food for the few waders which regularly feed there, such as Purple Sandpipers and Turnstones. Mussels are large bivalves found both on rocky shores and mud or sandflats. They are attached to the surface by strong anchor threads, in huge, densely-packed masses, often forming extensive banks across the shore. They are a primary food for many oystercatchers, which differ from other waders in their ability to gain entry to large molluscs; most species are obliged to swallow them whole and digest the shells away, and are consequently restricted to much smaller prey.

A few of the more aquatic waders may capture small fish, frogs or tadpoles. Since fish are alert and swift-moving prey, the only waders to catch them in any quantity are themselves agile and active, the Greenshank being a prime example.

Many waders spend their winters far from Europe in tropical or subtropical environments, yet the general range of prey available there is not too dissimilar from that of northern coasts and wetlands. Large crustaceans figure more prominently; fiddler crabs are numerous on intertidal mud on warm coastlines, and are taken in quantities by many waders. As these crabs have burrows to which they can retreat at great speed, both stealth and agility are needed to capture them. They and other shore prey are abundant in the vicinity of mangroves, and tropical shores have another rich habitat for which there is no real northern equivalent -- coral reefs, providing crabs and other crustaceans, large gastropods and small fish. Inland, tropical wetlands yield an abundance of insect larvae, often in such places as paddy-fields and irrigation canals, unlike anything to be found in temperate areas.

Numerous though these tiny creatures may be, they do not exist simply to provide food for waders, but have defences and behaviour geared to their own survival. The various feeding adaptations seen among waders have evolved in the course of this age-long battle between predator and prey, and as in any battle we have to consider both strategy and tactics. Strategy for survival centres around the crucial issue of energy, the balance between energy obtained as food and expended in acquiring it. With the latter, alternative strategies are either to sit and wait for prey to approach, or to go out and search for it. For waders, as much of their prey is subterranean and limited in mobility, the second alternative is usually inevitable, so most of them walk or run more or less continuously while feeding. As regards intake, the basic choice is between large but relatively scarce food items, or small but abundant ones. At one extreme are many plovers, which forage in a succession of short runs, interspersed with pauses to look for prey, and occasional captures of usually rather large worms, molluscs or insects. At the other are waders such as Dunlin or Redshank which feed as they walk, seizing tiny animals such as *Hydrobia* or *Corophium* with great frequency. Factors such as the weather (especially cold), tide and season all affect both birds and prey, shifting the balance one way or the other, in ways which ecologists are just beginning to understand.

As for the tactics of feeding, waders have two options open to them: to forage by sight or by touch. When hunting by sight, they simply have to see, either the prey itself or some trace such as a track or a cast. Hunting by touch is more subtle. It depends on special nerve endings, mainly concentrated in the bill tip, which are extremely sensitive to vibration. Waders hunting in this way make rapid, shallow probes into the mud surface as they walk along, and when telltale vibrations are detected a capture soon follows. Most species employ a mixture of techniques, according to circumstances, and may also resort to behaviour designed to make prey show themselves. Foot pattering on the mud surface, as performed by many plovers, or "dancing" through shallow water like a Greenshank, are examples.

The variety of bill lengths and head shapes seen among waders bears a general relation to methods of food finding. Short, stout bills like those of the plovers are characteristic of species hunting mainly by sight, while touch hunting generally requires a longer bill. At this extreme are species such as Woodcock, which have the bill angled downwards relative to the rest, in a permanently probing orientation, and the eyes shifted up and back, so that there is actually a wider field of view behind the head than in front. Most species lie between these extremes, but generally fall into two types as regards bill construction. Many, such as plovers and shanks, have upper jaws with a flexible zone quite near the head (though not right at the bill base as in most birds), permitting upward or downward bending. More specialised probers such as curlews, godwits, stints, snipe and Woodcock have the bending zone much nearer the bill tip, allowing just the tip of the bill to open underground to seize prey and permitting very delicate manipulation. The muscles which operate this are situated far back behind the eye, and their force is transmitted through an elegant system of bony levers.

Down curvature of the bill is shown to a greater or less extent by many probers. This shape allows a greater area to be explored underground in a single probe. However, for probers in very soft mud (e.g. snipe), this is evidently unnecessary, and a straight bill will suffice. Up curvature of the tip is often a feature of waders that frequently pursue active prey, such as the Greenshank, but in its most pro-nounced form in the Avocet it is connected with a distinct feeding method: sweeping from side to side through shallow water. Other feeders on tiny aquatic animals often have fine, needle-pointed bills (e.g.Marsh Sandpiper, Red-necked Phalarope). At the other extreme, the massively reinforced, chisel-ended bill of the Oystercatcher is used for opening large molluscs such as mussels.

MIGRATION

Although some facts about the arrival and departure of waders throughout the year must have been known from the earliest times by hunters who sought them for food, it is only in this century that accurate knowledge about their immense journeys has become available. This has become possible through the development of ringing as a technique for tracing bird movements; an account of its history can be found in the books *Bird Migration* by Chris Mead (Country Life Books, 1983) and *Enjoying Ornithology* by Ron Hickling (Ed. for B.T.O.) (T. & A.D. Poyser, 1983).

The earliest large-scale ringing of waders depended mainly on beach traps. Such traps are easiest to use on areas with little tide, such as the Mediterranean. The Baltic also has very little tide and the Swedish Bird Observatories have perfected these techniques to catch and ring very many waders since the war. Apart from ringing, these stations and others in Finland, Norway, Denmark and Germany have made systematic observations of visible migration which, coupled with regular counts, allow a description of the timing of migration for many species.

In contrast to their great success in Scandinavia these methods based on static tide-line traps were not very applicable to the birds of the large estuaries of western Europe, because of the great tidal range and the inaccessibility of feeding grounds. This was largely solved by two new techniques, the first being the introduction of Japanese mist-nets in the late 1950's. These fine nets, erected vertically between poles on flight lines near the high-water mark, allowed the safe capture of birds moving between feeding areas and roosts at night when the nets became difficult to see.

Secondly, around the same time large rocket-propelled nets developed by the Wildfowl Trust for catching geese were used at the Wash for catching large flocks of roosting waders. Both these techniques, the rocket-nets later being replaced by smaller and more manageable cannon-launched nets, were developed for large-scale ringing of waders by the Wash Wader Ringing Group, led by Dr. Clive Minton. These methods are now being used on many estuaries in the British Isles, mainly by amateur ringing groups which cooperate informally through the Wader Study

Group of the British Trust for Ornithology, and by groups in Norway, the Netherlands, France and South Africa.

Mist-netting of waders at several inland sites in Europe and on the lakes of East Africa has also been conducted for several years now. Through measurements of birds caught and recoveries of ringed waders, these studies have yielded a great deal of information about migration routes, but suffer from the considerable problem that recoveries can only come from areas where literate people are present to report the findings. Indeed, for many species, maps of recoveries tend to reflect the distribution of people rather than of the birds. Similarly, measurements are only available for comparison with each other from areas where birds have actually been caught.

It was to try to fill these gaps in our knowledge of the migration of the waders wintering or passing through Europe that a series of expeditions was organised. Two Cambridge-London/Iceland expeditions to study spring and autumn migrations in 1970 led to further Cambridge expeditions there in 1971 and 1972. Studies of migration to the southern moulting and wintering areas were initiated by the University of East Anglia expeditions to Morocco in 1971 and 1972, leading to further visits in 1972 and 1973. Also in 1973 studies were extended to the very important wintering grounds of the Banc d'Arguin by the Oxford and Cambridge Mauritanian Expedition.

In 1974, following a prospecting visit in 1972, large-scale ringing studies reached the high arctic breeding grounds with the Joint Biological Expedition to North-East Greenland, incorporating biologists from Dundee University and members of the Wader Study Group. In the same year, an Oxford University expedition studied waders in northern Norway, and a team from the Canadian Wildlife Service began wader ringing studies in the high arctic, which soon resulted in the exchanges of ringed birds between there and Europe.

This remarkable level of cooperative studies, conducted largely by amateurs, working near to home or on overseas expeditions, has greatly clarified our knowledge of migration routes and the geographical relationships between different wader populations. For several species it has become clear that waders from different parts of the breeding range did not simply spread at random over the winter range, but tended to occur in particular wintering areas. Knots from Greenland and the Canadian arctic islands of Ellesmere and Devon spend the winter on estuaries of the North Sea, Irish Sea and Bay of Biscay while those breeding in Siberia rapidly pass through this area on migration to winter in Morocco, Mauritania and southern Africa. With the Dunlin, the situation is reversed, with the nominate race *Calidris alpina alpina* from northern Scandinavia and Siberia wintering in north-west Europe, and *C.a. schinzii* from the Baltic lands, Britain and Iceland moving to north-west Africa.

Some migratory systems are very complex. Ringed Plovers, for example, have a "leap-frog" migration pattern. At the southern limit of their breeding range, British birds probably remain fairly near their nesting areas for the winter, while those from Scandinavia move to West Africa and the birds from farthest north-east in Siberia travel the greatest distances to winter in southern Africa.

We have dealt up to now with wintering areas on a rather large scale, but recent intensive ringing work in N.W. Europe, partly resulting from the need to predict likely effects of proposals for industrial use of estuaries, has shown important smaller-scale differences too. Oystercatchers overwintering on the west coasts of Britain are primarily from Iceland, the Faeroes and Scotland, while those on the east coast of England come principally from Norway. Further birds from Norway, and from the eastern Baltic and Russia, winter in the Waddenzee.

With the Curlew, ringing has shown a difference between birds breeding in northern Britain, which spend the winter on the west coast of this region and in Ireland, and those from central and southern Britain, which move to the south-west coast and to France and Spain. Similarly, Curlews moving into Britain for the winter show differences in origins, those from Norway occurring mainly in the north and those from the low countries and Germany mainly in the south, while birds from the Baltic area are more widely spread.

Many of the longer-distance migrants also show interesting movements when examined on a smaller scale. For example, the Knots and Dunlins wintering in north-western Europe show a tendency to move westwards during the winter. Although Knots and Dunlins are present in these areas from autumn to spring, the peak numbers gradually move from the Waddenzee in autumn, through the Wash in early winter, to the Irish Sea estuaries in late winter. This tendency seems to be less pronounced in mild winters. It seems possible that the movement may have developed to allow the birds to feed in the milder west coast conditions in cold years when food becomes very hard to obtain in the colder eastern areas. For most species for which information is available it is clear that several more or less distinct populations tend to breed and winter in fairly restricted parts of the range, but it must not be assumed that this necessarily applies to all species. The Lapwing provides a striking example of a species in which there appears to be a very high degree of mixing throughout both the winter and the breeding range. Many chicks ringed in western Europe have been found breeding in later years well to the east.

We have very little knowledge of the migrations of many other waders which breed and winter largely in inland areas. This is both because of the concentration of studies in Europe, particularly the west, and from the lack of techniques for mass-ringing in inland habitats. This is typified by the Redshank and the Black-tailed Godwit. The Icelandic populations of both these species are known to winter primarily in the British Isles and on the adjacent continental coasts, while the breeding birds of the western seaboard of Europe move to N.W. and W. Africa. Work is in progress to extend the mass ringing methods from the coastal to inland areas. Additionally, for some species well represented in museum collections, it may be possible to use measurements of preserved skins to relate summer and winter distributions of different populations.

Waders are among the longest distance migrant birds and several species are known to make non-stop flights of tremendous lengths, such as over the Greenland ice-cap and over the sea from Greenland and Iceland to Europe. For several species, such as Knot and Sanderling there are suggestions that even longer non-stop flights may occur, but conclusive evidence is lacking. Several ringed birds have been recovered only a few days later at considerable distances from the ringing site.

An important new technique, supplementing ringing by rapidly providing information on migration routes and timing in well-watched regions, is plumage-dyeing. This was pioneered for waders in a study of migration at the Swedish bird observatory at Ledskar. The advantage is that the birds do not need to be caught again or found dead, the markings being clearly visible in the field until the colour fades or the feathers are moulted; but because the birds are not individually marked, great care is needed in planning the use of this technique. The method has since been used with much success, notably by the expeditions to Greenland and by workers in South Africa and Canada. The Greenland expedition marked breeding waders of several species in late June, July and August 1974, and by the middle of September seventeen of the birds had been seen in Britain.

For several species, ringing has shown that particular individuals return annually, not only to the same breeding area but also to the same moulting and wintering areas and even the same "staging-posts" on their migration routes. Clearly, considerable navigational ability must be involved, but little work on this has been done on waders and our knowledge is based mainly on passerines, pigeons, and to some extent ducks and seabirds.

As described above, because of their need of wetland habitats, many waders move a long distance from breeding grounds in western Eurasia to western Europe and Africa. This introduces the question of whether the birds follow compass directions or are able to take the shortest route between two areas. The shortest distance between any two points on the earth is a line which, when extended, divides the earth into two equal hemispheres and is termed a "great circle". Because of the distortions inherent in presenting the earth on a flat surface, this is not clear on most map projections. Lines of longitude are all great circles, but lines of latitude, except the Equator, are not. The problem in following a great circle, apart from the special cases of lines of longitude and the equator, is that it involves a continuously changing compass direction, and we do not know if birds are capable of such behaviour.

Because the difference between compass-line courses and great circle routes becomes greater at high latitudes and when migrations include large east-west components, Palearctic waders may be among the best birds in which to study the problem. Good evidence is not yet available, but it may be significant that the route taken by Siberian Knots, moving from the Taimyr Peninsula and farther east to their first migration staging post at the Waddenzee, appears to approximate to a great circle rather than to follow a compass direction.

Radar studies of spring departures of waders from the coast of Ghana revealed that all headings could be projected on great circle routes to reach the breeding areas of these species in the USSR. More work on this is needed.

Over shorter distances, wader studies in northern England and southern Scotland have shown that waders appear to move on direct lines between estuaries, presumably "knowing" where they are heading for and ignoring topography, generally following neither coasts nor valley systems unless these lie along the direct route.

An interesting aspect of wader migration is that with many species adults precede juveniles on autumn migration. Some authors have suggested that the early departure of the adults from the breeding grounds is to reduce competition with their offspring for food. It is also possible, however, that the adults leave as soon as the young are independent so as to reach their moulting or wintering grounds as soon as possible, to complete moult and winter preparations before winter sets in. It is also notable that in some species one of the parents departs much earlier, leaving the other to rear the young.

The early departure of the adults leaves the young to find their own way to their winter quarters. In this respect waders differ from those other arctic breeding birds geese and swans – in which family parties stay together on migration and in the winter. Presumably juvenile waders inherit a tendency to migrate to the appropriate wintering area, but it seems unlikely that a "knowledge" of particular sites is instinctive, especially given the transitory nature of many wetland habitats. In view of such considerations, it is not surprising that juvenile waders are more frequently found away from their migration routes than are adults.

Curlew Sandpipers, Little Stints, and several other Siberian waders normally pass to the east of the British Isles, but in some years easterly winds over northern Europe result in "invasions", usually mainly of juveniles of these species. Similarly, it is normally only juvenile Knots and Bar-tailed Godwits which occur in autumn on the northern parts of the Moroccan coast, an area avoided by overflying adults. The change in habitat from breeding to wintering areas for such fast-moving arctic breeding species must be quite drastic and juveniles sometimes appear to try out several areas before finding suitable feeding grounds. At a coastal wetland in southern Morocco, recently arrived juvenile Knots have been watched trying to feed on barren cliff-sides instead of flats. By later in the autumn, however, young birds are rarely found away from the typical range of feeding habitats for their species.

It is probably errors in navigation and bad weather conditions which result in occasional "vagrants" (see below) from America or Asia appearing in Europe well away from their usual migration routes. Such "lost" birds tend to alight at the first land sighted, making our headlands and offshore such popular places for rarity-hunters. These "errors" may be important in extending the range of some species. The spread of Lapwings has already been mentioned, and it is noticeable that in 1975 American Spotted Sandpipers were found breeding in Scotland, although an isolated event does not, of course, constitute colonisation.

A final special type of migration must also be mentioned: hard-weather movements. The degree of westward migration of Knots already described is possibly a type of this, but usually this kind of movement is less regular, occurring only when spells of freezing conditions make feeding difficult and energy requirements high. Inland areas suffer quite frequently from hard frosts and cold-weather movements of Lapwings are well-known. Freezing of salt water in western Europe is less common. For several species, British ringing recoveries showed a more south-westerly distribution in that winter than in most years. Many birds had moved in this direction to try to benefit from milder areas adjacent to the coasts receiving the warmer water of the North Atlantic Drift. Other birds moved well to the south and cold weather arrivals were noted as far south as Morocco.

Vagrants. Under the heading Distribution in the main text, the number of records for the British Isles up to 1986 are given in ( ) as an indication of further sightings.

COURTSHIP DISPLAYS

Waders show great diversity and often complexity in their social and breeding behaviour, although most of the main groups resemble each other in several features. In this section are described the main types of display and mating systems and some of the distinctive features of the main groups.

The displays and aggressive behaviour patterns of the **Charadriinae plovers**, as typified by the smaller ringed plovers, are closely similar. The males indulge in territorial advertisement by performing conspicuous butterfly-like display flights over their territory. On the ground, aggressive encounters emphasise the facial pattern and breast-band, and the tail is often fanned and sometimes tilted at the adversary. Nest and scraping behaviour is all important in strengthening the pair-bond and also in the final selection of the nest-site. In the Ringed and Little Ringed Plovers the female approaches the scraping male by moving under his tail before settling into the scrape, although the female Kentish Plover enters the scrape mostly in front of the male's breast. At least five ringed plovers exhibit similar precopul-

PAINTED SNIPES   Family Rostratulidae

Medium-sized waders in which the female is slightly larger and more colourful than the male; she initiates courtship, but incubation and care of the young is generally by the male only. Painted Snipes superficially resemble true snipes, but are not closely related. In general somewhat rail-like; large eye suggests partly nocturnal habit.

Range. Africa, southern Asia to Indonesia and Australia; also in South America.

Number of species. World, 2; western Palaearctic, 1.

PAINTED SNIPE   *Rostratula benghalensis*

Du – Goudsnip
Fr – Bécassine peinte
Ge – Goldschnepfe
Sp – Rostrátula bengalesa
Sw – Rallbeckasin

Pl. 1

Identification. Length 9-10in. Strikingly patterned wader with marked sexual plumage differences, although outside the breeding season the sexes are more similar. About the size of snipe, but with longer, heavier, pale grey-greenish legs, shorter bill, markedly decurved at tip, and distinct creamy V on back. Flight action differs from Snipe in being slow and weak, almost rail-like, with broad rounded wings (showing rows of large buff spots across flight feathers), and dangling legs obvious. Both sexes have well-marked head and uniform face and neck, separated from dark upperparts by obvious broad white 'shoulder-strap' extending down to white breast. Plumage of breeding female more colourful than male's. Dark brown crown divided by buff crown stripe, and dark chestnut face with white 'spectacles' surrounding eyes. Throat and neck also dark chestnut, edged with a blackish brown bar below, separating white under-parts. Hind-neck chestnut with browner back, and bronze-green scapulars with fine barring – white feathers concealed under scapulars. Male has chestnut areas replaced by brownish-grey, also whitish throat and broad buff barring on the wing-coverts and scapulars. Juvenile resembles adult male, but lacks the clear-cut dark band across the chest.

Voice. In breeding season advertisement call of female (which carries over 1km) consists of five or six preliminary low '*vot*' notes, followed by up to 50 '*kot*' notes in succession. Given march-October; first heard in evenings, then in daytime from late April onwards. Calls are uttered at a constant rate of four to five a second – more frequent after sunset, or hour before dawn. Various growling and grunting calls are given by both sexes, and in alarm a deep, throaty hiss has been recorded. Flushed bird calls with a low '*kek*'.

Habitat. Mainly in swamps with pools, soft muddy patches and thick shrubbery vegetation or reed beds.

atory behaviour, where the male approaches the female from behind in a horizontal posture before becoming taller and "goose-stepping" and finally mounting.

Of the six species of **Lapwings** (*Vanellinae*), the Lapwing is undoubtedly the best known and most studied. In the spring, the male performs spectacular advertising and aerobatic displays over his chosen territory. When he is joined by his mate, his greeting-display is a ritualised form of scrape-making. The male displays at dozens of different sites before the female finally selects one. The behaviour and displays of the remaining five species are less well known, although the Spur-winged Plover has a scraping ceremony similar to the Lapwing's and like that species this probably plays an important role in courtship behaviour.

The displays of the many small species of the **arctic sandpipers** belonging to the *Calidridinae* also show very similar patterns. Typically, males perform display flights over their territories to advertise for a mate, while this behaviour is also commonly linked with aggression. The display flight of the male consists of rising and circling about on rapidly beating wings, interspersed with slower, bat-like wing-beats or combined with gliding or hovering flights, and giving various trilling or buzzing calls. Often the flights end in the bird gliding back to earth with outstretched or "V" wings. On ending the flight some species perform a wings-high display, e.g. Knot, Dunlin and Purple Sandpiper. In the Little Stint the display flight may be performed by both sexes, and the species appears to be less territorial than Temminck's Stint, defending no clearly-defined areas, so that the display flight is performed for sexual attraction only.

In ground displays, the white rumps of the White-rumped and Curlew Sandpipers are conspicuously exposed as each species moves back and forth, with wings held stiffly outward or raised. The breeding males of the Pectoral and Sharp-tailed Sandpipers have a swollen balloon-like breast-sac which they are able to inflate during display flights or ground displays in the presence of the female. The Pectoral produces a loud pumping series of hoots and the Sharp-tailed has equally loud distinctive notes. However, the ultimate in Calidridine display is given by the Ruff, with its highly ritualised ground displays and lekking activities. Its nearest relative, the Buff-breasted Sandpiper, also shows some of the beginning of the Ruff's complex social organisation.

While the males of the **snipes** have spectacular aerial flights and diving displays, which combine drumming and/or calling over their territories, mostly during the daylight hours, the Great Snipe forms leks during the more twilight hours. Males gather together and perform much singing, posturing and strutting in a small area and attempt to mate with any female that visits the lek. Although the species is promiscuous, no further displays are known to take place between the sexes once the females have left the males' lekking area. Nor are any pair-bonds formed, unlike the other snipes.

Nothing is known of the ground-displays of the two species of **dowitcher**, although they are known to perform song-flights over their territories, the males hovering on quivering wings and singing all the while. Differences, in any, in their ground-displays would be an interesting study.

Around dusk the roding male **Woodcock** performs a searching and self-advertising display-flight at tree-top height, while the female rests on the ground in cover. When the flying male is called to earth by the female, he may perform strutting displays not unlike a Snipe's, with drooping wings and raised, spread tail.

The self-advertising switch-back display flights of the several species of **Tringa sandpipers** are all rather similar, although each species has its own characteristic flight-song. In the Redshank a successful switch-back display flight usually attracts the female into the air. Earlier in the season the male may also attempt to secure a mate by persistent ground-chasing. In their courtship several species may perform a wings-high display, exposing the white underwing, e.g. Redshank, Spotted Redshank and Marsh Sandpiper. Conversely, the display flight of the Common Sandpiper is often performed close to the surface of the water, giving sudden rapid bursts of very shallow wing-beats, interspersed with stretches of gliding on down-curved wings. In ground displays the male holds his wings up in a brief double salute, and copulation follows ground-chases with extended wing-saluting and song by the male. However, the closely related Nearctic Spotted Sandpiper shows very different behaviour. The female is the more dominant partner courting the male, and while one of the pair may perform wing-fluttering actions, there is apparently no wing-saluting in this species.

The larger **godwits** have rather similar high climbing display-flights, ascending on rapid wing-beats, then changing to slower and more clipped beats or circling on stiff down-curved wings, twisting, turning and pitching before gliding down and settling to give an extended wings-high display. Both sexes may also indulge in pursuit flights.

The Black-tailed Godwit has several threat display postures, performed towards rivals on the ground, including tail-spreading, ruffling the back feathers and bill-crossing. The male may also include several of these elements, including wing-raising in his display towards females. There is also a nest-scraping ceremony in which the male runs to a depression in the grass, crouches in it, tilts his tail high in the air and rubs his breast against the ground. Sometimes the pair nest scrape alternately.

The conspicuous display flights and bubbling calls of the **Curlew** are well known. The male rises steeply, hovers for a moment, then glides down with wings held in a shallow "V", before repeating the whole action. On the ground, the male approaches intruders in a "hunched threat" posture, with slightly drooped wings and a raised and fanned tail. Courtship may begin with rather similar postures to the "hunched threat", leading to more elaborate displays and eventually copulation. Displays are more marked in birds pairing for the first time than in established pairs reuniting on the territory.

In the **Whimbrel**, display flight, ground-threat and advertising postures are similar to the Curlew's, and tail-fanning and exposure of the white rump are a feature of courtship. Nothing is known of the displays and behaviour of the much rarer Slender-billed Curlew, though presumably these would be much like those of the other larger curlews. The Little Whimbrel indulges in much higher display flights than other curlews, performing an alternate wing-shivering and slow-sailing flight, and after giving a short melodious fluting trill the male may close his wings and plunge downwards like a snipe, at the same time producing a whistling sound with his flight and tail feathers. Then he climbs up again to his original level to repeat the display.

Finally, in the **Phalaropes** the sex roles are reversed, with the female performing most of the courtship and aggression. The female is the larger and brighter of the sexes, and she initiates pair-formation either by performing advertising flights, or settling close to the male on the water and adopting an alert or imposing posture, or giving wing-whirring displays in the males's presence.

MATING SYSTEMS

Wader species have a considerable variety of mating patterns – monogamous, polygamous (both polygyny and polyandry) and promiscuous.

Monogamy. Seasonal monogamy is probably the most common pattern of mating in shore birds, i.e. two birds mate with each other only, but separate after the breeding season and re-pair at the start of the following season. Indefinite monogamy is rarer, although it does occur, e.g. the European Oystercatcher forms a life-long pair bond. Of the species of Palearctic and Nearctic waders analysed by Glutz et al. (1975, 1977), at least 24 were classified as seasonally monogamous for the most part, while 7 others exhibit at least brood monogamy and 4 have seasonal pair-bonds of uncertain type.

Polygyny. Here a male maintains two or more females simultaneously or successively during one breeding season, each female caring for her own brood of young without any help from the male. Of the Palearctic and Nearctic wader species analyzed by Glutz et al. (1975, 1977), 7 species were classified as polygynous or promiscuous, and successive polyandry was noted as occasional or regular for several species, but it is probably not universal in any.

Promiscuity implies no social bonding between the sexes other than that directly associated with copulation. Promiscuous matings occur in several Palearctic or vagrant Nearctic waders, including the Great Snipe, European Woodcock, White-rumped Sandpiper, Buff-breasted Sandpiper and Ruff. The Sharp-tailed Sandpiper exhibits either polygyny or promiscuity, and the Pectoral Sandpiper has a mating system that ranges from somewhere between monogamy, polygyny and promiscuity.

Polyandry. This is the least common kind of mating system – where the female maintains two or more males simultaneously or successively during one breeding season, each male usually caring for his own brood of young without any help from the female. Examples are the Painted Snipe and the phalaropes. The American Spotted Sandpiper often has a polyandrous mating system which is in sharp contrast to the closely related Common Sandpiper of the W. Palearctic, which has a monogamous system.

Multi-clutch breeding system. Here the females lay two or more clutches in rapid succession, with the female and her mate each incubating separate clutches of eggs and each usually caring for its own brood of young. This is found in e.g. Sanderling, Little and Temminck's Stints.

OYSTERCATCHERS   Family Haematopodidae

Large, sturdy, pied or all-black waders, often with prominent white wing-bar, or totally dark. Sexes alike, with only minor seasonal variations in plumage. Bill, legs and feet red, pink or orange, orbital rings usually bright orange. Bill long, stout, blunt and laterally compressed – used for chiselling molluscs off rocks, opening bivalves or dismembering crustaceans.

Range. Widespread on world coasts.

Number of species. World, up to 11 species currently recognised, comprising some 21 forms, but possibly a single superspecies of four or more species, though species limits still uncertain. Western Palaearctic, 2.

OYSTERCATCHER   *Haematopus ostralegus*

Du – Scholekster   Fr – Huîtrier pie
Ge – Austernfischer
Sp – Ostrero   Sw – Strandskata

Pl. 1

Identification. Length 16–18in. Unmistakable – large black-and-white portly shore-bird, with conspicuous white wing-bars, long orange-pink bill, red eye and red-pink legs. Sexes similar. White throat-band in winter, Juvenile like non-breeding adult but distinguished by faint pale fringes on feathers of upper-parts and dull greyish legs. Flight strong with rather shallow wing-beats and distinctive '*kleep*' calls often given. A noisy, excitable and wary bird.

Voice. The contact call is a loud, shrill and penetrating '*klee-eep*' or '*peek-kapeek*', also a short, sharp '*pic-pic*'. The most distinctive sound heard on the breeding ground is the noisy, shrill 'piping' display call. The 'piping performance' is a development of the ordinary call into a trill and is heard regularly from late February to late July and, exceptionally, into the autumn.

Habitat. Breeding habitat chiefly coastal, nesting on shingle beaches or nearby stony ground with short vegetation. Occasionally on rocky outcrops, broken walls or posts. Also nests inland in some areas beside lakes, streams or wide shingly rivers, as well as in grass or crops. Both in and out of the breeding season it is chiefly found on the sea shore, resorting alike to rocky coasts, pebble ridges, sandy shores and estuarine mud-flats, but will also occasionally forage for worms in nearby fields.

Distribution. The race *H.o.ostralegus* breeds in Iceland, the Faeroes and northern Europe, southwards along the coast of France, the north-western Mediterranean, north-eastern Adriatic south to northern Greece and the Aegean coasts of Turkey. It also breeds in some inland areas of Scotland and Ireland, southern Sweden, the Netherlands, Turkey and Russia. *H.o.longipes* breeds in Asia Minor, south-central Russia and western Siberia. Map **2**.

Movements. Mainly migratory, although small numbers are dispersive to resident in western Europe. Some Icelandic birds stay to moult and winter on the coasts there, but on the whole Icelandic, Faeroes and birds breeding in northern Britain winter mainly around the Irish Sea and on other western coasts of Britain and Ireland. Norwegian birds winter on both sides of the North Sea. Baltic and Russian birds winter on the Dutch–German Waddenzee and southern British and Dutch birds winter between their breeding grounds and Iberia, with a few in Morocco. There is some overlap and the origins of birds found in West Africa and the Gulf of Guinea are not known. The small numbers which breed around the northern Mediterranean and the Adriatic probably winter in Tunisia and Libya. Post-breeding birds from all western European populations arrive on their moulting and wintering grounds from late July, mainly August–September, returning to breeding grounds late January–April, and later for Russian birds. Birds wintering in East Africa, Arabia and western India are probably the south-eastern population, *H.o.longipes*.

Feeding. Feeds both by touch and sight, and the method of feeding varies greatly with time and place and between individuals. Predominantly bivalve molluscs, particularly cockles, mussels and baltic tellin; mainly earthworms inland. Cockles discovered by probing mud, and in feeding for them at night the bird makes 'sewing' movements to a depth of 2cm, (bill inserted deeper for baltic tellin). There are two main techniques for opening bivalves: *hammering*, whereby one shell of the mussel is broken by a series of short, thrusting blows, the bill is inserted and the adductor muscle cut; *stabbing*, the bill is inserted between gaping valves, the adductor muscle is severed, the various members are then systematically chiselled out and the flesh is shaken free. Individuals specialise in one technique, which they learn from their parents and improve with practice. Small cockles up to 8mm, mussels up to 12mm and small crushed crabs or lugworms may be eaten whole. The food is often washed before eating. Shells may be carried to hard sand or rocks for hammering. Limpets, periwinkles, dog whelks and other molluscs are also dealt with.

Social and breeding behaviour. Threat behaviour, including the all-important piping display, by one bird or several, is seen to some extent in winter feeding flocks or roosts. However, the most distinctive patterns are more clearly related to advertisement and defence of territory during the breeding season. Many pairs visit their territories from early March onwards, and territorial encounters between neighbouring pairs or interlopers are common at the beginning of the season until the boundaries are fixed. The chief activity is the piping display, which is given with the bill pointing downwards and mandibles partly open, sometimes vibrating. Either or both of the pair may meet an intruder in this excited frenzy of high-pitched piping. Apart from intimidating the intruder, this piping display acts to strengthen the pair-bond. During the spring, the male performs a display or song-flight in which he flies buoyantly with slow, stiff wing-beats, giving a wailing '*kweea-kweea*'. Normally copulation is without preliminaries or special invitatory posture adopted by the female, with the male taking the initiative. The species has a monogamous mating system and pair-bonds are typically long-term. Gregarious after breeding, forming large flocks at favoured roosting spots.

Nest, eggs and young. Nests on or near shore, on shingle beds, among rocks, in sand-dunes, or among grassy banks or crops. Nest is a shallow scrape, sometimes lined with small stones, shells or rabbit droppings. Both birds make a number of preliminary scrapes. Eggs 3 (2–4), buffish-yellow to stone, spotted black-brown. Incubation period 24–27 days, by both sexes, but greater share by female, beginning with last egg. Young cared for by both, brooded while small, and fed by both parents for a variable period. Fledging period 28–32 days, with age of independence varying from soon after fledging to 26 weeks or more. Age of first breeding normally four years.

AFRICAN BLACK OYSTERCATCHER   *Haematopus moquini*

Fr – Huîtrier de Moquin
Ge – Schwarzer Austernfischer

Identification. Length 17in. An all-black or blackish-brown oystercatcher, sometimes revealing a small white flash on the inner primaries. Differs from the American Black Oystercatcher (*H.bachmani*) in having a red (not yellow) iris, and is less brown on the mantle. It has a red bill with an orange tip, the eye-ring is broad and orange, and the legs are pink. The juvenile has distinctive pale fringes to the plumage, a duller bill, a brown iris and grey legs.

Voice. Frequently gives a clear and shrill '*Klee-weep, Klee-weep*' or '*tsa-peee, tsa-peee*'; in alarm, a sharp '*kik-kik-kik*'.

Habitat. Frequents all shore habitats, from sandy beaches to rocky coasts.

Distribution and movements. Nominate *moquini* occurs on the coasts of southern Africa from Angola to Natal. In the western Palaearctic, *H.m.meadewaldoi* was formerly endemic on Graciosa, Lanzarote and Fuerteventura in the eastern Canary Islands and the evidence generally points to this shorebird being extinct. Until 1968 there had only been one certain record and two sightings by naturalists this century and, despite several intensive searches in recent years, the established haunts of this species have proved vacant. However four apparently genuine records of 'Black Oystercatchers' (two on the coast of West Africa) since 1968 offer the slimmest hope of its survival. Sight records from Tenerife, 1968 and 1981.

Feeding. Feeds along the water level, prising mussels from the rocks, breaking them in crevices, or taking prey from sand banks and beaches. Also feeds actively at night. An active and agile bird, working quickly on exposed rocks or probing to the full length of its bill in soft sand. Mainly molluscs, crustacea and annelid worms are taken.

Social and breeding behaviour. No data available on the breeding biology of the isolated *meadewaldoi.*

Nest, eggs and young. Seldom seen by visiting ornithologists and no nests or young were ever found.

A pair of Oystercatchers respond to an intruder on their territory with the piping display.

STILTS and AVOCETS   Family Recurvirostridae

Stilts and avocets are fairly large pied waders with long slender bills that are either straight or recurved, and have long necks and legs. Bodies relatively slim and graceful, while stilts have proportionately smaller heads. When feeding, they seize food by quick pecks, or sweep bill from side to side. Sexes alike or nearly so, but some species show seasonal plumage variations.

Range. Almost world-wide in temperate and tropical zones.

Number of species. World, 7; western Palaearctic, 2.

BLACK-WINGED STILT   *Himantopus himantopus*

Du – Steltkluut
Fr – Echasse blanche
Ge – Stelzenläufer
Sp – Cigüenuela
Sw – Styltlöpare

Pl. 2

Identification. Length 14–15½in. A slender long-necked wader with enormously long pink legs trailing nearly six inches beyond tail in flight; straight black needle-bill and boldly contrasted black-and-white plumage make the stilt quite unmistakable. Flight action free and rapid on long, black, pointed wings. On the ground a high, graceful carriage, often wading deeply. Summer male has blackish back to head, ashy-brown in winter. Juvenile much browner, with pinkish-grey legs.

Voice. A sharp contact call '*kek*' or '*krek*'. Alarm and mobbing calls (also given in flight) are a more urgent repeated version of the contact call, an incessant monotonous '*kik-kik-kik*', becoming a rapid '*kiwikiwikiwiki*' under excitement.

Habitat. Breeding habitat is typically shallow still water, either brackish or fresh, in wet marshes, lagoons and open pool systems. Also deltas, estuaries, coastal lagoons, saltpans, irrigation areas or ricefields.

Distribution. An opportunistic species, breeding more or less irregularly throughout its range, depending upon the stability of its habitat. In recent years there have been clear signs of an increase in Spain and Italy, contrasting with some signs of a decline in populations further east. In western Palaearctic, nominate *himantopus* breeds mainly in France, Spain, Tunisia and Morocco, Italy and Sardinia, Greece, Hungary, Bulgaria, Turkey, Israel and southern Russia, north of the Volga to 48°. Also irregularly in Holland and other parts of Central Europe to Yugoslavia, Jordan and Cyprus. Accidental in the Atlantic islands and most European countries, including the British Isles (186). Map 3.

Movements. Mainly migratory. The main winter quarters of western Palaearctic birds are in Africa north of the Equator, and to a lesser extent in the Middle East. Many birds are thought to penetrate the northern tropics to reach West Africa, Chad, the Sudan and Eritrea, as there are generally rather few wintering in North Africa. There is no conclusive evidence of birds' occurring in East Africa south of Ethiopia. However, small numbers winter in southern Spain. Movements away from the breeding sites begin in late July. The western Mediterranean population moults in southern Spain and Morocco. Other large autumn concentrations are reported from the southern Caspian, from mid-August to October, probably another major region for moulting birds. Return passage mainly in March to April, or May in Europe and Siberia. Instances of irregularly breeding well outside the normal range occur from time to time in central and north-western Europe; bred central England (1945) and unsuccessfully 1983.

Feeding. Able to wade into deeper water than other waders. Most commonly seizes food by quick pecks from the water's surface or below it. Sometimes completely immerses head and neck. Bends legs to pick up food from vegetation or from the ground. Takes chiefly insect adults and larvae, particularly beetles, caddisflies and dragonflies; also small crustaceans and molluscs, worms, tadpoles and small fish.

Social and breeding behaviour. Typically gregarious. Nests in large or small colonies, often associating with those of other *Charadrii*, gulls or terns. Prior to nesting, a few birds occasionally congregate in shallow water, calling loudly. Calls attract others, who fly in slowly over them, alighting nearby. The group interact in mildly antagonistic encounters, with mantle feathers raised. Fighting may break out before the encounter ends as suddenly as it started and they disperse. Pairing is achieved passively by the female persistently associating with the male, who is intially hostile. Eventually the male ceases to attack, accepts her, and they then both defend the feeding area. Pairs maintain individual distance-spacing, except in copulation or nest relief; too close an approach by one of the pair induces the typical upright display (neck extended and head held high), head-bobbing, or both from the mate, as in antagonistic encounters – causing the other to respond similarly before one moves away.

The mating ceremony is initiated by the female adopting the soliciting posture. As the full ceremony develops, the male strides from side to side of the female, passing behind, pausing each time to perform the 'dip-shake-and-preen' display opposite the female's shoulder (two to five times); then male briefly performs 'giraffe' display and mounts female, balancing by waving wings and flexing legs so that the whole length of the tarsi rest on the female's back. After copulation the pair may more usually stand close together in upright posture before performing a post-copulatory run with bills crossed, male's wing extending over female's back and a run or walk of about 1m before separating. The species has a monogamous mating system. Outside the breeding season usually occurs in small flocks.

Nest, eggs and young. Nest on ground, usually in the open surrounded by shallow water, but can be in low vegetation; often on small islet or mound in water. Nest may be a shallow scrape with little lining, to a substantial nest of available vegetation, lined with finer materials. Built probably by both sexes. Eggs 4 (3–5), pale buff-brown, lightly marked with black spots. Incubation period 22–25 days, by both sexes. Fledging period 28–33 days, young becoming independent about 2–4 weeks after fledging. Age of first breeding normally 3 years.

AVOCET   *Recurvirostra avosetta*

Du – Kluut   Fr – Avocette
Ge – Säbelschnäbler   Sp – Avoceta
Sw – Skärfläcka

Pl. 2

Identification. Length 16½–17¾in. Beautiful snow-white plumage, boldly patterned with black, slender, up-curved bill and long lead-blue legs make the Avocet unmistakable. Seen from below in flight, appears mainly white, with only black wing-tips apparent, but from above it is boldly marked. Flight action free, rapid – and, mainly outside the breeding season, flocks fly up and down with more unified movements. Distinctive flight call, *'kluit-kluit'*. Sexes similar. Juvenile resembles the adult but the black is less intense and scapulars streaked sepia and brown.

Voice. Gives a clear, liquid *'kluit'* or *'klooit'*, and in alarm this is repeated more rapidly. Newly formed pairs give a soft *'cuck-cuck'* early in the season. A weak-sounding *'cwit-cwit-cwit'* is uttered rapidly during aggressive encounters. A higher-pitched *'cree-yü'* alarm note is used around the time the eggs are laid, and is used exclusively against gulls. Birds performing distraction-threat displays at nest utter *'kwit-kwit-kwit'* calls or *'krreewer'* calls (when adult with a hatched chick). Attack call during intra-specific aerial attacks, *'cut-cut-cut'* given as bird swerves off.

Habitat. Breeding habitat chiefly saline lagoons, delta marshes, brackish lagoons and pools on salt marshes, with open sandy flats or expanses of dried mud on which to nest. More rarely, borders of inland lakes, especially saline, where suitable conditions exist. Outside breeding season, in similar habitat, although choice now widened to mudflats and shallow waters farther from suitable nesting sites.

Distribution. In Europe breeds locally on coasts of North Sea and Baltic, Britain, Denmark, France, Portugal and Spain, Sardinia, Italy, Greece, Hungary, Bulgaria, Rumania, USSR: Estonia and Volga delta. Also Turkey and Tunisia. Map **4**.

Movements. Migrant in northern parts of breeding range. Spring passage begins late February–early March, but later in cold spells, with the majority arriving in April, but later in Russia. In Europe autumn passage is predominantly SW–SSW. Dispersal from breeding grounds begins in mid-July and August–September. Large numbers of Swedish, Danish, German and Dutch birds arrive to moult in the Heligoland Bight and Dutch delta region. Many birds move on in October, although many may still be present in November. Juveniles move south before adults complete their moult, indicated by August recoveries in southern France and Iberia. In mild winters significantly large numbers remain in the North Sea countries, e.g. Britain, France and The Netherlands. The main wintering areas are from the Mediterranean basin to the southern Caspian and south to the African Sahel, West Africa, Sudan, Eritrea, Arabia and India. Birds wintering in the eastern Sahel (Chad-Eritrea) probably refer to central and eastern European populations – numerous on passage in the Black Sea and western Anatolia.

Feeding. Food obtained from shallow water by sweeping bill and head from side to side in a regular movement, prey being located by touch. Also occasionally by stirring movements with the bill. Bird takes visually located prey in clear water, or off the mud by picking. Food mainly small crustaceans, molluscs, insects comprising adults, pupae and larvae of flies and beetles, tubificid worms, polychaete worms and small fish.

Social and breeding behaviour. Pair formation probably starts in late winter, as many birds are already paired on arrival at their breeding grounds. They tend to remain in small groups after spring arrival until pairs have established their feeding territory and nest sites. Though pairs are hostile to all birds of their own and other species coming close to their nests, colonies are often near to, or mixed with, the nests of the smaller gulls, terns or other waders. When disturbed, the adult adopts an alert, upright posture, head high, with head-bobbing and calling. In intra-specific encounters a formal bowing posture is adopted by both sexes, with the legs bent, body slanted forward obliquely and bill held near the ground or water. Encounters with other pairs, with much posturing, seem to play a considerable part in strengthening the pair-bond. Usually three to six, but occasionally up to 18 birds assemble in groups, sometimes arranging themselves in a circular pattern with heads inward in bowing attitude, which may also be accompanied by straw-throwing, water-pecking, head-shaking and vigorous bill-sweeping. These grouping ceremonies begin at the same time as pair courtship, soon after their arrival on the breeding grounds. The gathered birds often engage in antagonistic behaviour, leading to fighting, and paired couples endeavour to keep side by side, pressing close together (bowing and pressing together are also associated with nesting activities). Such gatherings are usually short, with the participants dispersing.

Copulation takes place in shallow water and is preceded by both birds pecking into the water and then resorting to formalised preening of the feathers of the neck and breast. Either sex may initiate this behaviour, and the dipping of the bill into the water becomes faster as the excitement increases. After a while the female assumes the invitatory attitude, with neck lowered so that the head lies flat on the water, legs wide apart. The male runs behind the female from one side to the other several times, finally springing on to her back. After copulation both birds run side by side for a short distance, the male with half-open wings – one sometimes extending over her back – necks stretched out close together and bills crossed. The species has a monogamous mating system.

Gregarious for most of the year, in flocks of five or six to 20–30 birds, sometimes larger. Outside the breeding season they often loaf, roost and fly in flocks. Birds will assemble quickly at times to feed co-operatively on shrimps at the edge of a rising tide.

Nest, eggs and young. Nests in colonies of varying size – nest a shallow scrape on open ground near water, composed of stems, roots and leaves added to form rim and lining of scrape, or merely a slight hollow quite unlined. Both sexes participate, forming scrape with breast and foot movements. Eggs 3 or 4, pale buff or brownish-buff, variably spotted black with some small blotches and greyish markings. Incubation period 23–25 days, by both sexes. Young cared for by both parents and brooded while small. Young self-feeding, fledging between 35 and 42 days. Age of first breeding normally in second year.

CRAB PLOVERS   Family Dromadidae

Medium-sized robust wader with body shape and stance recalling Stone Curlew, though pied plumage reminiscent of avocets. Essentially a maritime species, and its diet of crabs confines it to tidal zones exposing mudflats and sand banks. Breeding habits unique in Charadriiformes, nesting in sandy burrows close to the sea, with young remaining in burrow for some time after hatching and food brought by parents.

Range. Persian Gulf, coasts and islands in the Indian Ocean, south to Madagascar. Coasts of Red Sea and East Africa.

Number of species. World, 1; western Palaearctic, 1.

CRAB PLOVER   *Dromas ardeola*

Du – Krabplevier   Fr – Drome ardéole
Ge – Reiherläufer   Sp – Cigüenuela cangrejera
Sw – Krabehackare

Pl. 1

Identification. Length 13–14in. Large, mainly white wader with a thick, short, black bill (with pronounced gonys), heavy head, looking out of proportion to the rest of the body, and long blue-grey legs. Mantle and flight feathers are black (under-wings white). Sexes similar. Juvenile duller, with less striking pattern. Carries head low at rest, but extends it when alert. Flies with neck and legs extended, flight call '*chee-ruuk*'. When flying to roost or on migration flocks fly in flight formation, low, fast and in straight lines.

Voice. A shrill '*ki-ki-kew-ki*', a barking '*crow-ow-ow*', a harsh tern-like '*krerrk*' and a musical '*prooit*', besides the flight call mentioned above.

Habitat. Its diet of crabs etc. confines it to tidal zones where there are exposed mudflats, coral reefs, lagoons or estuaries.

Distribution. Estuary of the Shatt al Arab in Iraq, islands in the Persian Gulf, southern coasts and islands in the Red Sea, islands in the Indian Ocean, south to Madagascar. East coast of Africa. Also winter visitor to the coasts of Pakistan, western coasts of India, Laccadive, Maldive, Andaman and Nicobar islands, straggling to western coast of Malaya.

Movements. Partially migratory and present all year in Kuwait (largest numbers August) and Masirah Island (Oman) – largest numbers in autumn-winter. These probably include birds from the Persian Gulf which have finished their breeding activities. There is an influx in Aden from mid-August, increasing September–early October, but moving on by mid-November. The species has been reported as not uncommon on the Arabian side of the Red Sea and winter flocks occur in coastal Eritrea, but are uncommon on the Sudanese coast, and only straggle to Egypt. Breeding not confirmed south of the Equator, so that birds found on the East African coastline south to Natal and on islands in the Indian Ocean, must be migrants. Large numbers occur on the Somali coasts from March to October (breeding) and the species is common on the coasts of Kenya and Tanzania from September to April. Madagascar and Aldabra islands are both important wintering areas, October to March.

Feeding. Usually feeds in flocks of 20 or more – mainly on crabs caught on mudflats at low tide, or in shallow water. Often crepuscular, feeding after dark. Feeds by picking and probing and by slow stalking. Breaks open crab shells easily with powerful bill. Stabs into water with bill open, emerging with crab, which is then crushed and eaten. Also takes other crustaceans, small molluscs, marine worms and other invertebrates.

Social and breeding behaviour. Normally gregarious all seasons and forms large flocks outside breeding season. Winter flocks noisy, often restless. Breeds colonially with nesting burrows set close together. Nothing known about heterosexual behaviour or parental care. Incubating birds hiss at intruders from their burrows.

Nests, eggs and young. Nest is a chamber at the end of a tunnel, varying from 1 to 2.5m in sandy ground close to the sea. Building probably by both sexes, using bill and feet. 1 egg laid (rarely 2), white. No data on incubation period. Young after hatching remain in burrow for some time and food is brought by parents. Also fed by parents after leaving the burrow – juveniles approach adults with head held low and forward and body hunched, giving a plaintive call.

STONE CURLEWS   Family Burhinidae

Medium to large terrestrial or littoral waders, with highly cryptic plumages, large yellow eyes and crepuscular or nocturnal habits. Large headed, with rather stout, short bills, often yellow or greenish with swollen black tip, and tarsal joints obvious (hence nickname 'thick-knee'). They are active, mobile and noisy at night (giving wailing or curlew-like cries), but also feed by day. Flight fast, on rapid wing-beats, often low over the ground and silent, legs stretched out behind.

Range. Mainly temperate and tropical parts of the world, except North America, New Zealand and the Pacific islands.

Number of species. World, 9; western Palaearctic, 2.

STONE CURLEW   *Burhinus oedicnemus*

Du – Griel   Fr – Oedicnème criard
Ge – Triel   Sp – Alcaraván
Sw – Tjockfot

Pl. 2

Identification. Length 16–17in. Plumage markedly cryptic and habits cause bird to be easily overlooked. A large, sandy-brown streaked bird distinguished from all other waders by rounded head, large staring yellow eyes, short, stout yellow-and-black bill and long, heavy, pale yellow legs. In flight reveals a conspicuous wing pattern, with two bold whitish wing-bars. Flight direct, usually low with deliberate wing-beats, occasionally long glides. When standing still, carriage may be remarkably upright – when moving, body more horizontal, or if alarmed, moves furtively – body hunched, head lowered and neck withdrawn – with short, pattering steps. Distinctive call, a plaintive shrill '*kur-LEE*'. (Curlew's call – '*COURL*i' – is low-pitched and more musical.) Chiefly vocal at dusk or after dark.

Voice. Most familiar calls consist of shrill ringing variants of the basic '*kur-LEE*' (repeated three to six times). Choruses begin shortly after sun-set; single bird or pair calls and neighbouring birds join in – calling finishing mostly by dawn. Many calls highly variable and include '*whit-whit-weet-weet*' notes, high, almost trilling 'kikikikee' calls, several '*kurEEu*' notes, short whistles, '*chhwhik*' notes, mellower '*ku-ik*' and rapid musical '*kururulik*' etc. from bird in flight over some distance. Flushed or startled birds utter loud '*krieehk*', '*whee*' or '*klui*'. Can also make loud hissing noises. From early autumn a tittering or bubbling call is employed.

Habitat. Frequents and breeds in extensive dry, stony, sandy or chalky areas, heathland mixed with short grass and bare patches, extensive sand-dunes with bare sand and short herbage, poor stony pastures, steppe and shingle spits. Also adapts to cultivation where undisturbed.

Distribution. Marked decline in typical race which breeds in north-western and central Europe, due to loss of habitat since mid-19th century. From Britain ranges south to Iberia and the Mediterranean, east to Rumania and the Black Sea, the Caucasus and Turkey. Birds from south-eastern Russia, from the lower Volga eastwards and south to Iran, Afghanistan and Baluchistan are *B.o.harterti*. North Africa, the Middle East, including Egypt and the northern Sudan are *B.o.saharae* and two insular races are resident on the Canaries. Map **5**.

Movements. Flocking occurs after breeding at traditional pre-migration gathering sites in mid-August, although a few birds may remain in vicinity of nesting areas till October. Mainly a migrant in northern and eastern Europe and western Siberia, but varying – some resident where milder winters. Iberian birds considered resident; a few winter in south-west France and many more in southern Europe. Substantial numbers of European birds (typical form) cross the Mediterranean to winter in North Africa and the Afrotropical region (Senegal to north-eastern Zaire, the Sudan, Eritrea, Uganda and north-western Kenya). Mediterranean and Sahara believed to be crossed on a broad front. Breeding areas are reoccupied in mid-March, with passage continuing into April or later in eastern European populations. The eastern *harterti* breeds in western Siberia and Iran to north-west India, and probably migrants winter in the southern parts of their breeding range and may extend into Iraq and Arabia.

The southern birds, *saharae*, of North Africa and the Middle East, are mainly resident for most of the year – but migrants reach north-east Africa in the Sudan, Eritrea and northern Kenya and Somalia (though unknown whether from western Palaearctic).

Feeding. Mainly crepuscular and nocturnal feeder, foraging mostly in darkness, but may also feed in daylight in breeding season. Prey approached by heron-like stalk and swift stab; distant prey on the ground approached at a run, or bird can chase and catch flying insects; even adapted to following a ploughing tractor to pick up exposed invertebrates. Food mainly insects and their larvae, earthworms, snails, small lizards, amphibians, fieldmice, voles and eggs of ground-nesting birds.

Social and breeding behaviour. Pairs established shortly after arrival on breeding ground. In spring, occasionally, some or all pairs in area may gather at a site some distance from the nearest laying area to indulge in group display. Birds run about calling loudly, performing leaps, charging one another and strutting in upright posture; however, this performance may be a more normal crepuscular activity. Wing-waving behaviour occurs at the approach of dusk, indicating restlessness prior to departure for feeding areas. In aggressive encounters the bird adopts a high, upright posture – body almost vertical. While no special courtship display before female by male has been established, dancing and running movements in front of one or more females have been recorded. A male has also performed giving quick runs, jumps and skips with wings hanging or half raised, body feathers fluffed out, tail spread, raised and lowered, with neck and head turning and twisting. In pre-laying period two important displays occur between the pair, the deep bow and neck-arch. The former is associated with scrape-making and nest-site selection and may continue over long periods as promising nesting sites are investigated. The neck-arch is basically a greeting ceremony used during the pre-laying period and occurs when paired birds meet each other after separation. The neck-arch may be followed by copulation (ceases after incubation). Copulation can also follow the deep-bow and nest-scrape activities. In nest relief an adult may either be relieved at the nest by its mate or leave on its approach – done inconspicuously and without ceremony. The species has a monogamous mating system. Mainly gregarious, forming flocks in autumn and winter.

Nest, eggs and young. Nests on open ground, making fairly deep scrape lined with stones, shells or rabbit droppings. Eggs 1–3, usually 2 – very pale buff or stone, variably marked with brown and purple-grey streaks or blotches. Incubation period 24–26 days, by both sexes. Fledging period 36–42 days; young also cared for by both parents; food brought to young at early stages. Normally breeds in third year, although recorded in first.

SENEGAL THICK-KNEE *Burhinus senegalensis*

Du – Senegalese Griel   Fr – Oedicnème du Sénégal
Ge – Nordafrika Triel   Sp – Alcaraván senegales
Sw – Senegal tjockfot

Pl. 2

Identification. Length 13–15in. Similar in plumage to Stone Curlew, but differs in being slightly smaller, longer billed and with more white around the eyes, giving it a paler-faced appearance and greyer back. Pattern of folded wing also differs in lacking black-margined white band across coverts and showing more uniform pale grey shoulders. In flight wing pattern obviously different, only showing a single wide pale grey panel, and white patch at base of primaries smaller. At all ages bill mainly black, with yellow restricted to base of upper mandible, whereas Stone Curlew also has yellow on lower mandible for two-thirds of its length, with black tip.

Voice. Calls are similar to Stone Curlew's, but less strident and more nasal. Song described as a series of mournful, ringing whistles, rising in pitch and volume, then falling and fading – 'pi pi pi-pi-pi-Pll-Pll-Pll-pii-pii' or more disyllabic 'ku-Lll Ku-Lll Kulii' etc. Also '*Plkop-Plkop-Plkop*', '*tche-u*' and piping calls.

Habitat. Similar requirements as Stone Curlew – arid or dry open regions in savanna and thorn-scrub country. However, differs from Stone Curlew in avoiding deserts and preferring vicinity of water, especially sandy or rocky river beds. Also adapted to nesting on flat-topped roofs in Egypt.

Distribution. The form *B.s.inornatus* is found in Egypt from the delta of the Nile and from Ethiopia south to Kenya and Uganda. Map **6**.

Movements. Resident in Egypt, but subject to local movements in rainy season or floods – moving to drier areas.

Feeding. Mostly insects and crustaceans, molluscs, worms, frogs and small rodents. Often crepuscular foraging in small groups, and regularly a mile or more away from water.

Social and breeding behaviour. Mainly active by night, but also by day. Commonly in pairs, or four to five, occasionally 30 birds. No information on heterosexual behaviour although the species presumably has a monogamous mating system. Young brooded by both parents and remain in nest for a few days after hatching. Both parents accompany young, which are self-feeding.

Nest, eggs and young. Nest shallow scrape with little or no lining. Eggs 2, dull ochre, lightly marked brown and grey. Incubation and role of sexes not known.

COURSERS and PRATINCOLES   Family Glareolidae

COURSERS (Subfamily Cursoriinae) are small to medium terrestrial, plover-like waders with relatively long legs, pointed bills and no hind toe, and are agile runners with characteristic upright stance. Sexes alike. Except for the Egyptian Plover, all are mostly sandy-coloured or brown, have a pectinated middle toe, and live on semi-desert, bare ground or short grass. The very strikingly patterned Egyptian Plover is a riverine species and has peculiar habits, burying its eggs in the sand, or similarly burying its young when danger threatens.

PRATINCOLES (Subfamily Glareolinae) are graceful, long-winged waders of plains and dry wastes, mostly highly aerial –resembling terns or large swallows, taking insects on the wing and ground. They spend more time on the wing than do coursers. Bills are short and somewhat curved, with a wide gape, facilitating aerial capture of prey. Bodies more elongated, with longer forked tails than coursers. Carriage also more horizontal, and distinctly shorter legged, middle toe long and pectinated. Sexes similar.

Range. Temperate and tropical Europe, Africa, Asia and Australia.

Number of species. World, 16; western Palaearctic, 4.

EGYPTIAN PLOVER   *Pluvianus aegyptius*

Du – Krokodilwachter   Fr – Pluvian d'Egypte
Ge – Krokodilwächter   Sp – Pluvial de Egypto
SW – Krokodilväktare

Pl. 3

Identification. Length 8½in. A strikingly patterned plover-like bird, with short, stout, black bill and bright blue-grey legs. Plumage basically pale blue-grey above and buff-white below, with black crown and upper cheeks divided by a long white supercilium (to nape), and prominent black necklace. Mantle and centre of back glossy black, and grey tail broadly tipped white. In flight the bird unfolds its strikingly patterned black-and-white cape-like wings. The primaries are mainly white, showing a black wing-bar, and the leading and trailing edges are also black. Sexes similar. The juvenile shows rusty-brown fringes to the smaller wing-coverts and rump, and the breast-band is narrower.

In flight it has a characteristic flutter on take-off, combining fast, flickering wing-beats low over the sand or water. Movements on the ground are quick and jerky, but it often stops suddenly to scratch at the ground. It is exceptionally tame.

Voice. In aggressive encounters gives a rapid, harsh '*cherk-cherk-cherk*' or '*chur-chur-chur*'.

Habitat. Frequents sandy margins, islands and sand banks of large rivers, normally avoiding salt water. Outside the breeding season also on lakes and other fresh waters, occasionally on fields, and may feed around human settlements near rivers. Breeds on sand-bars when rivers are low in the dry season.

Distribution. Formerly not uncommon in Upper Egypt, but no recent records and may now be considered rare, or extinct in the western Palaearctic. It is found in the southern Sudan, Ethiopia and northern Uganda, north-eastern Zaire and the Kasai, to the

Cuanzo River in northern Angola, and westward from the Congo (excluding the heavily forested regions) to West Africa, north to Senegal. Has occurred in Libya, Palestine and the Canaries.

Movements. No information on former Egyptian population. In the northern tropics of Africa, the birds make irregular movements with changes in water levels. It is perhaps a seasonal migrant in Nigeria, where birds move away from southern rivers in the wet season (June–October), when the sand banks are covered by floods, and peak numbers occur at Lake Chad, Kano and Sokoto in northern Nigeria. In Chad the species also disappears from Fort Lamy district (May–September) and makes irregular movements to temporary wetlands in the Sahel zone.

Feeding. Chiefly insects and other invertebrates, taken mainly from the ground, foraging on shores of rivers and lakes. Picks prey from surface of ground or from vegetation, after careful searching. It stalks winged insects in heron-like manner and may also flush them by running with the wings slightly spread. Also probes damp sand to the depth of the bill, and will excavate holes with the bill to obtain prey. Can also dig in sand with both feet and overturns debris to expose prey.

Social and breeding behaviour. After the birds have paired, courtship activity and precopulatory displays are simple and minimal. Scrape-making is one of the earliest and most persistent of breeding activities. Dozens of scrapes may be made (both sexes participating) and the highly ritualised associated postures suggest that this activity has developed into an important social ceremony for which the burying of eggs and chicks is so vital. Scraping is usually preceded by a V-tilt display, after which the bird walks about rather stiffly before starting to scrape. Little ritual involved prior to copulation, and the female sinks slowly into a low crouch without any apparent signal. The male mounts directly from behind, often running up a short distance. The species has a monogamous mating system. They are moderately gregarious at times and may be found in small flocks, generally up to 20.

Nest, eggs and young. Nest on a small island, on ground in the open. Scrape made in loose sand and no material is added. Eggs 1–3, light yellow-brown, with many small red-brown to grey spots and speckles. Incubation period 28–31 days, by both sexes. The eggs are completely covered by sand when the bird is not incubating. During hot periods the parents soak the eggs and covering of sand at intervals by wetting the feathers of their under-parts and sitting on the nest for brief periods. Fledging period 35 days, young cared for and fed by both parents.

CREAM-COLOURED COURSER   *Cursorius cursor*

Du – Renvogel   Fr – Courvite isabelle
Ge – Rennvogel   Sp – Corredor
Sw – Ökenlöpare

Pl. 3

Identification. Length 8½–9in. A tall, graceful, sandy-isabelline plover-like bird of almost Dotterel size, with a short, sharp decurved bill and long, thin, whitish legs. At a distance may look uniformly sandy, but closer inspection reveals striking head pattern – parallel streaks of white and black run from behind the eye to meet in a V on the nape. Rear crown blue-grey and under-parts dull pink-buff, paler than upper-parts. Black primaries partially obscured in folded wing show as a black line. Tail short, with black subterminal band with white tips, conspicuous at sides. In flight the bird produces a startling effect, as both surfaces of the wing show striking pattern. Above, black primaries (including secondary bases) contrast with sandy coverts. Below, whole under-wing uniform black except for sandy leading edge and white tips to secondaries. Flight direct with well marked wing action, and legs extending one to two inches beyond tail. The bird runs swiftly, usually in short bursts, keeping a measured distance between itself and an observer. Juvenile has less contrasting head pattern, while sandy upper-parts and upper chest show irregular wave marks and spots.

Voice. Commonest call a sharp, piping whistle and a distinctive, penetrating *'praak-praak'* in flight. Other notes recorded range from a whiplash-like *'quit-quit'*, *'woo'*, *'wee'* or *'too-li'*, also *'pwuk'* calls, followed by the occasional *'AAArka'*.

Habitat. Essentially arid, very warm, sandy desert, semi-desert and arid steppes with sparse vegetation – avoiding damp depressions, wadis or areas of tall plants or scrub.

Distribution. Cape Verde islands, Canaries and Sahara east to Egypt, Sudan and Somalia. In the Middle East from Palestine through Syria, Iraq, Iran, Arabia and Baluchistan to north-western India. Accidental in most European countries, including the British Isles (33). Map 7.

Movements. Extensive movements, including seasonal migrations, occur in Saharan and Arabian birds (nominate form). From mid-September to October, trans-Saharan autumn movements towards winter quarters take place – the species is scarce in winter in the northern Sahara, although found in the coastal plain in southern Morocco. In the northern Middle East the main autumn departure is in late September, although some birds are resident north to Israel, Jordan and Iraq, but many move south into Arabia for the winter. In Africa the winter range extends south to Sahelian and Sudanese zones, along the southern side of the Sahara, to Senegambia, Mali, Chad (where widespread October to February) and Sudan (common). The main northward movement in the Sahara occurs March to April, birds moving on a broad front in small parties. After the breeding season flocks form and wander extensively, and not infrequently reach the Mediterranean coasts – probably the origin of many vagrants reported in Europe from time to time.

The Cape Verde islands endemic race *exsul* is resident. The eastern race *bogolubovi*, of Transcaspia, eastern Iran and Afghanistan is partially migratory, wintering in southern Iran and north-western India, and birds recorded in south-eastern Arabia in winter may include this race.

Feeding. Forages on foot, making short dashes to pick off prey spotted some distance away. Chiefly insects and their larvae, also spiders, snails and larger prey, i.e. small lizards, or grasshoppers and mantids up to 8cm long.

Social and breeding behaviour. Gregarious even when breeding – usually flocks of five to 20 birds in loose association. Several nests may be found within a short distance of one another. Details of courtship and pair formation, scrape-making and nest relief not known. The female has been observed to crouch motionless on the ground while the male (attempting copulation) stood upright two to three feet behind for about 30 seconds, finally mounting with outstretched wings. After the female rose they both assumed the upright posture, then hopped from foot to foot, bobbing heads. They picked up small stones and twigs from the ground and dropped them again, sometimes sharing the same item, and still with hopping movements.

In a display flight, a bird circled high in wide spirals on quickly beating wings, giving a display call *'quit-quit-whow'*. Another bird was seen to give a Woodpigeon-like display flight – climbing to 15m, giving a bubbling call '*lu-lu-lu*', then single '*wheck*' notes, before gliding down on slightly decurved wings, continuing to call for a further two minutes. Presumed males in aggressive behaviour faced each other one metre apart, both standing upright and with chest thrust out, head drawn back – each moving chest rapidly up and down.

Nest, eggs and young. Nest is a shallow scrape on bare ground, no nest material. Normal clutch is two eggs, rarely three. Both birds probably incubate (period not known). Young cared for and fed by parents, becoming self-feeding before fledging. Fledging period not known. Breeding recorded in first year.

COLLARED PRATINCOLE   *Glareola pratincola*

Du – Vorkstaartplevier   Fr – Glaréole à collier
Ge – Rotflügelbrachschwalbe   Sp – Canastera
Sw – Vadarsvala

Pl. 3

Identification. Length 10in. Distinctive swallow-like shape and flight action, with deeply forked black tail and broad white base, serve to distinguish it. The buoyant flight, forked tail and sharp rippling '*kikki-kirrik*' calls equally recall terns. On the ground a mainly dark olive-brown, rather short-legged plover-like bird, with remarkably long pointed wings and even longer tail streamers (extending 1–3cm beyond tail at the rest in fresh adults) giving it an elongated appearance. The chin and throat are creamy, offset by a narrow black border in summer, which in winter is more or less streaked. Wing in flight shows distinctive contrast between blacker primaries and paler inner wing and mantle, accentuated by the white trailing edge of the secondaries. By comparison the Black-winged Pratincole has a more uniform appearance in flight, with the secondaries black like the primaries and rather dark wing-coverts and mantle. The chestnut axillaries and underwing-coverts (black in *nordmanni*) can be surprisingly hard to determine even when the bird is overhead. Bill short, black with red base; legs black. The juvenile resembles the non-breeding adult, but throat lacks any outline and feathers of upper-parts have paler fringes.

Voice. Calls variable but typically shrill, harsh and chattering – often tern-like. Calls most frequently on the wing, but also given on the ground, and loud twittering sounds produced by a nesting colony were audible at some distance. Various calls described, from '*kikki-kirrik*' to '*kitty-kerrick-kerticktick*' used in joint courtship flight, '*chitti-chitti*', strident tern-like '*tit-ir-it*' and '*kirriririk*' in alarm.

Habitat. Shows rare combination of ground-living and more markedly aerial habits. Frequents open, bare areas and sites, i.e. stretches of sun-baked mud in marshy places, river deltas, borders of lagoons, lakes or river flats, plains and semi-desert.

Distribution. Nominate *pratincola* breeds in Europe in southern Iberia and France, Italy, Corsica, Greece, Hungary, lower Danube and southern Russia, Turkey, Palestine, Jordan and Iraq. Also in North Africa, in Morocco, Tunisia and Egypt. Small numbers which breed in Pakistan, winter in India. Accidental in the Atlantic islands and many European countries, including the British Isles (69 of 104 pratincoles). Map **8**.

Movements. Summer visitor to Europe, Asia Minor, Russia and Iran – these populations (nominate *pratincola*) wintering in Africa. Main wintering areas thought to lie along southern edge of Sahara from Senegal to Ethiopia, mixing with local African races.

Southern winter limits not known, as not readily separable from local birds, but doubtful if the nominate form reaches the Equator, thereby differing from *nordmanni*, which is a trans-equatorial migrant wintering in large numbers, mainly in South Africa.

At the end of the breeding season large flocks form around lake margins, saltpans etc. prior to departure. Autumn migration in the Mediterranean basin and the Middle East is mainly from late August to October, and Palaearctic migrants are present in the Sudan from October to March. Return movements occur in North Africa during April and breeding areas are reoccupied in April–early May.

Feeding. Most active morning and evening, foraging in flocks. Hawks insects, particularly swarming species, in powerful swallow-like flight. Food mainly locusts and grasshoppers, beetles, flies, bugs and moths.

Social and breeding behaviour. Breeds in scattered loose colonies, where nests may be three metres, or more normally 12–15m, apart. Very noisy and demonstrative at nesting places, flying close to an intruder and frequently settling close by on the ground. Each pair maintains a small nesting territory within the colony which it defends against its own or other species. Soon after arrival pairs may engage in flying in wide circles, calling loudly and performing sudden swoops and climbs. On the ground the pair greet each other in a bowing display – neck stretched forward and head arched down, with wing nearest partner hanging limp. After a few seconds both stand upright. Body-tilting also noted in display, with wings spread and tail almost vertical. Birds may also approach directly, or circle partner, and then face each other, raising head, displaying throat-patch and calling. Breeding birds may perform group ceremonies on a neutral piece of ground, there indulging in communal bowing and calling. Mating and courtship feeding also involve bowing; then, with female turning back on male, neck feathers are ruffled and head extended, she runs a few steps then stands still before male finally runs up, mounts and copulation takes place. The species has a monogamous mating system.

Gregarious, feeding in flocks even in the breeding season. Post-breeding flocks sometimes very large, about 5,000 in August (Algeria).

Nest, eggs and young. Nests in colonies, often in the company of other waders etc. Nest is a shallow scrape, or hoof-print, with little or no lining, on bare open ground, occasionally in very short vegetation – often near water. Eggs, 3 (2–4), creamy with black or dark-brown blotches, spots or streaks. Incubation period 17–19 days, by both sexes. Young leave nest after two to three days and are cared for by both parents, who regurgitate food for first week; young then self-feeding. Fledging period 25–30 days. Probably breeds in first year.

BLACK-WINGED PRATINCOLE   *Glareola nordmanni*

Du – Steppenvorkstaartplevier	Fr – Glaréole à ailes noires
Ge – Schwarzflügelbrachschwalbe	Sp – Canastera alinegra
Sw – Svartvingad vadarsvala	Pl. 3

Identification. Length 10in. Very similar to Pratincole, but distinguished by black instead of chestnut under-wing, and upper surfaces of wings show less contrast, also lacking white trailing edge to secondaries present in former (more fully described above). Distinction from Pratincole never easy, but flight silhouette subtly different, with slightly longer primaries giving shorter-tailed appearance. At rest, folded primaries of spring adult extend well past the tip of the tail than in Pratincole, and the tail has a shallower fork. Also lacks distinctive eye-ring, has less red at base of bill and is longer legged and a darker bird above. Juvenile lacks narrow black border to throat, and has extensive buff tips and dark subterminal black bands to feathers of mantle. Best distinguished from juvenile *G. p. pratincola* by narrow pale buff tips to secondaries rather than wider and paler ones, by black axillaries and under wing-coverts and less red to base of bill.

Voice. Different from Pratincole and apparently lower pitched. On migration, as well as at breeding colony, '*kirlik-kirlik*' and '*kip-ip*' calls heard. Autumn vagrants' calls range from '*kitt-kitt*', '*sriik*' and '*keek*' to a shrill '*kettret-kettret*'. Alarm call near nest very different from Pratincole's – always lower in pitch – '*pwik-pwik-pwik*', then '*pwik-kik-kik...pwik...pwik-kik-kik*' – all clearly separated notes.

Habitat. Confined to steppes, often adapting to taller or denser herbage, i.e. grassy meadows, saline vegetation and even fields cultivated with flax, maize or millet. Also salt flats, borders of salt lakes or sand spits. Larger breeding colonies require presence of water nearby, also damp meadows or marshes overgrown with tall grasses.

Distribution. Breeds in S.E. Europe in Rumania and southern Russia; also occasionally or rarely reported nesting as far west as France and West Germany – also Hungary and Syria, and present in Iraq in summer. Accidental in Iceland and most European countries, including the British Isles (21). Map **9**.

Movements. Migratory, wintering entirely in Africa, mostly below Equator, although recently recorded in Ethiopia in some numbers. Large flocks form at the end of the breeding season (late June to mid-July) and adults moult mainly before migrating. The main departures occur in August–September, with some continuing till early October in Transcaucasia. Migrates from breeding grounds in S.W. Asia and S.E. Europe through Iran, Iraq, Turkey and northern Arabia. It is scarce on passage in Cyprus and is noted on passage through Egypt and the Sudan. Elsewhere wintering reported from Chad and northern Nigeria. The majority of birds continue south to south-west from the Sudan, crossing the Central African Republic, Zaire, western Zambia and Angola to winter in large numbers on the plains of Botswana, Namibia and south to northern Cape Province. Some autumn migrants occur as far west as Togo, Cameroun and Gabon. Return movements noted from early March (Zambia) and the first half of April (Zaire), with the first birds reappearing in the USSR from mid-April and main arrivals in May.

Feeding. Feeds mostly morning and evening, hawking insects, especially swarming species. In Africa recorded feeding in flocks of hundreds, or thousands on locust swarms. Also congregate to feed on flying ants and termites.

Social and breeding behaviour. Gregarious – but flocks often larger than Pratincole, with flocks of up to 10,000 recorded passing over western Zambia October to November and again on return north in March. Nomadic in winter quarters (see *Feeding*). Breeding behaviour poorly known, but probably basically similar to Pratincole, which also has a monogamous mating system; hybridisation with the latter has occurred in the Camargue, southern France. Calls are different (see above).

Nest, eggs and young. Nests in colonies from under ten pairs to several thousand. Nest shallow depression, lined with small pieces of vegetation, sometimes sparse, but generally more than in Pratincole. Building probably by both sexes. Eggs 4 (3–5), olive to olive-green, well marked with blackish spots, streaks or blotches. Incubation, no data. Young tended by both parents and independent at five to six weeks.

PLOVERS and LAPWINGS   Family Charadriidae

PLOVERS   Subfamily Charadriinae

Small to medium waders, smaller than most Lapwings. Plumages often with one or two dark bands on the breast, with white neck band, black crown patch and black line through the eye. Show well shaped, rounded heads, large eyes and short necks and bills. Feed with characteristic movements; they walk or run a few steps, pause upright, then tilt forward to jab at prey before moving on. May also run swiftly in short bursts. Larger *Pluvialis* plovers usually have black under-parts in summer plumage. Sexes alike, or nearly so. Flight fast and direct, and they typically form flocks of their own species, or with others. Some species are spectacular long-distance migrants, e.g. American Golden Plover. **Range.** Worldwide. **Number of species.** World, 42; western Palaearctic, 14.

LITTLE RINGED PLOVER   *Charadrius dubius*

Du – Kleine Plevier   Fr – Petit Gravelot
Ge – Flussregenpfeifer   Sp – Chorlitejo chico
Sw – Mindre strandpipare

Pl. **4**

Identification. Length 5½–6in. Plumage pattern typical of ringed-plover group. Differs from similar Ringed Plover in smaller and trimmer appearance, mainly black bill, bright yellow orbital ring, flesh-coloured legs and white line behind black forecrown. In flight lack of white wing-bar and distinctive call readily distinguish it from the latter. Call a whistling '*PEE-u*', with emphasis on first syllable, unlike equivalent liquid call of Ring Plover's '*too-LEE*' – emphasis on second syllable. Juvenile has distinctive hooded appearance and eye-ring duller yellow.

Voice. General alarm or contact call '*PEE-u*', uttered singly or repeatedly and used equally on ground or wing – or a more persistent '*pee-pee-pee-u*'. Single '*prip*' note given repeatedly by adult with young, also, if danger threatens, a repeated '*cru*'. Threat call is a ringing musical '*gree-gree-gree*' – increasing in intensity – given by both sexes in breeding season. Song is a strongly rhythmic '*gria-gria-gria*' repeated by male during 'butterfly-type' flight display over breeding territory – most common first half of April. Parents summon chicks after disturbance, or for brooding, with a fast, continuous '*pip-pip-pip*'.

Habitat. Found in vicinity of fresh water with shallow muddy edges for feeding and, unlike Ringed Plover, rarely coastal. Frequents sand and gravel banks on rivers, stony river beds and gravel pits. Sometimes also saline inland pools and flats, or, when found breeding on coast, usually at the mouth of a river or stream.

Distribution. In western Palaearctic, race *curonicus* is widespread in Eurasia, from S.E. Norway, Sweden, Finland and Russia to about the Arctic Circle on the Kanin peninsula and to about 65° on the Pechora, south, including Britain, to the Mediterranean and some of its islands, northern Africa in Morocco, Algeria and Egypt in the Nile delta. Also in Asia Minor, Iraq and Iran. The nominate form occurs from the Philippines south to New Guinea and New Ireland and *C.d.jerdoni* is found in India and S.E. Asia. Map **10**.

Movements. Migratory, with majority of western Palaearctic birds wintering mainly in northern tropics of Africa, also sparingly in Persian Gulf and southern Arabia. In Africa, winters from Senegal to Somalia, north to Mali, Lake Chad basin and Nile valley at Khartoum in the Sudan – only a few crossing Equator to winter in eastern Zaire and Tanzania. Autumn passage begins in earnest in mid-July, with August peak in Europe. Few left after mid-September. In western Europe, autumn passage S.S.W.-S.S.E., with birds reaching Mediterranean between Portugal and Italy – avoiding Atlantic seaboard. Only a few Iberian ringing recoveries, compared with many in France, seem to indicate a major overland route through France, with birds crossing the Mediterranean between eastern Spain and southern Italy to make landfall in the Maghreb. Fenno-Scandian ringing recoveries indicate south-east movement through Russia toward Black Sea – possibly wintering in Persian Gulf, although one bird ringed in Kenya was found in the Caucasus in May. A few birds are probably resident in the southern parts of their breeding range, i.e. the Mediterranean basin and the Middle East. Return movement from Africa begins in late February, and some early arrivals may reach Britain by the second week of March. Main return is April-early May, or later in northern Russia.

Feeding. Chiefly insects and their larvae, picked from surface or just below ground, usually in damp or wet areas. Occasionally takes small snails, crustaceans and plant seeds.

Social and breeding behaviour. At least in Britain the sexes arrive on their breeding grounds separately, with males generally preceding females by about one to three weeks – few arriving already paired. Breeding pairs highly territorial and nesting territories also defended up to about 30 metres in the air. Often noisy and demonstrative when breeding. Soon after arrival in spring, males start to perform song-flight (see *Voice*) and scraping displays. The latter is an important aspect of courtship (similar to Ringed Plover); as female approaches nest scrape, male turns away while raising and spreading tail. The female then enters nest scrape by passing underneath the male's tail. Copulation occurs near nest scrape and is preceded by the male's approach in a horizontal position, gradually becoming more upright and also increasing the speed of his footsteps, which become progressively shorter and higher – 'goose-stepping' – while his body posture assumes a more vertical, full-chested, upright aspect as he stands by female marking time on the spot. When female crouches horizontally, male mounts and copulation takes place. The pair then separate and run away from each other in a gliding run. Copulation occurs exclusively in the nesting territory. A monogamous mating system is the rule. Less gregarious outside breeding season then Ringed Plover, but about 50 not uncommon in a traditional gathering-spot in autumn. More normally, one to six birds observed together.

Nest, eggs and young. Nest is on bare ground or among low vegetation, rarely far from water and often on small islands in rivers or lakes. The male makes one of several shallow scrapes during courtship and the female selects one for the nest. Eggs, 4 (3–5), stone or buff, well marked with small brown spots or streaks. Two broods, but in Britain rarely two, and in Scandinavia only one. Incubation 24–25 days, by both sexes. Young cared for by both, and young self-feeding. Fledging 25–27 days, and young independent from 8–25 days. Normally breeds in first year, but often not until second.

RINGED PLOVER   *Charadrius hiaticula*

Du – Bontbekplevier   Fr – Grand gravelot
Ge – Sandregenpfeifer   Sp – Chorlitejo grande
Sw – Större strandpipare

Pl. 4

Identification. Length 7–8in. Larger than Little Ringed or Kentish Plovers and more robustly built than either. Breeding adults have brightest legs, orange-yellow, and two-tone coloured bill, orange with black tip. In flight, longer wings showing striking white wing-bar, and distinctive liquid call, '*too-LEE*', readily separate it. Juveniles lack black breast-band of adult, which is brown, often reduced to lateral patches, and legs are dull orange-yellow. Similar-plumaged Kentish Plover has black legs (beware of mud adhering to legs, making them look dark). Juvenile Little Ringed Plover has pale flesh-coloured legs, but looks less hunchbacked, is slimmer and has obscure brown head markings, giving it a hooded appearance, and lacks white wing-bar.

Voice. Mainly short simple calls, from melodious '*too-LEE*' (all seasons) to liquid piping '*kluup*' or '*queep*'; also '*queeo*' and a less liquid musical '*turrrp*'. A short '*pip*' or '*pritt*' given in agitation – may be repeated continuously. Threat call a melodious, repeated '*teLEEa-teLEEa…teLEE-teLEE…lee-lee*' – reducing, and ending in monosyllables – used mainly during horizontal crouch displays. Similar '*tee-leea*' or '*leea*' uttered by male in song flight. Scraping call is a rhythmical '*pju-pju-pju*', leading to sharper, higher '*pipipi-pipipi*' calls.

Habitat. Essentially a coastal species during breeding season, nesting on sandy, pebbly or shell beaches, along coastal tundra pools or lakes. In some areas breeds inland on fallow land or sandy heaths and on rivers or lakes with pebbly margins. It leaves inland sites after breeding and then has a more normal coastal distribution, feeding on sandy or muddy shores. On passage it also visits inland sewage farms and reservoirs.

Distribution. The nominate form breeds from north-eastern Canada, Greenland, Iceland, Spitsbergen and the Faeroes to the British Isles and the coasts of western Europe, also breeding inland in Norway, Sweden, Finland and Poland, and in small numbers on the north-western coast of France, rarely Spain. The more northern *C.h.tundrae*, which averages slightly smaller and darker, breeds on the coasts and tundras of Russia and Siberia. Map 11.

Movements. Largely migratory, although some British birds are resident. Most northerly populations winter furthest south. Birds breeding in extreme north-eastern Canada and Greenland winter in the Old World – some visiting Iceland, the majority passing through Britain and Ireland (mainly mid-August to mid-September and last half of May). Some autumn movement from Greenland also reaches the western coast of Norway. These birds probably moult after reaching coastal Morocco and Mauritania, before passing on to winter further south in West Africa. Young Icelandic birds have been recorded on passage in France, Iberia and Morocco, and heavy passage through western Britain in April–May are probably Icelandic birds (normally arrive back in early May) returning from wintering areas, probably including West Africa. British-bred birds are resident, or short-distance migrants, some breeding on North Sea coasts – wintering on the Irish Sea or English Channel, others moving to Ireland, France or Northern Spain. Birds return to breeding areas February–May, but mainly March–April. Birds breeding on the coasts of Scandinavia, the Baltic and from East and West Germany south-westwards move widely to wintering areas extending from the British Isles to West Africa. More northern and eastern European birds cross the Continent to winter in the Mediterranean basin and on the Atlantic coasts. The northern *tundrae* populations of Russia also have extensive overland journeys through Siberia and Europe – probably the longest of all – wintering in eastern and southern Africa. Breeding areas reoccupied mainly during the second half of May and June, having similar schedule to Greenland birds.

Feeding. Feeds almost entirely on animal matter, including a diverse array of molluscs, crustaceans, insects, annelids and other invertebrates. It feeds in a stop-run-peck manner, typical of most plovers. It frequently uses foot-trembling movements during pauses between pecking, probably causing prey to rise to the surface.

Social and breeding behaviour. Nesting territories established in March (England) and breeding pairs are highly territorial. Behaviour quite similar to that of Little Ringed Plover, including hunched display during low-intensity skirmishes on ground – tail often fanned and sometimes tilted at adversary when threatening laterally. Aggressive behaviour patterns similar to other 'ringed' plovers, emphasising facial pattern and breast band. The territorial advertisement 'butterfly flight' is performed by the male, three to 10 metres above the ground – mainly after the establishment of a pair-bond and territory. Nest and scraping behaviour similar to Little Ringed Plover, where female approaching nest enters it by moving under tail of scraping bird. The displaying male approaches the female in much the same way as described for the Little Ringed Plover, shifting from his low and horizontal attitude to a progressively more erect and intimidating one, and 'goose-stepping'. The male grasps the nape of the female while mounted and copulation lasts 15–20 seconds. The species has a typical monogamous mating system.

   More gregarious than Little Ringed Plover, although parties of 20–30 are commoner than very large flocks. Except when in territory, typically feeds, moves and roosts in flocks.

Nest, eggs and young. Nest, shallow scrape lined with tiny pebbles and débris, or unlined depression in sand, never far from water. Eggs 3–4, variably marked – buff or stone with spots and black blotches, and some grey spots. Two, sometimes three, broods – except in northern areas, where one. Incubation period 23–25 days, by both sexes. Fledging period about 24 days, young cared for by both. Breeds in first year.

SEMIPALMATED PLOVER   *Charadrius semipalmatus*

Du – Amerikaanse Bontbekplevier   Fr – Gravelot semipalmé
Ge – Ringregenpfeifer   Sp – Chorlitejo semipalmeado
Sw – Amerikansk strandpipare

Identification. Length 6¼–7in. Nearctic counterpart of similarly marked Ring Plover, but careful comparison shows it to be somewhat smaller, less robust, less attenuated at rear of body and appearing noticeably shorter-tailed in flight, with less striking wing-bar, which is narrower and shorter. Has a smaller rounded head and pattern also differs, with white marks behind and below eye reduced, or not visible. The black chest-band and white collar are also thinner. The immature has a more hooded appearance (supercilia more obscure) and at rest shows more contrast between paler wing-coverts and mantle.

The bill is stubbier, looking shorter and more swollen, with slightly less orange at the base of the black bill. The slightly paler flesh-to-orange legs have small webs between the toes, particularly outer and middle toes, more evident at close range. Voice quite distinct from Ringed Plover's – a plaintive, repeated '*che-wee*' and a piping '*chip-chip*' in anxiety.

Voice. Distinct from Ringed Plover's, with usual flight and alarm calls more reedy – lacking fluting quality of latter. In summer, familiar call a plaintive '*che-wit*' or '*ke-ruck*'. Other calls include '*tu-whee*' and a soft, whistled '*tyoo-eep*' and rougher '*keup*' notes which may be given in a rapid series when nervous.

Habitat. Similar to Ringed Plover, and found on both fresh and salt mudflats, beaches, margins of lakes, rivers and lagoons and in the breeding season on sparsely vegetated low gravel ridges, gravelly plains and dunes. Breeds extensively inland in Canada.

Distribution. Breeds in Alaska and northern Canada east to Victoria, Southampton and South Baffin Island (where it locally overlaps with Ringed Plover), south to Nova Scotia, James Bay, Great Slave Lake and British Columbia. Winters on Atlantic coast from south Carolina to Patagonia, and on various islands such as the West Indies; on Pacific coast from about San Francisco to Chile. Accidental Azores (adult, September 1972); Scilly Isles, Britain (1) (juvenile, October–November 1978).

Movements. Adults depart from Canadian breeding areas from early July, and the species is a common migrant through most of southern Canada, although it is more numerous in the maritime provinces in the autumn than in spring. It is probable that some birds make a long sea-crossing of the western Atlantic from the Canadian maritimes to the Lesser Antilles and north-eastern South America (where arrivals noted from September to early November). In the U.S.A. peak numbers occur in the autumn from late July to mid-September and return passage is from April, with a peak in the second and third weeks of May. Southern breeding areas are reoccupied by the end of May, and during the first ten days of June further north.

Feeding. Foods and foraging methods similar to Ringed Plover. the ecological significance, if any, of their differences in foot palmation is not known.

Social and breeding behaviour. Pair-forming behaviour on breeding grounds very similar to Ringed Plover, and where the two species overlap, they occasionally form mixed breeding pairs. There are fairly elaborate displays, both terrestrial and aerial. The male performs a buoyant, slow, butterfly-like flight, as in Ringed Plover, giving a more chattering '*too-wat-wat-watwatwat*', increasing in tempo, and sometimes altering to a prolonged, even liquid, trill. Outside the breeding season occurs in flocks of 40 or less, commonly associating with other shorebirds. On the mud runs rapidly, stops abruptly and, if alarmed, bobs head.

Nest, eggs and young. Apparently semi-colonial. The nest is a slight hollow, sometimes with small pieces of débris added. Eggs 4, ground colour usually buff, overlaid with spots, streaks and blotches of blackish-brown. Incubation period 23 days, by both sexes. Fledging period probably between 22 and 31 days.

KILLDEER   *Charadrius vociferus*

Du – Killdeerplevier   Fr – Pluvier vocifer
Ge – Keilschwanzregenpfeifer   Sp – Chorlitejo culirroja
Sw – Skrikstrandpipare

Pl. 4

Identification. Length 9–10in. Distinguished from all other ringed plovers by larger size, longer black bill, double black breast-bands (in all plumages) and long, wedge-shaped tail with black-and-white surround and obvious rufous rump. In flight reveals a broad and long white wing-bar. Flight free, rapid and often erratic, with classical '*kill-dee*' calls uttered either on ground or in flight. Legs dull yellowish to flesh, orbital ring red. Sexes similar. The juvenile resembles the adult but shows fewer black marks on the face and has an incomplete upper chest-ring and yellowish-grey legs.

Voice. '*Killdeer*' or '*kill-dee*', '*dee-dee-dee*' calls, short '*deet*' and '*kill-er-dree-eet*' – and many variants.

Habitat. Frequents meadows and dry uplands, arable and cultivated land; also on golf courses, airports and similar areas of open turf, often near water. During the winter more closely associated with water and found along beaches, watercourses and mudflats, as well as in open fields.

Distribution. *C.v.vociferus* breeds in North America from Canada south to central Mexico. Other races occur in the West Indies and in coastal Peru and northern Chile. Accidental in Iceland, the Faeroes, Norway, the British Isles (42), France, Switzerland and the Azores.

Movements. Nominate *vociferus*, which breeds in North America to central Mexico, is migratory in the northern half of its range. On migration it occurs commonly near the Atlantic seaboard, and also has extensive broad-front passage overland through U.S.A. in spring and autumn. Autumn passage through U.S.A. begins in early July, but is drawn out, continuing into November or even December. The bird is one of the earliest returning spring waders, with movements begining in the south in February, and the more temperate areas of its breeding range reoccupied in March or early April. Winters from British Columbia, Colorado, Ohio valley and Long Island (New York) southwards through the West Indies and central America to Colombia and western Ecuador. Also regular on passage and in winter on Bermuda.

Feeding. Foraging is done in the usual plover manner of quickly running forward, stopping and suddenly seizing a prey object from the surface, rather than probing for food. The Killdeer's large eyes also enable it to feed actively at dusk. Beetles and other mostly terrestrial insects make up the bulk of its diet, with a variety of other invertebrates forming the remainder.

Social and breeding behaviour. Apparently little pair formation occurs before the birds arrive in their breeding quarters. Territorial advertisement consists of the bird's standing in a conspicuous spot and calling loudly '*di-yeet*' every few seconds. Periodically the bird makes runs or short flights, or high, circling flights giving the highly variable '*kill-deer*' calls. Often these flights are marked by slow, deep wing-beats, and are usually performed by males. On the ground the birds perform nest-scraping displays, with trilling calls combined with the lowering of the body. During pair formation the male digs a succession of scrapes, in the last of which the eggs are laid. The species has a monogamous mating system and double-brooding is apparently common over much of the breeding range. Outside breeding season only semi-gregarious, ranging from single birds to loose flocks of up to 50 birds.

Nest, eggs and young. A shallow scrape, unlined, or lined with nearby material – small pebbles or plant fragments. Eggs, 4 (3–5), creamy-buff, heavily marked with spots and scrawls of blackish-brown. Incubation period 24 days, by both sexes. Young leave nest shortly after hatching and begin to forage for themselves, guarded by the adults, flying at about 40 days.

KITTLITZ'S PLOVER   *Charadrius pecuarius*

Du – Herdersplevier   Fr – Gravelot pâtre
Ge – Hirtenregenpfeifer   Sp – Chorlitejo de Kittlitz
Sw – Kittlitzpipare

Pl. 4

Identification. Length 4¾–5½in. Small, neat and compact plover, distinctly smaller than Kentish Plover, with banded head pattern similar to other ringed plovers, but lacking black breast-band or lateral patches. A black line extending from the eye runs down the side of the neck, differing from all its congeners, and the head and upper-parts show more unusual feathering where feathers tipped sandy or pale sandy-rufous. Wing-coverts and tertials also strongly patterned, lacking uniformity of ring plovers, and also showing a dark shoulder patch. Chin and throat white, contrasting with orange-buff under-parts. In flight shows an ill-defined wing-bar and the black-centred tail is broadly tipped and edged white. The juvenile lacks any distinct dark facial markings, although has pale supercilium. Bill black, legs grey-green.

Voice. In flight gives a plaintive '*tee-peep*' or '*trit-tritritritrit*', and '*chrit*' or '*prit*' in alarm.

Habitat. Favours dry sandy or stony soil with sparse growth of grass. Less attracted to coasts than Ringed and Kentish Plovers, although visits sandy foreshores and mudflats. Often near margins of lakes, reservoirs and small pools or salt pans, also on sand banks and along sandy river beds.

Distribution. In W. Palaearctic restricted to Egypt, where reported fairly common. Vagrant to Eilat Oct./Nov. 1986. Map **12**.

Movements. Resident in breeding areas in Egypt. In Afrotropical region reported as locally making seasonal movements of undetermined nature.

Feeding. Its food is the usual array of insects and their larvae, crustaceans and molluscs taken in typical plover-like action. Foot-trembling and then lunging forward to catch prey recorded.

Social and breeding behaviour. Pairing takes place commonly in groups of birds, three to four weeks before territories are occupied, when flocks are more compact than usual at this period. Birds dash about with feathers fluffed out, making buzzing sounds and chasing each other, both on the ground or in the air. The pattern of the mating ceremony is typical of the better known *Charadrius* plovers, i.e. the male approaches the female from behind and performs the usual marking-time foot movements and upright posturing prior to copulation. The species has a monogamous mating system. Flocking in the non-breeding season is regular, the birds often foraging in small flocks, and occasionally associating with other wintering waders – e.g. Little Stints, Curlew Sandpipers and Lesser and Greater Sand Plovers.

Nest, eggs and young. Nesting pairs may be solitary or in loose groups, sometimes nesting fairly close together, but more normally at least 20m apart. Nest is a shallow scrape on open, usually bare, ground and lined with available material. Eggs 2, sometimes 1 – creamy-buff more or less obscured by fine sepia lines and heavier black streaks. Incubation period 23–26 days, by both sexes. Fledging period about 25 days. Some birds breed in first year.

KENTISH PLOVER   *Charadrius alexandrinus*

Du – Strandplevier   Fr – Gravelot à collier interrompu
Ge – Seeregenpfeifer   Sp – Chorlitejo patinegro
Sw – Svartbent strandpipare

Pl. 4

Identification. Length 6–6¾in. Smaller than Ringed Plover, more compact appearance and snowy-white breast and under-parts combine to give 'snowball' appearance on fast-running legs. Plumage differs from Ringed Plover in having paler upper-parts, blackish legs and bill, and the black markings are less extensive and fainter. The pectoral band is reduced to a vestigial blackish or dusky patch on the sides of the breast and the black is limited to a bar on the forecrown (not reaching eyes). Male in summer has crown more rufous than back. Female has no dark mark on forehead and the breast patches and band through the eyes are dusky-brown. In winter both sexes become duller, male losing rufous crown and jet-black head markings and female showing even fainter head and chest markings. The juvenile is paler, with scaled upper-parts and mottled breast patches. Juveniles of Ringed and Little Ringed Plovers require to be separated, and although both have paler legs, they may appear darker when coated with mud. Distinctive call of Kentish readily separable from other two, an emphatic but quiet '*whit*', also '*chirr*'. In flight shows a narrow white wing-bar and pure white sides to tail-coverts contrast most obviously with brown rump and tail centre than in Ringed or Little Ringed Plovers.

Voice. Frequently repeated '*whit*' or '*whit-whit*' notes are given in flight and on the ground. Calls intermingle in flying flocks, sounding like '*pittittittittit*'. Other notes recorded include a hard '*prrr*' and '*tweet*' or '*hooeet*' in excitement; also '*kittup*' and purring '*trrr-trrr-trrr*'. Main threat call (song rattle) is a metallic '*dwee-dwee-dweedweedwee*'. In song flight male gives a loud, sharp, rhythmical '*TJEKke-TJEKke*' – alternating with song rattle.

Habitat. In breeding season frequents shingly and sandy beaches or flats primarily along sea coasts, but it is also found far inland by lakes, lagoons depressions and saline sites. Prefers smooth surfaces of sand, silt or dry mud, avoiding windy, exposed coasts.

Distribution. Nominate *alexandrinus* breeds on European coasts south of southern Scandinavia to the Mediterranean, also in northern Africa, south to Mauritania, the Gulf of Aden, Socotra and western India, east to south-east Transbaikalia (USSR) and Inner Mongolia. Also breeds inland in some areas of Austria, Hungary, Spain, Turkey and the Middle East. Other races occur in China and Japan, and in North and South America. Winters regularly from southern Iberia, southern France and Italy to Greece, Turkey and central Iraq. Also winters coastally further south to Gulf of Guinea in West Africa, Somalia, southern Arabia, southern Iran, India etc. Smaller numbers winter inland in northern tropics, i.e. lakes of northern Nigeria and Chad, the Nile Valley in the Sudan, and Eritrea. In Britain a few pairs bred in the south-east up to 1956, and a pair bred in Lincolnshire in 1979; scarce migrant (mainly east coast), April–May and August–October. Map **13**.

Movements. The western race, nominate *alexandrinus*, is mainly migratory north of a line running from about central Spain to northern Greece. Further south it is dispersive, or perhaps resident locally, i.e. in North Africa and Arabia. Dispersal from breeding areas starts in late June. North-west European adults moult in late summer around the Waddenzee and southern North Sea. Birds begin to move in August, but mostly in early

September, appearing on passage in Morocco in September, and largest numbers reported in October, further south on the Banc d'Arquin, Mauritania. In the Near East movements also occur through the area in September, although large numbers winter north in Turkey etc. Breeding areas in north-west Africa are reoccupied in late February, though spring passage in Europe, and probably also in Russia, is mainly during March–April, falling off in May.

Feeding. Feeds by typical plover run-and-peck method of visual foraging, also indulging in 'pattering' or foot-trembling, encouraging prey to move and thus reveal itself. Also probes in wet sand or mud. Food chiefly insects and their larvae, flies, caddisflies, earwigs, ants etc. and various invertebrates. In coastal areas mainly polychaete worms, crustaceans and molluscs.

Social and breeding behaviour. Pair formation normally occurs after the birds have returned to breeding areas. Territories are established by the male and are advertised in 'butterfly flights' similar to Little Ringed Plover, but performed less frequently. Once paired, both participate in territorial defence, often driving off larger birds than themselves. The male selects the nest-scrape, and the nest-scrape ceremony is probably an important pair-forming and pre-copulatory display, as the latter is restricted to the vicinity of the scrape. As the female approaches a scraping male he typically steps out of the scrape, side on to her, near wing closed and far wing held out slightly and pointed upwards, while tail raised and fanned open and closed rhythmically. The female enters the scrape mostly in front of the male's breast and not under the tail as in Ringed and Little Ringed Plovers. The mating ceremony usually follows when the female leaves the scrape, standing with back to male. The male approaches with progressively shortening steps – but 'goose-stepping' movements not so high or exaggerated as in Ringed or Little Ringed Plovers. If the female is receptive she raises her tail, displaying the white-bordered cloaca, after which the male mounts. A monogamous mating system is the rule, although sequential polyandry has occurred (where the female who hatched a clutch changed mates before re-nesting). Gregarious outside the breeding season, but flocks seldom large.

Nest, eggs and young. May nest solitary, but more normally in semi-colonial clumps, where most nests 20m or more apart, though in many cases only 2–5m. Nest is a shallow scrape, either lined or unlined with shell fragments or small pebbles. Eggs, 3 (2–4), creamy-buff and spotted with black-and-grey markings. Incubation period 24–27 days, initially by both sexes. Fledging period, between 27 and 31 days. Age of first breeding, one to two years or older.

LESSER SAND PLOVER   *Charadrius mongolus*

Du – Mongoolse Plevier   Fr – Gravelot de Mongolie
Ge – Mongolenregenpfeifer Sp – Chorlitejo mongol chico
Sw – Mongolpipare

Pl. 5

Identification. Length 7–8¼in. Only marginally larger than Ringed Plover with similar body size, but has relatively longer blackish legs, shorter tail and all-black bill. Whilst distinctive enough in summer plumage, with broad, bright, rufous-cinnamon breast-band, black facial mask and forehead (western *atrifrons* group), in winter adults and juveniles are drab brown and white. The Greater Sand Plover in winter is similarly plumaged, so that both require to be separated with care. However, the Lesser is the smaller of the two, with proportionally smaller and less bulbous bill, which is closer to or only slightly longer than a Kentish Plover's in length, although obviously more robust. It is also shorter legged, lacking the more stilt-like appearance of its cousin. Both show white wing-bars in flight, both have black bills, but the legs of the Lesser are generally darker, lead-grey to blackish, although there may be some overlap. Flight call is a short, clear '*trik*' or '*chitik*', distinct from Greater's louder and longer '*treeep*' or more trilling call.

Voice. Commonest call in flight a short, clear '*trik*' or '*drrit*', also a soft '*tikit*' and dry trills. Territorial males call in flight as well as on the ground with a melodious '*kruit-kruit*' repeated, and in song flight utter a two-syllabled '*tekr-ryuk*'.

Habitat. In the breeding season primarily an alpine species, that inhabits mountain steppes and deserts, sometimes occurring on alpine tundra at 4–5000m, or 5,500m in Tibet. However, the eastern race *stegmanni* also breeds on sandy dunes near the sea in the Commander Islands. Wintering habitats are mostly tidal sands and mudflats associated with bays, inlets and estuaries.

Distribution. Central Asian populations, ranges as follows: Western race, *C.m. pamirensis*, breeds northern and western parts of Central Asian mountain ranges – winters in western India, Pakistan, Arabian Sea, Persian Gulf, Seychelles and East Africa south to Cape Province and Namibia. Himalayan race, *C.m. atrifrons*, winters from Pakistan, Indian subcontinent and Bay of Bengal to Sumatra. Western Chinese race, *C.m.schaeferi*, winters in Gulf of Siam, Malaysia and western Indonesia. In western Palaearctic (some racial mixing occurs in Indian Ocean winter quarters) – regular on passage in Kuwait and Persian Gulf, with flocks of up to 5,000 on Masirah Island, Oman. Accidental in Norway, Austria, Russia, Turkey, Syria and Israel.

Movements. In Russia, western race *pamirensis* begins to form flocks in early July, departing in early August–early September and arriving very shortly (probably by unbroken flight) in their winter quarters from early to mid-August, with numbers increasing to mid-September. Main departure from wintering grounds is in the first half of April and northern breeding areas are reoccupied in mid-April to early May. East Siberian birds (races *mongolus* and *stegmanni*) depart from breeding areas August–early September, and migrate coastally through the Sea of Okhotsk and the Soviet maritime territories. Large numbers also pass overland through Transbaikalia and Manchuria. These eastern birds winter from south-eastern China to Australia. Breeding areas are reoccupied from late May to early June.

Feeding. Terrestrial insects appear to be the primary summer foods, but wintering birds are reported to eat small molluscs, amphipods, small crabs and marine worms. Runs quickly in short spurts, bending forward to pick up prey.

Social and breeding behaviour. Social behaviour has been little studied. Courtship begins with the arrival of the birds on their breeding grounds and lasts until about mid-June. Males perform a territorial flight, flying in broad circles at great heights on rapid wing-beats, or performing slower, more gull-like flights. Birds are highly territorial, with little or no tendency to form colonies, although in Pamirs colonies of 3–10 birds have been reported. Forms flocks on migration, often mixing with Greater Sand Plovers and other shore birds in winter quarters.

Nest, eggs and young. Nest is a shallow scrape or hollow, lined with dried stems and leaves, or frequently with fragments of dried cow dung. Eggs 3, creamy-buff, peppered with small brown or grey spots. Incubation period 22–24 days. Fledging period 30–35 days.

GREATER SAND PLOVER   *Charadrius leschenaultii*

Du – Woestijnplevier   Fr – Gravelot de Leschenault
Ge – Wüstenregenpfeifer   Sp – Chorlitejo mongol
Sw – Ökenpipare

Pl. 5

Identification. Length 8½–9½in. Stands taller and is larger bodied, longer legged (shows a greater extent of bare tibia) and has a proportionally longer, more robust bill (appears more dagger-shaped), than the Lesser Sand Plover. Allowing for individual variation, the Greater's bill is longer than the distance from the base of the bill to the rear of the eye, whereas that of the Lesser is about the same length. However, the western race *columbinus* has a short and slender bill, with less bulbous tip, so that shape of bill resembles that of the western *atrifrons* group of Lesser Sand Plover and may cause some confusion where identification is based on bill shape only. The plumage (all ages) is very similar to that of the Lesser, but the upper-parts are rather paler. This may be of limited value in the field, as both sand plovers tend to become paler in winter through abrasion and sun-bleaching, causing some individuals to show strikingly paler upper-parts than normal. The male's breeding plumage pattern is like the Lesser's, but it has more white on the forehead, the black patch through the eye and the rufous breast-band are narrower, the latter more restricted and paler. In winter the male becomes pale drab brown above and strikingly white below, with grey-brown lateral breast patches. Unlike the Lesser Sand Plover, the female Greater lacks a distinctive breeding plumage, or at the most may resemble a dull breeding male. In flight the Greater generally shows a more prominent and extensive white wing-bar, with more white on the sides and tips of the tail; the feet extend further and the upper tail-coverts are mottled paler grey and white, contrasting with the more uniform dun-brown rump. Both call differently: the Greater utters a trill-like '*treeep*' three or four times, while the Lesser typically calls '*chitik*', which is more like a softer version of a Turnstone's call. Leg colour may be yellow-grey, olive-grey or leaden grey, so that it is not safe to identify a lone sand plover by leg colour alone.

Voice. Flight calls similar to Lesser Sand Plover, but it trills louder and longer, with rippling '*treep*' or '*trrrt*' or '*drrit*'. Trilling becomes longer and louder in disputing winter birds – '*drri-drrii-drrii-drri*', or rattling '*triiiii-ou*', and also a loud 'tittering'. It may also give a *phylloscopus*-like '*hooit-hooit*' etc. in anxiety, or a harsher single '*tirrip*' or '*irrp*' – which may be repeated with increasing intensity in great excitement. Male utters a rather Golden Plover-like '*pipruirr-pipruirr-pipruirr*' in display flight.

Habitat. In breeding season found only in open, flat, uncultivated and treeless areas, where surface consists of dried mud, silt, clay, saltpan or other arid soils interspersed with stony ridges or sparse desert growth of salt-tolerant shrubby vegetation. Outside the breeding season it is almost entirely a shorebird.

Distribution. Breeds from Armenia, west through Transcaspia and Russian Turkestan to the steppes east of the Aral Sea. Also breeds in the steppes of the south-eastern Russian Altai, and in Mongolia east to 111°E. Winters from the Persian Gulf east to the Indo-Chinese countries, Taiwan and the Philippines, south to southern Africa and Australia. In the western Palaearctic the small-billed western population *columbinus* breeds from the western Caspian to Turkey, Syria and Jordan, and winters mainly on the Red Sea and the Gulf of Aden. Accidental in a number of European countries, including the British Isles (7). Map **14**.

Movements. Mainly migratory, and wide-front autumnal movements occur overland across southern and south-west Asia. The few inland sightings suggest that flocks fly non-stop between breeding areas and winter quarters, as in Lesser Sand Plover. Post-breeding flocks gather from mid-July to early August, eventually migrating. In early August the first adults arrive in Pakistan and India. Peak movements occur in the southern Caspian in the second half of August, and in Turkey, continuing till late September. First arrivals in Africa occur in August, with numbers increasing in September–October. Return movements are early, with birds arriving in late February and early March in Iraq, Syria, Turkey and Afghanistan. Passage through the southern Caspian occurs mainly in the first half of April, and departures from East Africa continue well into April. Breeding grounds are reoccupied by the first half of May.

Feeding. Feeds singly, or in loose flocks that are often well scattered over mud, in typical *Charadrius* stop-run-peck movements. Takes mainly insects, especially beetles, also ants, larvae of flies, crustaceans and worms. In winter quarters insects, small crustaceans and marine worms.

Social and breeding behaviour. Knowledge of the bird's social behaviour is incomplete, but it seems that breeding probably occurs in the second year, with first-year birds summering on their wintering grounds. Pairs are formed before arrival on their breeding grounds, or soon after. The birds are territorial and the male performs a song-flight, circling 30–50m above the ground. The territorial song is given as the bird flies on slow, owl-like wing-beats, which alternate with more rapid wing-beats, and renewed ascent. Breeding pairs are separated some 150–200m, with few colonial tendencies. Courtship of the female by the male may involve running towards her, lowering front part of body, then assuming erect posture with stiff neck and breast thrust out – parading slowly with typical high-stepping gait, recalling pre-copulatory behaviour of other ringed plover types. Copulation not observed. The species has a monogamous mating system. Gregarious for most of the year, typically in flocks outside the breeding season.

Nest, eggs and young. Nest a shallow scrape on open ground or in low vegetation, with variable amounts of lining – fragments of vegetation and twigs. Eggs 3 (2–4), dark brownish-yellow with olive tinge, evenly marked with small black spots, coarser at larger end. Incubation period at least 24 days, by both parents. Fledging period not known. Age of first breeding, probably two years.

CASPIAN PLOVER *Charadrius asiaticus*

Du – Kaspische Plevier   Fr – Gravelot asiatique
Ge – Wermutregenpfeifer   Sp – Chorlitejo asiático
Sw – Kaspisk pipare

Pl. 5

Identification. Length 7½–8in. The Caspian Plover resembles both sand plovers, but on the ground it is much more slender and attenuated, with more upright carriage and long-legged appearance which, combined with the large eye, give it the look of a Golden Plover or small *Vanellus* plover. Its black bill is smaller in proportion to its head, less robust-looking towards the tip, lacking the more bulbous bills of either the Golden

Plover or the Greater Sand Plover. In summer plumage the adult male has a white forehead, lores and supercilium, chin and throat. The crown, ear-coverts and entire upper-parts are sandy brown. Below the white throat is a deep rusty-rufous breast-band, terminated posteriorly by a narrow black band, with the rest of the under-parts white. The female resembles the male, but chest-band is mostly grey-brown and black lower border indistinct or absent. In winter plumage the bird has a dusky wash right across its breast, unlike both sand plovers, whose chest-patch is neatly defined, and also has a more scaled back pattern. In flight a short, whitish wing-bar is centred on the inner primaries, while broad, rather short and square tail is fringed white, and toes project beyond tail-tip. Underwing dirty white with brownish axillaries.

Juveniles have extensive pinkish-buff fringes to the feathers of the upper-parts, creating beautiful scaled pattern like Dotterel. The breast-band varies from buffy to greyish-brown, and the legs may be more yellowish than those of the adults, which are yellow-brown to olive-grey or dull green. In contrast to the sand plovers, in winter it seeks inland areas (see Habitat) and may then require to be separated from Dotterel. The latter, however, is more compact in flight, with broader body and rump and relatively short wings, and on the ground its mottled, dusky upper chest is divided by a white line, from the faintly streaked dusky fore-belly and flanks.

Voice. In flight, a sharp, whistled '*ku-wit*', '*kwhitt*', also a piping '*klink*', give a far-carrying twittering sound. Song-flight call of male is a sharp, whistling '*zzheeoo-zzheeoo-zzheeoo*', and either same or another variant – a melodious '*tyurlee-tyurlee-tyurlee-tyurlee*'.

Habitat. Breeds on dry steppes and semi-deserts of Central Asia and, unlike the two sand plovers (which overlap in range and breeding habitats), it is not associated with coastal habitats on its wintering grounds, being found on arid inland plains that are dominated by grasses, and especially where recently burnt.

Distribution. Breeds from the region north of the Caucasus and the southern Volga-Ural steppes, eastwards to the Aral Sea and the vicinity of Lake Balkash. Winters in East Africa south to Namibia. Forms a superspecies with the Oriental Plover *C.veredus*, which breeds in Mongolia, Transbaikalia and Manchuria, and which is sometimes regarded as conspecific. Accidental in Britain May 1890, France, West Germany, Norway, Italy, Malta, Bulgaria, Rumania and the Middle East. Map **15**.

Movements. After breeding, flocks form and wander over steppes before finally migrating in August. The main movement is south-west across western Iran, Iraq and Arabia, then across the Red Sea on a broad front (Sudan–Somalia) to winter in East Africa, generally arriving in the last half of August, with main arrivals in September–October, and fewer in November. Large numbers migrate through Iraq in autumn (mid-August to October) and the species is even more apparent in spring (late March to early May), with the birds breaking their flight there between their breeding grounds and winter quarters in Africa. Within Africa there is a general trend southwards, the birds moving to take advantage of local dry seasons, and with the most southerly wintering areas not being occupied until mid-December, or even late February. Return movements start in late February in eastern and southern Africa, with the main departure in late March and early April. Spring migration rapid, as despite stops in Middle East, the foremost birds reach their southern breeding areas in early to mid-April.

Feeding. Feeds in typical *Charadrius* stop-run-peck manner, primarily feeding on insects and their larvae, occasionally plant material and seeds. In winter also chiefly insects, especially beetles, termites and grasshoppers.

Social and breeding behaviour. Pairs may nest singly, but tend to breed in loose colonies of up to 10–25 pairs in favourable areas. In the male's display flight he rises steeply to 50–60m, then circling on descent, uttering characteristic call, or performing swooping, diving flights with erratic turns and also calling. Flights most intense during egg-laying period or warmer weather, and are performed most at sunset, occasionally on moonlit nights. After song flight the male was seen to approach and run round the female with fluffed plumage. A group-display, involving about 20 birds, has been observed on the breeding grounds, but details of pair-forming and copulatory behaviour have been little studied. Monogamous pair-bond reported. Gregarious even in breeding season. In winter nomadic, in flocks of 20–100 birds, often tame, and also remain in flocks several weeks after return to breeding grounds.

Nest, eggs and young. Nests solitarily or in loose groups. Nest, shallow scrape on ground in open or among low vegetation. Eggs 3, pale ochre, tinged olive-green with many black and grey spots and blotches. Incubation and fledging periods not known. Young cared for by both parents. Probably breeds in second year.

DOTTEREL   *Charadrius morinellus*

Du – Morinelplevier   Fr – Pluvier guignard
Ge – Mornellregenpfeifer   Sp – Chorlito carambolo
Sw – Fjällpipare

Pl. 5

Identification. Length 8½–9in. Breeding adult unmistakable, but winter and juvenile can be confused with Caspian Plover (see that species). Breeding plumage pattern distinctive (female brighter than male), with elongated blackish-brown crown contrasting with long white supercilia meeting in a V on the nape, and lower flanks and belly deep rufous, becoming black in the centre and rear of the belly, with conspicuous white vent. A narrow blackish line and white bar separate the pink-grey breast-band. The face, sides of neck, chin and throat are white. Legs dull yellow. Winter adults are much drabber, with only the pattern of the breeding dress faintly retained on the head and lower chest. Juveniles have a more distinctive pattern than the adult, with a darker brown crown and back, and broad golden-buff fringes to the feathers. The more strongly marked brownish-buff chest is also crossed by an indistinct whitish line. The flight is strong and rapid, on quick wing-beats, showing a dark belly in summer but a dark chest in autumn and winter. The wings lack any kind of wing-bar, unlike Golden Plover, and the tail is bordered white, with a dark sub-terminal band.

Voice. Usual call in flight is a sweet, trilling twitter, not carrying very far, and a soft, penetrating '*pweet-pweet-pweet*', also heard in flying parties. The take-off call is a trilling and clear-ringing, repeated '*pyurrr*', and '*tititititi*', also given by low-flying courting parties. A soft, tinkling, rising '*wit-wit-wit wita-wita-wita-wee*' in alarm, and a sharp '*ting*' in excitement. Couples give a soft '*peep-peep*' in breeding season. The song-flight call of the female is a quick rhythmical '*peep*' or '*pit*'. Scraping male calls '*pu-pu-pu*'.

Habitat. Typically associated with northern tundra, heaths and sparsely vegetated barrens, particularly where there is a combination of mossy vegetation and scattered boulders, not far from the tree line. Although northerly in distribution, it is perhaps more a mountain species, although since the 1960's it has been found breeding on the rich soil of the new polders of Ijsselmeer (Netherlands) four metres below sea-level. In winter it frequents open arid areas and semi-desert, including barren plateaux. In spring, or after breeding, small flocks or 'trips' make halts on passage on barren areas on or near the coast, heathlands or ploughed fields.

Distribution. Breeds from the Scottish Highlands and Scandinavia, east through northern Russia to the Kola and Kanin peninsulas, the Urals, the Taimyr peninsula, east to eastern Siberia in the Chukotski peninsula, and the estuary of the Anadyr. Also in southern Siberia, north-western Mongolia and the Russian Altai. Sporadically breeds in the mountains of central Europe and Italy, and probably also in Alaska. Winters from north-western Africa and the Mediterranean basin (a few winter in Spain), east to Iraq and the Persian Gulf. Map **16**.

Movements. Migratory. The main departure from breeding grounds in the Scottish Highlands is in the first half of August, although a few young birds may linger till the end of the month. In Siberia females may leave from mid-July, with the males and juveniles following in early August. Autumn passage in western Europe lasts from mid-August until late September, a few lingering until October. In Russia many stop to moult around the north Caspian, and the autumn exodus continues into October or early November. Birds arrive in their winter quarters in the Middle East and North Africa from September. In spring, passage through western Europe is mainly from mid-April to mid-May, with a tendency to few stopping places, although there are traditional halting sites, which are used for around one to three days each year. Return to breeding grounds in Scotland is from early May, in southern Scandinavia, mid- to late May, and in Lapland and Russia, late May to mid-June.

Feeding. Feeds mainly on insects and spiders, occasionally molluscs, earthworms and plant material, including berries. Most food taken from the ground, probing and pushing the bill into moss for cranefly larvae, or picking beetles or spiders from between stones.

Social and breeding behaviour. The roles in courtship are reversed, and the care of the eggs and young is done exclusively by the male. Shortly after arrival on the breeding grounds the female starts calling and displaying, typically from a newly snow-free ridge. She will pursue the male with much wing-raising in order to try to isolate him from the other birds, and she may also squat and perform nest-scraping behaviour. Often a newly formed pair will perform a rapid display flight with synchronised turns, or fly with slow wing-beats, similar to the display flight of the Ringed Plover, sometimes with legs dangling. Mating occurs usually near the nest scrape, and is preceded by the female squatting and upending her tail in a rather submissive display. Pair-bonds probably last until the clutch is completed and the male begins to incubate. Afterwards females leave and form unisex groups that roam about foraging. The Dotterel is normally monogamous, although in a few instances polyandry has been reported, and may be not uncommon locally. Often gregarious; outside breeding season usually in small groups, or 'trips' of three to six, or up to 20 birds. Well known for its tame disposition.

Nest, eggs and young. Nest is a shallow scrape in short vegetation, or on bare gravel or soil, often in a small hollow, and lined with moss or lichen. Nests may be solitary, or loosely grouped, occasionally within 100m of each other. Eggs 3, buff tinged olive-green, or brown heavily marked blackish or red-brown. Incubation period 24–28 days, normally by male, although polyandrous females take greater share of incubation with second clutch and any subsequent ones.

AMERICAN GOLDEN PLOVER   *Pluvialis dominica*

ASIATIC or PACIFIC
GOLDEN PLOVER   *Pluvialis fulva*

Du – Kleine Goudplevier
Fr – Pluvier fauve
Ge – Kleiner Goldregenpfeifer
Sp – Chorlito siberiano
Sw – Tundrapipare

Pl. 6

Until recently these two forms were regarded as races of a single species, i.e. Lesser
Golden Plover, *Pluvialis dominica*, with the Asiatic race *P.d.fulva* represented in
northern Siberia and western Alaska. However, it has recently been demonstrated that
they nest side by side in western Alaska, without interbreeding – thus fulfilling the criteria
for specific separation. In this account these two are considered together, but the
differences between the two species are explained.

Identification. Length $8\frac{1}{2}$–$10\frac{1}{4}$in. Smaller and slimmer than (similarly plumaged)
Golden Plover, with finer bill, less rounded belly, longer legs and larger-headed
appearance, resulting from a slimmer, waisted neck; also narrower wings extending well
beyond the tail at rest. Distinguished in all plumages by dusky or fulvous-grey under-
wing, with smoky-grey axillaries (European Golden has mainly white under-wings).
Adult in summer closely similar to Golden Plover (*P.apricaria*), but shows more black
on the upper- and under-parts, and the under tail-coverts are mostly black and not white,
with flanks usually lacking white borders. Has two well marked forms – in Asia (*fulva*)
and North America (*dominica*), which can often be distinguished in the field. The Asiatic
form (smallest) looks distinctly smaller than Golden Plover, although by virtue of its
longer legs it stands equally as high. The American form is larger, approaching Golden
Plover in size. It is the blackest of the three golden plovers in breeding plumage,
and has a large white oval-shaped patch at the side of the breast. Asiatic birds,
however, especially first-year birds, are closely spangled with yellow, like Golden Plover.
In winter both adults and juveniles show a pronounced supercilium, whitest in American
dominica, which are often very grey, or grey-brown, below, with distinct soft barring
present on the breast of juveniles. Under-parts of Asiatic birds are brighter yellowish-
buff or yellowish-white in juveniles, with limited soft streaking on the breast. In flight
both forms show an indistinct whitish wing-bar, less obvious than shown by Golden
Plover. Bill black, legs dark grey or black. Distinctive call a sharp '*klee-eet*', distinct from
Golden Plover's plaintive '*tlui*'.

Voice. No clear distinction between the calls of either form. Commonest call is a soft
melodious '*quee*', rather similar to Golden Plover's '*puie*'. Also a whistled '*too-loo-ee*'.
Most distinctive note is a sharp '*kloo-it*' or '*chu-wit*' recalling Spotted Redshank. Various
other calls used mainly outside breeding season include '*tu-ee*', '*ki-wee*', '*kleee-yee*' and
'*queedel-ee*'.

Habitat. Breeds mainly on dry tundra, usually uplands, and usually where ground cover
is lichens and mosses. In winter found regularly on short-grass fields and cultivation,
occasionally on the shore.

Distribution. *P.dominica* breeds from northern and central Alaska east to Baffin Island,
and winters in the interior of South America, from Bolivia and southern Brazil to central
Argentina. *P.fulva* breeds in northern Siberia from the Yamal peninsula to the Chukotskiy
peninsula, Anadyr basin, and in western Alaska. Winters chiefly from Pakistan and
south-east Asia to Australia and Polynesia.

Both species have occurred as vagrants in the western Palaearctic under *P.d.dominica* or *P.d.fulva*, i.e. Lesser Golden Plover, but forms not always separated. Accidental in Iceland, several European countries, including the British Isles (112), Cape Verde islands and as far south as South Africa.

Movements. Both species are migratory, travelling great distances between breeding and winter quarters. The American Golden Plover's migration pattern is elliptical, with autumn passage extending from early August to early November, and juveniles leaving after adults. Adults cross Canada and pass through a corridor stretching between west Hudson and James Bay, continuing south-east on a narrow front extending from western New England to Delaware and onwards, on a great circle course to the Lesser Antilles and northern South America. They may stop over for a short period, then continue south to the pampas, birds arriving in Argentina from late August. Some young birds do not follow the adults, but prefer to follow the reverse spring route through the interior. From early February birds begin moving north and fly up through the interior, over Central America and across the Gulf of Mexico, with stopovers in southern Texas, then passing on to reach the upper prairies of Canada about the middle of May – finally reaching various breeding grounds in the third week of May into June.

The Asiatic Golden Plover, breeding in northern Siberia and western Alaska, leaves the tundra in late July-early August and many birds migrate south to south-east into the central Pacific, or others move south to SSW into southern Asia and even the fringes of the Indian Ocean. Also occurs on passage and in winter in Oman and Aden and sparingly in East Africa, and presumably these regions are reached by overland passage across western Siberia. In trans-Pacific migrations, spring departure from southern wintering areas begins in March, with major staging posts in Hawaii in April and the Pribilof Islands in the first half of May, and the tundra finally reoccupied during the first half of June.

Feeding. In breeding season feeds mainly on insects, including beetles, the larvae of lepidopterans and the like. Also small molluscs, crustaceans, spiders, small worms, and berries such as crowberries. Large numbers of terrestrial insects such as grasshoppers, crickets and locusts are eaten by migrating birds.

Social and breeding behaviour. Birds arrive singly, in pairs, or in small parties of up to about six, some of which appear to be already paired on arrival at their breeding grounds. At that time much of the tundra is covered in snow, but males soon start to perform their territorial aerial display flights over the snowy ground. The flight display is performed at 60–90m above the ground, on long circling flights, with slow wing-beats while giving a repeated '*ktoodlee*' call. The bird makes a fast gliding descent, which may also be followed by a rapid climb and continuation of the flight. Territories are quite large, covering up to about half a square kilometre in area. A captive male displayed to his mate with sleeked plumage, body held low, wings closed and tail pointing upwards with neck stretched downwards. A long trill is uttered and the male usually displays in full view of the female, sometimes running in small circles in front of her. From limited studies it appears that copulation is probably independent of nest-scrape ceremonies in this species. At present, analyses of the behaviour of the two species are unavailable – in future these may show important differences.

Gregarious outside the breeding season, often forming sizeable flocks.

Nest, eggs and young. Nests where gravel and lichens cover the ground in relatively dry and high areas. A shallow depression lined with lichens, dry grasses or leaves. Eggs 4 (3–5), buff, heavily marked with spots and small blotches of black, and lighter shades of grey. Incubation period 27–28 days, by both sexes. Young cared for by both and able to fly at about 22 days.

GOLDEN PLOVER   *Pluvialis apricaria*

Du – Goudplevier
Fr – Pluvier doré
Ge – Goldregenpfeifer
Sp – Chorlito dorado commún
Sw – Ljungpipare

Pl. 6

Identification. Length 10–11½in. Distinguished from American and Asiatic Golden Plovers by larger size, white under-wing and axillaries, proportionately shorter legs, less bold supercilium and, in all seasons, more golden-spangled back (but see *P.fulva*). Northern birds in summer normally have jet-black face and under-parts, clearly divided by broad white stripe from forehead down the neck and along the sides of the flanks, with vent and under-tail white. More southern birds show less contrast, with partly obscured black face and under-parts, and the white blurred and yellowish. In winter plumage the black is lost and the under-parts are whitish, with golden and dusky mottling. Can be confused with immature Grey Plover, which is yellowish, but larger size, prominent black axillaries, bold white wing-bar and white rump readily separate it from Golden Plover. The juvenile plumage is distinctive, having the gold spotting on upper-parts a little paler and duller than the adult, with breast, mantle and scapulars showing distinctive spots, and the belly and flanks white, but extensively tipped pale brown. In flight shows a whitish wing-bar most obvious across the primaries while rump and tail look dark. Legs grey-green, or greyish-black.

Voice. On the wing migrant flocks give a liquid '*too-ee*' or '*puie*' and use '*tee*' or '*too*' notes prior to take-off. In excitement gives a '*whee-whee-hee-oo*', in alarm a shorter, higher '*pluué*' and a harsher '*a-chryolee*' in alarm-threat, whilst on the ground. The song is a wailing, plaintive '*a-PHEE-oo-a-PHEE-oo*' or '*per-PEE-oo-per-PEE-oo*' and associated with 'butterfly-type' flight – synchronised with wing-beats. Also a rippling, warbling, trilling song, quickly repeated, '*a-tyrolee*', and given in normal flight during display flight.

Habitat. Hilly and lowland moors, and in the arctic on coastal and riverain tundra, avoiding terrain over which it cannot easily run and preferring flattish or gently sloping ground. In winter on fields or open farmland, also seashores and estuaries, but less so on tidal flats of mud and sand.

Distribution. The southern race *P.a.apricaria* breeds in the British Isles, Denmark, western Germany and southern Scandinavia. The northern race *P.a.altifrons* breeds in Iceland, the Faeroes, northern Scandinavia, and east through northern Russia and Siberia to the Taimyr Peninsula. This form, or both, winter from the British Isles and the southern end of the North Sea to the Iberian Peninsula, and in the Mediterranean basin, including large numbers in North Africa; also winters in small numbers eastwards to Turkey and the southern Caspian coast, rarely beyond. Map **17**.

Movements. Migratory, except in Britain and Ireland, where partially migratory. In autumn Icelandic birds use western route through Ireland, western Britain, western France and Iberia, with very large numbers wintering in Ireland, presumably mainly Icelandic birds. Portugal and western Spain are apparently the chief wintering areas, south of Ireland. Icelandic birds flock in July–August with main departures from late September to early November, and the main arrivals in Ireland occur in October–November. Return movement in Ireland begins in March, with some indication of birds arriving there in March–April, presumably Icelandic birds which wintered further south in France and Iberia. Icelandic breeding areas reoccupied mid-April to early May. In Britain only a few normally emigrate and most internal movements are of a limited nature, SSE–SW. In Britain breeding grounds are vacated from early July, with return normally starting from February. In winter, peak numbers occur in southern England December–February, with many staying into April, indicating their more continental origin. The majority of the birds breeding mainly in Fenno-Scandia and Russia migrate south-west in autumn, to winter in the western maritime countries and the western Mediterranean basin. Between November and April many are found in Britain (not Ireland), Belgium, France, Iberia and Morocco, and those wintering in southern England are believed to be mainly continental birds, and it is apparent that this stock also predominates in Maghreb winter quarters. In autumn adults depart late-July to late-August (juveniles October–November) to moult in northern Europe. The main southward movement through Europe is October-December, with arrivals in Morocco from November (peak January). Return – mid-February in Mediterranean basin, and in north-western Europe numbers build up to peak in early May, prior to onward movement. Breeding areas reoccupied during May, or early June on the northern tundra.

Feeding. Prey normally located visually – most food taken from the surface, or by probing for 1–2cm. Repeatedly runs short distances when foraging, stopping to capture prey. Earthworms are grasped in the bill and pulled out of the ground almost vertically; worms often slip, and are then quickly grasped again, though sometimes break. Feeds singly, in pairs, but often in large flocks. Foot-trembling recorded. Food, mainly beetles, earthworms and other invertebrates, also some plant material, including berries, seeds and grasses.

Social and breeding behaviour. Birds arrive on their breeding grounds singly or in two's and three's, but mostly in large flocks. Pairing begins with the female more commonly visiting the male in his territory. The male chases the female, separating her from other birds by running after her in a low-hunched posture, with back feathers ruffled and tail fanned and gently bobbed. The chase may be prolonged, and if the female is forced to fly, the male pursues her closely, giving the trilling song-call, in an erratic chase involving switchback ascents and descents; at the end of which both dive steeply and skim low over the ground. The male may also climb high, circling with slow and buoyant wing-beats and giving his wailing song. Although the advertisement flight is an individual ceremony, several males may sometimes perform simultaneously, or may meet and perform together. Males establish display centres and advance on one another with wings raised and attack fiercely, sometimes leapfrogging one another. The mating ceremony begins a few days after spring arrival, when territory and pair-bond established. Mating typically follows scraping-display, with female running (in horizontal posture) a short distance to the side of the scrape, giving a soft 'too-too' call, then turning tail to mate and crouching. The male may fly on to the back of the female or mount from closer quarters. After copulation the female scrapes vigorously and the male may also assist in the ceremonial scrape-making. The species has a monogamous mating system. Gregarious throughout the year, especially outside the breeding season.

Nest, eggs and young. Nest is a shallow scrape, typically on moorland with short, tussocky vegetation, lined with a few heather twigs or lichens. Eggs, 4, yellowish-stone, heavily marked black-brown. Incubation period 28–31 days, by both sexes, and both parents care for young. Fledging period 25–33 days. Breeds in first year.

The forward-hunched posture (right-hand bird) is an aggressive display sometimes seen among birds in spring flocks.

GREY PLOVER   *Pluvialis squatarola*

Du – Zilverplevier   Fr – Pluvier argenté
Ge – Kiebitzregenpfeifer   Sp – Chorlito gris
Sw – Kustpipare

Pl. 6

Identification. Length 10½–11¾in. Larger, more robust, larger-headed and longer-legged than either Lesser or Golden Plovers, with stouter black bill, and in summer plumage silvery upper-parts, with extensive black on the face and flanks, but white on the under-tail coverts. In winter plumage black areas lost and upper-parts and coverts brownish-grey (more uniform than Golden Plover) with white fringes, and under-parts white. The plumage of the juvenile may be confused with Golden Plover, as the upper-parts and coverts are brownish-grey, boldly spotted pale gold or yellowish-white, and the white under-parts have very extensive buff-brown barring on the breast and flanks. In flight shows prominent black axillaries, contrasting with whitish under-wing, and bold white wing-bar and white rump are diagnostic at all ages. In Golden Plover rump and tail look wholly dark. Distinctive call, a far-carrying, mournful '*plee-uu-wee*'.

Voice. Common call a tri- or disyllabic '*tlee-oo-ee*'. Other calls on breeding grounds include '*tee-oo*', '*too-ree*' and a soft, mellow '*quu-hu*'. Song of male in display flight is a melancholy '*kudiloo*' or '*koodleeoo*', also a trilling song, composed of several trills – first a melodious '*pljujutipljuju*', then two to three hissing '*tiut-tiut*' calls, followed by a short, ringing, trilling '*prrlju-juju*', changing to '*tiu-li*'.

Habitat. Breeds in high arctic on lowland tundra. In winter found on sea coasts, on broad mudflats and sandy beaches, in contrast to Golden Plover. Only exceptionally occurs inland in Europe, i.e. at reservoirs or sewage farms etc., during hard weather or on migration.

Distribution. Breeds on the arctic tundras of North America and Alaska. In Russia and Siberia, from the Kanin Peninsula eastwards to the Chukotski Peninsula and the coast of Anadyrland. In western Palaearctic, breeds in extreme north-eastern part of European Russia. Map **18**.

Movements. Migratory, with the species' winter range extending to the coasts of South America, Africa, southern Asia and Australia. Birds wintering in the western Palaearctic breed in northern Russia, and many migrants passing through the western Palaearctic continue south to South African winter quarters, although there is no evidence for those using the western seaboard continuing further south than the Gulf of Guinea. The large numbers occurring in South Africa are believed to come from further east, with Russian birds using the great circle route (via Black Sea) between breeding areas and winter quarters. Adults leave their breeding grounds mainly in August, with juveniles following a month or more later. In Britain birds arrive from July onwards, through the autumn and winter. In Morocco they arrive from late July, but mainly September, in Ghana, late July and August, and in South Africa from September. Peak numbers occur on the Dutch Waddenzee in the first half of September and in England on the Wash in late August (juveniles begin to arrive in early September, i.e. six weeks after the first adults). Far more birds winter in Africa than in Europe, although many of the former stop over and moult in European estuaries. Spring departures from South Africa start February–March, in Morocco from early April, and generally from April till late May on the Wash, late March till early June on the Waddenzee and late May till early June on the White Sea. Non-breeders, probably first-year birds, are common in summer in usual wintering areas.

Feeding. On breeding grounds feeds mainly on insects and other invertebrates; on the shore outside the breeding season, chiefly polychaete worms, molluscs and crustaceans. Feeds mainly by sight in typical *Charadriidae* stop-run-peck manner, waiting motionless for several seconds before moving to new waiting position, or darting to peck at prey. Foot-trembling not recorded. Regularly washes prey items. Many bivalve molluscs seized by extended siphon and torn abruptly out of shell; crustaceans may be pecked apart. Detects marine worm near surface when notices small outflow of water made by worm in hole. Feeds in areas where available prey greatest, and some birds may hold winter feeding territory.

Social and breeding behaviour. On the breeding grounds birds return separately, whether or not paired in the previous year, and quickly occupy territory and pair or re-pair soon afterwards. Male indulges in 'butterfly-type' song display on shallow wing-beats, kept above the horizontal, giving wailing song and circling, then gliding to ground, giving trilling song-call. Before descending may also break into a fast zig-zag flight, towering and occasionally dashing headlong at ground. The song flight is more intense than those performed in autumn territories and differs in being directed at the female on the ground, while he displays overhead. Patrolling flights of male may also attract females. On the ground the male performs a variety of displays – typically with body low, neck outstretched and parallel to the ground – runs stiffly towards female, sometimes passing her or stopping abruptly in front of her, in low-hunched posture, with tail up and bill nearly touching the ground. The female may participate with him, and perform joint-runs, scrape-ceremonial behaviour and various gestures that indicate her willingness to copulate. Copulation usually occurs after a joint-run, or male has run at female from some distance in low-hunched posture, with wings dropping; he jumps directly on to her back, and she bends legs (not crouching). Male flies off after mating. The female deepens the initial scrape made by the male and lines it. The species has a monogamous mating system. Less gregarious than Golden Plover, often solitary or in two's and three's, or in loose flocks of up to 30, although very large flocks may form before spring migration. When defending winter territory (which owner may reoccupy in subsequent years) owner adopts a forward-hunched posture and trots towards intruder, who usually retires.

Nest, eggs and young. Nest is a shallow scrape, lined with a few small stones or pieces of vegatation. Eggs 4, stone to buff, with darker spots and blotches. Incubation period 26–27 days, by both sexes initially, as female normally leaves mate and brood when latter less than 12 days old. Fledging period 35–45 days. Age of first breeding, 2–3 years.

LAPWINGS   Subfamily Vanellinae

Most species larger than plovers, many having crests, colourful facial wattles and orbital rings. Wing-spurs present in some species, others have a bony knob beneath the skin on the carpal joint – features which correlate with their occasional aggressive nature. All species have black primaries, often with a broad white wing stripe stretching diagonally across the wing, and except in the White-tailed Plover, have a black band to the distal end of the white tail. Flight slower and more buoyant than that of plovers, some species having rounded wings. May frequent edges of rivers, lakes or marshes, but are equally at home well away from water, preferring open country, cultivation and fields. Often form large flocks. Noisy: many have screeching or strident calls.

Range. Almost worldwide; absent from North America and islands in the Pacific.
Number of species. World, 24; western Palaearctic, 6.

SPUR-WINGED PLOVER   *Hoplopterus spinosus*

Du – Sporenkievit
Fr – Vanneau éperonné
Ge – Spornkiebitz
Sp – Avefría espolonada
Sw – Sporrvipa

Pl. 7

Identification. Length 10–10½in. Distinctive-looking plover, often seen standing in rather hunched attitude, with black cap of head separated by white collar from buff-grey mantle. Black nape and crown with loose crest, contrast with white face and sides of neck. A bold black line runs from bill down foreneck into black flanks and lower chest, with lower belly and under-tail coverts white. In flight shows bold upper-wing pattern with buff-grey wing-coverts separated from black flight feathers by a prominent white wing-panel extending right across the coverts to the inner secondaries. From below, wing pattern even more striking, with black flight feathers contrasting with white under-wing. Noticeable white rump and all-black tail, and a small curved black spur is present on the carpal joint. The juvenile is more blackish-brown, with extensive buff fringes to the coverts. Sexes similar, no seasonal variation. In flight, long black legs extend beyond tail. Flight rather slow.

Voice. Commonest call, a constantly repeated sharp '*kik*', also a loud, screeching '*did-he-do-it*', not unlike the call of the Red-wattled Plover. Alarm call is a loud, sharp, metallic '*tick*' or '*teek*'.

Habitat. Breeds in marshy areas and other wetlands, and in Egypt, mainly on flooded or irrigated inland farms. Also occurs round reservoirs, lagoons, lakes, riversides, coastal marshes and deltas.

Distribution. From eastern Greece (where bred for the first time in Europe in 1959) to Turkey, northern and eastern Syria, Israel, Jordan, Iraq and Egypt. Further south, in the Sudan and eastern Africa, south to Kenya, and west in the dry belt south of the Sahara to Senegal. Mainly sedentary in Africa. Accidental, Spain, West Germany, eastern Europe and USSR, also Lebanon, Kuwait and Malta. Map **19**.

Movements. Migratory north of Lebanon, and a summer visitor to Greece and Turkey, with migrants crossing to Cyprus in spring, in small numbers (mid-March to mid-April), and also reaching Turkey in same period. Autumn departure from Turkey is in August–September, with flocks of 100 reported in river deltas of southern Turkey (third week September). A few birds reported in Cyprus (mid-August to early October). Winter quarters of these birds are unknown.

Also breeds in Levant and Middle East and probably resident or dispersive, wintering occasionally north to Syria. Movements in Iraq are fairly extensive and probably also involve birds from other areas. Whilst Israeli birds are resident, small numbers of migrants pass Eilat in Gulf of Aqaba (September–October), and there are other autumn records from southern Sinai whose origins also are not known. The species is resident in Egypt, and it is unusual for flocks in winter to move away from their breeding areas.

Feeding. Feeds by sight, making a few quick paces before lunging at its prey. Food mainly insects, including beetles, adults and larvae of midges, and ants. Also spiders, worms, molluscs, tadpoles and small fish.

Social and breeding behaviour. No information on pair formation, but in typical courtship male assumes a horizontal posture with head drawn well in, patters up to female and begins to circle her clockwise, with slow, stiff, deliberate steps, for many minutes. The circling is only occasionally interrupted by the male adopting a high-upright posture, with wings tightly folded and tail spread. After a pause, circling may start again, or also lead to pre-copulatory behaviour, or nesting displays. Prior to copulation, both stand side by side and bob, then turn sharply to face each other, with male stretching himself up in a high-upright posture, after which he circles again. When the female assumes the forward-stretched posture, the male runs towards her and, with a light spring, mounts her back and copulates. Afterwards he may continue circling the female again. The scrape display of the male is evidently similar to the Lapwing's and, as in that species, it probably also plays an important role in courtship behaviour. The species has a monogamous mating system. Occurs singly or in pairs, with small flocks mostly forming at the end of the breeding season.

Nest, eggs and young. Nest is a shallow depression on the ground, usually near water, and lined with small pieces of grass and other debris. The male makes a number of scrapes and the female selects one. Eggs 4 (3–5), olive-buff, heavily blotched and spotted black-brown. Incubation period 22–24 days, by both sexes, and young cared for by both. Fledging period 7–8 weeks. Age of first breeding not known.

The high-upright posture is a high intensity threat-display used in territorial disputes.

BLACKHEAD PLOVER   *Hoplopterus tectus*

Fr – Vanneau à tête noire   Ge – Schwarzkopfkiebitz

Identification. Length 11in. About the size of Spur-winged Plover, with a distinctive short black crest and a red wattle in front of the eye. Head, black except for white above and below the bill, contrasts with a long white supercilium. The black neck extends as a narrow black line down the centre of the breast and the remaining under-parts are white. The upper-parts and sides of the breast are pale brown, and the wing-coverts are also brown, with the greater coverts tipped white. The primary coverts and bases to the primaries and secondaries are also white, and the remainder of the wings are black. In flight the broad white wing-bar and the white bases to the black primaries are conspicuous, as is the black distal half of the white tail. From below the white under-wing is offset by black tips to the primaries and black rear edge of the secondaries. Sexes similar. Juveniles resemble adults, but have the upper-parts edged buff. Iris yellow, bill red with black tip, legs carmine.

The flight is slow, and they are noisy, giving rasping cries.

Voice. Gives a shrill, two- or three-note whistle, usually heard at dusk or at night. Also a rasping cry, similar to Spur-winged Plover, but less harsh.

Habitat. An arid-adapted species, usually frequenting dry sandy country covered by low bushes with scattered grass tufts, or arid thorn-bush country. Largely nocturnal, and when encountered during the day, is usually seen in pairs or small parties in the shade of acacia trees. Also partial to airstrips where they exist.

Distribution and movements. Nominate race breeds from Sénégal to Ethiopia, Uganda and western Kenya; in Chad has penetrated north to Ennedi. The eastern race *latifrons* breeds in Kenya east of the Rift Valley, and in southern Somalia. Evidently this species is a local migrant, and is sometimes found in small flocks. The only record of the species' occurrence in the western Palaearctic is of a bird collected at Wadi Araba, Jordan–Israel frontier in 1869.

Feeding. The birds are evidently not attracted to water for foraging, but instead tend to feed in dry and sandy areas. Probably much of the feeding is done at night and includes various insects and molluscs.

Social and breeding behaviour. The birds are relatively tame, occurring in pairs or small parties, from five to 10 birds. In alarm birds bob erect and depress the head, neck and crest, and flirt the tail. Relatively little is known of the species' nesting biology.

Nest, eggs and young. Nests are simple scrapes, typical of Lapwings, but are well lined with grass, or sometimes almost any available material. Eggs 2–3, clay-coloured, with black spots and blotches. Incubation and fledging periods not ascertained.

RED-WATTLED PLOVER   *Hoplopterus indicus*

Du – Indische Kievit   Fr – Vanneau de l'Inde
Ge – Rotlappenkiebitz   Sp – Avefría de curuncula
Sw – Flikvipa

Pl. 8

Identification. Length 12½–14in. Body size as Lapwing, but stands taller, with black-tipped red bill, long yellow legs and sizeable red wattle in front of eye. Cap, face, throat and breast black, with rest of under-parts white, and variable amounts of white on ear-coverts and sides of neck. Upper-parts pale brown, with strong green suffusion. In flight shows broad areas of white across wings, with black primaries and secondaries, with some white on the inner secondaries. Upper tail-coverts and tail white with broad black tailband. Juvenile resembles adult, but head markings duller, with white on the throat and lower face. Flight action recalls Lapwing, but wing-beats are stronger and more regular, so that its flight speed is more rapid and direct.

Voice. Typical is a loud screeching '*did-ye-do-it*'. In alarm a '*trint-trint-trint*' and, more excitedly, a '*krededeedeer*' or '*did-did-did-did*'. The nocturnal song flight (heard February–March) may be heard up to three hours after sunset, or again before dawn.

Habitat. Mainly inland, near water, i.e. jheels, mudbanks, ditches, canals and rivers and, particularly in cultivated land, large irrigated gardens, and on wasteland, either grassy or rough and stony.

Distribution. The race *H.i.aigneri*, occurring in the western Palaearctic, breeds in Iraq, and this race extends eastward through Iran and Afghanistan to north-western India. Also in north and south-east Turkmeniya (USSR), eastern Arabia and Trucial Oman and Muscat. In 1983 at least 2 pairs were holding territory in south-east Turkey. This constitutes a recent expansion of range northwards, probably from central and eastern Iraq. Elsewhere other races occur east to the Indo-Chinese countries, Malaya and south-western Yunnan. Map **20**.

Movements. Migratory in Russia (eastern Turkmeniya), although resident or dispersive elsewhere. In Middle East, resident in Iran, Iraq and eastern Arabia, although locally some birds may be dispersive, i.e. in Iraq (autumn and winter) birds disperse to river edges in late summer as temporary flooded areas dry out. There are several records of birds in the Persian Gulf (mainly October–February), whose origins are not known. Whilst the species also breeds nearby in the United Arab Emirates and north-eastern Oman (where resident), this does not exclude the possibility that some Iranian birds may move south towards the Gulf.

Feeding. Walks in short spurts on long legs, leaning forward to pick up prey. Feeding essentially nocturnal, although active in the day but not for foraging. Takes mostly ground-living invertebrates, including beetles, ants, grasshoppers and termites, also molluscs, worms and crustaceans.

Social and breeding behaviour. Behaviour studies incomplete. Mates feed close together at dusk, and during the day often bow to each other in territory, with the male calling.

Pairs are very noisy at night, but accompanying behaviour not known. The male initiates the mating ceremony by calling loudly, with the female eventually replying. Calling between the pair increases, and the male then approaches the female with his crown feathers raised in a tuft. When the female moves away he follows her, and as the calls reach a climax, they cease abruptly. The male then offers the female some nesting material in his bill, she accepts and crouches, and the male then mounts. The species has a monogamous mating system. Often in pairs throughout the year, and outside breeding season solitary, or in groups of two to three, or occasionally in small parties of from six to thirty.

Nest, eggs and young. Nests on ground in open, usually near water; a shallow scrape, lined with small stones and debris, or may be unlined. Eggs 3–4, buff tinged yellow or green, well marked with black-brown spots and small blotches. Incubation period 26 days, mainly by female – and young cared for by both. Fledging period and age of first breeding not known.

SOCIABLE PLOVER   *Chettusia gregaria*

Du – Steppenkievit   Fr – Vanneau sociable
Ge – Steppenkiebit: Sp – Chorlito social
Sw – Stäppvipa

Pl. 8

Identification. Length $10\frac{1}{2}$–$11\frac{1}{2}$in. Slightly smaller than Lapwing, but with longer black legs. In summer plumage reminiscent of Dotterel, with black cap of crown separated by broad white supercilia meeting in a V on the nape, and a black stripe through the eye to the rear of the ear-coverts. The cheeks and lower throat are warm buff, merging into a pinkish-grey breast, with lower black belly patch shading into darker chestnut, contrasting with white under tail-coverts. Upper-parts are grey-brown, with folded wings showing as a black line along the flanks, edged white by the secondaries above. Unmistakable in flight, with pattern recalling Sabine's Gull, i.e. all-black primaries contrasting with all-white secondaries, forming a white wedge to carpal joint and contrasting with greyish-brown wing-coverts. In flight from below, more like Avocet, i.e. black primaries contrast with remainder of white under-wing. Tail and upper tail-coverts white, with black sub-terminal tailband (two outer pairs of tail feathers white). In winter plumage a drabber-looking bird, with duller head markings and paler face, neck and chest (latter visibly streaked dark brown at sides), and rest of under-parts wholly white. The juvenile is similar to non-breeding adult, but with more contrasting head pattern, darker, buffier under-parts with distinct V-shaped flecks on the breast and upper-parts with more extensive buff fringes to feathers. Flight free and graceful, recalling Lapwing, but wings narrower, slightly longer and less rounded.

Voice. Generally noisy in breeding season, but outside rather quiet. Commonest call is a rasping '*etch-etch-etch*', and this may be speeded up into an angry chattering, '*etchetchetchetch*'. Also a softer '*krek*', and a series of '*kjek*' calls when more alert.

Habitat. Breeds in rather steppe-like country, and is found mainly in areas of transition between denser grasses and continuous cover of wormwood or sagebrush. In winter favours sandy or grassy plains, wastelands near cultivation, ploughed fields and stubble. Also occurring near coasts.

Distribution. Breeds on the steppes of central Russia and Kazakhstan, south nearly to the Caspian and Aral Seas and Lake Balkash. Appears to have decreased in Europe and elsewhere, due to cultivation of steppe areas. Winters in western India, Pakistan, Baluchistan, Iraq, Arabia (few) and north-east Africa. Accidental in the Middle East and in several European countries, including the British Isles (28). Map 21.

Movements. Migratory, and leaves steppe breeding areas from early August, but movements are slow and lengthy, with exodus from Turkmeniya still continuing mid-November. Those birds wintering in the eastern parts of their range (India etc.) are presumably from Kazakhstan, although more westerly breeders occur on passage in the Ural valley and Volga delta, with a well defined movement west of the Caspian through Transcaucasia, irregularly reaching the Black Sea in the Ukraine. These movements (mainly second half of September) continue through Turkey and Syria, in small numbers, to wintering grounds in Iraq, Arabia and north-east Africa. In Africa it is a scarce winter visitor to Eritrea and the arid parts of the Sudan (from late October). Birds leave their winter quarters in March to early April, passing through eastern Turkey and the Caucasus, also Alma Ata in Kazakhstan, from the second half of March. The southerly breeding areas are reoccupied mid-April, and the more northern steppes mid-May.

Feeding. Feeds by sight, and actions typical of genus, but the dip to pick up food is emphasised more by its longer legs. Birds have been seen pattering or trampling the ground with their feet while foraging. Diet is almost entirely made up of insects, particularly beetles, weevils, grasshoppers and moth larvae, also some vegetable matter.

Social and breeding behaviour. Breeding behaviour not well known. Shortly after arrival on breeding grounds males have been recorded gathering and engaging in aggressive bouts, in presence of females, often leaping at each other with mantle and scapulars ruffled, delivering blows to their opponents with feet and wings. Pair formation assumed to occur during spring gatherings. In presumed courtship of female (who was nest-scraping), the male ran swiftly and gracefully around her with slightly open wings. Breeding occurs in loose colonies, from a few to several dozen pairs, but within the colony each pair maintains a small but exclusive territory. A monogamous mating system is indicated.

Gregarious. Generally in small flocks outside breeding season, but post-breeding flocks sometimes reaching several hundred birds. Large flocks reported on wintering grounds in Iraq, Iran and Pakistan, although migrant flocks are much smaller, and up to 15–20 birds.

Nest, eggs and young. Nest is a shallow scrape on open ground, or in short vegetation, lined with grass and leaves. Eggs 4, warm buff, spotted and streaked black. Incubation period 25 days, probably by both parents. Fledging period 35–40 days. Age of first breeding not known.

WHITE-TAILED PLOVER *Chettusia leucura*

Du – Witstaartkievit Fr – Vanneau à queue blanche
Ge – Weissschwanzkiebitz Sp – Chorlito coliblanco
Sw – Sumpvipa

Pl. 8

Identification. Length 10½–11½in. About the size of Sociable Plover, but with longer bill and very much longer yellow legs. The head is mainly buff-brown, with the face and throat paler and the forehead creamy. The neck is buff-brown, contrasting with a strongly grey breast, and the centre of the belly is rosy-buff, becoming whiter towards the all-white tail. Upper-parts grey-brown, with a strong lilac sheen. In the closed wing, the black primaries and white secondaries show as a line along the body, with the white line narrowly bordered black above, producing a black-and-white sandwich effect. In flight unmistakable, showing all-white tail and large areas of white extending from the secondaries across the wings to the carpal area, contrasting with black primaries. In flight from below, shows front half of body dark grey-brown, contrasting with white rear half, and the whole underwing pure white, contrasting with black primaries, with long legs extending about 3in beyond tail. In winter the adult is duller and whiter around the face and throat. The juvenile is similar, but the upper-parts show dark centres to the feathers and have paler margins.

Voice. Generally noisy in breeding season, but rather silent afterwards. On breeding grounds gives a rapid, squeaking '*pet-EEwit pet-EEwit*', bearing some resemblance to the calls of a Lapwing. Also has a high-pitched, vigorous call like spring flight-song of the latter. Alarm calls '*ker-wirrah*' and '*kee-vee-ik*'.

Habitat. On breeding grounds, found in damp areas near water, fresh or salty, overgrown with wormwood and other plants. Also winters on marshes, flooded fields, ponds, and along the swampy or grassy shores of brackish lakes and jheels.

Distribution. Breeds from Transcaspia and Russian Turkestan, south-west to Iran, southern Iraq, and east across Kazakhstan to the vicinity of Lake Balkash. Also breeds occasionally in central Turkey. Winters from north-western India to Afghanistan, and in northern Egypt and the Sudan. Accidental in several European countries, including the British Isles (4), also in the Middle East and North Africa. Map **22**.

Movements. Migratory in Russia, but resident in the Middle East. In Russia, birds leave their nesting areas (in small groups) in Uzbekistan between late August and late September. Migrants cross Iran and Afghanistan to winter in north-west India, Pakistan and Baluchistan, with the occasional migrant turning up in the Persian Gulf, to reach Oman. The Iraqi population is resident, whilst making some local movements, but it is not known whether those birds wintering in Iraq and southern Iran include migrants from the north. More western birds, which winter in north-east Africa, probably also include some from east of the Caspian Sea. Birds depart from Turkey in early September. In Africa the main wintering areas are in the Sudan (October–March), although the bird has recently straggled west to Chad (January and October). In March birds leave their winter quarters in India and Africa – with spring migrants reaching Turkey in April, and also crossing Afghanistan in the same month. The main passage in southern Uzbekistan is in the first half of April, and by the end of the month all breeding areas are reoccupied.

Feeding. Probably mainly insects, especially beetles. Feeds by running and walking, and may pause with head upright or lowered, feeding both on land and in shallow water, occasionally submerging head. Also takes grasshoppers, worms, aquatic insects and small molluscs.

Social and breeding behaviour. Arrives at breeding areas in spring, in small parties. Often semi-colonial, nesting in small groups, but several hundred nests found together in Iraq (some only a few metres apart, on small islets). Commonly nests in association with birds like pratincole, Black-winged Stilt and terns. Little information on breeding behaviour, although 'nuptial flights' noted in one male of a pair. The male, whilst guarding his incubating mate on the nest, would duel in the air with any intruding males, sweeping and swooping like a Lapwing. A monogamous mating system and care of the young by both sexes is likely, as in other *Vanellinae*. Gregarious, collecting in flocks outside breeding season. Post-breeding flocks small, less than 20 (early July), but often in larger flocks on migration.

Nest, eggs and young. Nest is a shallow scrape, usually near water, with a little lining gathered from the available vegetation. Eggs 3–4, buff with dark brown spots and small blotches. Incubation period 22–24 days, young fledging in about 30 days. Age of first breeding probably first or second year.

LAPWING   *Vanellus vanellus*

Du – Kievit   Fr – Vanneau huppé
Ge – Kiebitz   Sp – Avefría
Sw – Tofsvipa

Pl. 7

Identification. Length 12in. A large plover with iridescent greenish-black plumage, long wispy crest and blackish breast-band, contrasting with white under-parts and cheeks. In flight has broad, very rounded wings, white tail with broad black terminal band and cinnamon under-tail coverts. In winter, adult becomes buff above the cheek line, and juvenile has stronger buff and less patterned face, brownish tone on the chest, pale crescentric markings to the feathers of the back and wing-coverts, and a shorter crest. In flight looks black and white – flocks normally travelling in loosely bunched parties, which may trail out into elongated formations, on rather slow and slightly erratic wing-beats. In full flight its broad, well rounded wings give it astonishing manoeuvrability. Bill black, legs dull reddish-flesh. Sexes similar.

Voice. Normal call, given chiefly on the wing, is a shrill, rather wheezy '*pee-wit*' or '*peeawee*'. Alarmed bird flying overhead calls '*cheew-ép*' or '*chaeew-ép*'. In anxiety (on the ground), a thin '*euwip*'. The spring song-flight of the male varies in detail, but typically '*chaaew-á-á-o-wee*', and wing-strumming of male sounds like '*wup-wup-wup*', and is produced by the vibration of 3–4 outermost primaries in alternating flight of song-flight. Mating call of male, a soft, rasping '*skrr-skrr*'.

Habitat. Predominantly a farm bird, favouring arable land, especially when newly ploughed or fallow, and other open areas which afford unbroken all-round views – avoiding uniformly tall, dense or rough herbage or crops. Visits margins of fresh water, such as lakes, rivers, floodlands and marshes. Along coasts and estuaries often breeds on saltings and, especially in cold spells, resorts to tidal mudflats.

Distribution. Europe, from the Faeroes and the British Isles eastwards to Ussuriland in the Russian Far East, and north to 70°N in Norway, north to 60°N in the Urals and western Siberia, but not much further north of Lake Baikal in eastern Siberia. Winters from the British Isles and W. Europe to the Mediterranean basin (including North Africa), east to Iran and Afghanistan. Elsewhere winters in the Indo-Chinese countries. Map **23**.

Movements. Mainly migratory, and Britain and Ireland constitute the northernmost regular wintering areas, although small winter flocks are present in Denmark and West Germany. Dispersal from breeding areas begins in late May and June, with many birds from central Europe moving west to north-west in early summer to the Low Countries and Britain, while others move south-west into Italy and southern France. Birds from the Baltic countries move south-west and also west to Denmark and Britain. Westward movements continue all summer from the Continent into Britain (majority adults), which merge gradually into autumn migration after September. British breeders generally make only short, localised movements, though some adults reach Ireland. Summer movements merge into autumn migration during September–November, as an increasing number of juveniles depart from their breeding grounds. Unlike the more leisurely summer movements, autumn passage is more urgent with the onset of the frost season. Birds move south-west along the western seaboard into Iberia and North Africa, with more eastern birds reaching Italy and crossing the Mediterranean. Those birds wintering in Turkey and the Middle East are assumed to include migrants from Russia. The British Isles are an especially important wintering area for Scandinavian birds. Important wintering areas for west and central European birds are found in western France, Iberia and the Maghreb. Cold easterly airstreams from northern Europe extending over the Atlantic have sometimes caused flocks to overshoot and cross the Atlantic.

Spring passage begins early – from late January in southern wintering areas, and reaches a peak in temperate Europe in early March.

Feeding. Feeds mainly by sight, but can also locate prey by hearing. It feeds by walking, or making a short run, then pausing and probing, with body tilted forward, pushing bill into surface of soil. Foot-trembling is also used, presumably to flush inconspicuous prey. Feeds chiefly on small invertebrates living on or in the ground – insects and their larvae, including beetles, flies, grasshoppers, moths, ants etc. Other prey items include spiders, earthworms, molluscs, frogs, small fish and some vegetable matter, including seeds.

The song-flight begins with a low-level butterfly-flight (**a**) grading into an alternating flight (**b**) with faster wing-beats and side-to-side motion, also including a dive. The bird then continues with a low-level flight (**c**) before rising for the high-flight, starting song as it does so (**d**). A vertical dive follows (**e**), and the song finishes as the bird levels out back into alternating-flight (**f**), after which it may land or repeat.

Social and breeding behaviour. Males arrive on their breeding grounds from mid-February and very shortly indulge in dramatic flight displays, with the purpose of discouraging other males and hopefully enticing a mate. The male's spectacular advertising display consists of rising, plunging, twisting, diving and rolling over his chosen territory, whilst calling and beating the air with his wings. When he is joined by a mate, his greeting display is a ritualised form of scrape-making. Typically he runs up to the female, with head and neck bowing before her, tail fanned and cocked, then sinks to the ground, paddling with his feet. Once the birds are paired much time is devoted to choosing the exact site of the scrape. The male may display at dozens of different sites before the female finally chooses one. Mating is often without prior ceremony and the intention of the male to mate is always indicated by a long series of mating calls, which are given as he flies or runs towards the female. The male usually mounts from a low-level flight on heavy wing-beats, prior to copulation. The species has a monogamous mating system.

Highly gregarious outside the breeding season, with flocks beginning to form in early to late May, and newly fledged juveniles flocking with adults from mid-June onwards.

Nest, eggs and young. Nest site on open, normally slightly raised ground; a shallow scrape lined with variable amounts of vegetation. Eggs 4, olive-brown, spotted and blotched black. Incubation period 26–28 days, by both sexes, and young cared for by both. Fledging period 35–40 days. Age of first breeding, usually two years.

SANDPIPERS and allies   Family Scolopacidae

Includes subfamilies Calidridinae (arctic sandpipers and allies), Gallinagininae (snipes and dowitchers), Scolopacinae (woodcocks), Tringinae (godwits, curlews and other sandpipers), Arenariinae (turnstones) and Phalaropodinae (phalaropes).

ARCTIC SANDPIPERS and allies   Subfamily Calidridinae

The true sandpipers of this group are the many species of *Calidris*. Most of them are small or very small (stints – 'peeps' etc), having cryptic brown or grey plumages, often with rufous or buff edgings to the feathers, and are fairly short-billed, although three species have long decurved bills. All breed in high northern latitudes and perform long migrations. Identification of the various members of this group of small sandpipers can often be difficult, offering the greatest challenge to the field observer – particularly the plumages of non-breeding birds or juveniles. Recognition mostly depends on size, length and shape of bill, colour and pattern of back, wings, rump and tail, also the pattern of markings on the breast, colour of legs and calls. It is particularly important to take field notes and not rely on memory, and a prerequisite to identification is to ascertain the age of the bird in question (i.e. is it a worn adult still showing some traces of breeding plumage on the mantle or scapulars, or is it a fresh and brighter-plumaged juvenile?), then make comparison with similarly aged and more familiar species. Other genera include *Tryngites* and *Philomachus* (i.e. Buff-breasted Sandpiper and Ruff), both of which show well developed lekking behaviour.

Range. Holarctic (mainly in the north), wintering south from temperate zones across the Equator to the southern hemisphere.

Number of species. World, 24; western Palaearctic, 21.

GREAT KNOT   *Calidris tenuirostris*

Du – Grote Kanoe   Fr – Grand Bécasseau maubèche
Ge – Anadyr-Knutt   Sp – Correlimos de Bering
Sw – Större Kustsnäppa

Identification. Length 10½–11½in. Larger than Knot with noticeably longer, thinner, more downwards-inclined bill, and longer wings. The species is more likely to be seen in winter plumage except in its far eastern Siberian breeding grounds. In winter it is grey above, with the under-parts white, and the breast is finely streaked and spotted dark grey. Head lacks a distinct white supercilium, but shows more blackish-brown streaking on the crown than is found in Knot. In flight shows white upper tail-coverts which appear as a narrow band, and has an indistinct whitish wing-bar. In summer it is readily distinguished from Knot by lack of red upper-parts, whilst the breast is heavily spotted, forming an almost blackish-brown band, the bold spots extending down the flanks. The head is streaked, more strongly blackish on the crown, with the hind neck streaked greyish-white. The scapulars and some tertials have large chestnut spots. The juvenile is distinctive, and is darker than the winter adult – upper-parts blackish-brown, with pale buff tips, and with black spots on the chest and flanks – very different from juvenile Knot, which has a faintly marked breast and distinctive sub-terminal dark lines on the scapulars and coverts. Bill black, sometimes with olive base; legs grey-green.

Voice. Rather silent – voice not well known. Gives a low, Knot-like '*nyut-nyut*'. Also a low '*chucker-chucker-chucker*'. In courtship flight male gives a gutteral '*kurru...kurru*' and later '*trry-ha...trry-ha*'.

Habitat. Arctic-alpine zones rather than tundra, breeding on inland barren upland ridges (4–600m), or on flat or gently sloping terrain, strewn with gravel or broken rocks, covered with lichen. In some areas up to 1,000m in the upper Kolyma basin. In winter resorts to mudflats and sand bars.

Distribution. Breeds in north-eastern Siberian highlands, and winters on the coasts of Pakistan and north-western India, migrating through eastern Asia, east to Micronesia to winter in Burma, Malaya and the Sundas to northern Australia. Accidental in Spain (April 1979), Morocco (Aug 1980), Oman (Sept 1982) and Eilat (Oct 1985). Vagrants have also been recorded in Alaska, Laccadives, Seychelles and Sri Lanka.

Movements. Migratory, but movements incompletely known. Departs from breeding areas late July (the females migrate southwards long before the males), with the main passage through south-eastern Siberia, Kuriles and eastern China (coastal) August–September. Birds normally arrive in northern Australia (where common and abundant top end of Northern Territory) from late August, departing in March. The Australian wintering population has recently been estimated at 253,500 (Nov–Dec). Spring passage on Chinese coasts is between April and early June, but mainly in the first half of May through Japan, arriving on Siberian breeding grounds by the second half of May. The Great Knot has been considered uncommon, but recent sightings during spring migration on the Kamchatka Peninsula revealed more than 20,000 birds at one site. No information on routes used by those birds reaching the most westerly wintering areas, i.e. coasts of Pakistan and north-western India.

Feeding. In summer, birds take dipteran larvae, beetles, spiders and berries or seeds.

Social and breeding behaviour. On the whole, very little is known about the breeding biology of this species. Its breeding grounds remained unknown until 1929, when a nest was found on a barren ridge near the mouth of the Kolyma River in north-eastern Siberia. Adults are reported to arrive on their Siberian breeding areas in late May or early June, as snow-melt commences. During courtship flights the males hover high over their territories uttering a repeated gutteral '*kurru*'. They also chase other birds with quickly repeated '*chirri*' calls, during a short glide with raised wings. Great Knots mate monogamously, both sharing the parental duties, until the female abandons the nest shortly before hatching, and only males have been found with broods of three or four young. Gregarious outside the breeding range, sometimes forming sizeable flocks. First-year birds may spend their first summer on their winter range.

Nest, eggs and young. Nest a depression in the ground, amid moss, on a high gravelly ridge. One nest contained 4 eggs, grey-yellow liberally speckled with red-brown markings. Males lead their broods from drier nesting sites to wetter feeding areas in mossy bogs.

KNOT   *Calidris canutus*

Du – Kanoetstrandloper   Fr – Bécasseau maubèche
Ge – Knutt   Sp – Correlimos gordo
Sw – Kustsnäppa

Pl. 9

Identification. Length 9½–10in. A robust, short-billed and relatively short-legged wader which may only be confused with the larger, more heavily marked and whiter-rumped Great Knot (see above). In summer the feathers of the upper-parts have black-brown centres with warm buff to rufous edges. Below the base of the bill it is pale pinkish, with the rest of the face and under-parts pink-cinnamon, barred black on the rear flanks, and with some white on the vent. Wing-coverts grey, forming a pale panel, primaries black, rump whitish-buff, closely barred black, and tail uniformly grey. In winter plumage, mainly grey above with thin white fringes, and whitish below, with grey suffusion and streaking on the breast. Has white supercilium and cheeks, speckled dark grey. Juvenile similar, but less grey and more brown above, finely scalloped cream and dark grey. In flight shows thin white wing-bar, and palish rump and tail. Feeds and flies in densely packed flocks, often numbering several thousand birds, even in mid-winter.

Voice. A low hoarse '*knut*', and 'twittering' from flocks, or a more whistled '*twit-wit*', especially in spring. Flight song on breeding grounds is a powerful, pleasing, fluting '*kouhi*', recalling Curlew, and ending as the bird descends with a deeper '*kouit-kouit*'. Alarm call given on breeding grounds, a resounding '*kve-kve-kve-kve*'.

Habitat. Breeding confined to high Arctic, mostly on peninsulas and large islands, usually near but not on the coast. Nests chiefly on barren and stony wastes, or dry ridges and fells, with scanty vegetation. In winter moves to large, flat, muddy and sandy beaches that are uncovered at high tide.

Distribution. *C.c.islandica* breeds in north Canadian Arctic on Axel Heiberg and Ellesmere Islands, also in northern Greenland. Nominate *canutus* breeds Taimyr Peninsula and Servernaya Zemlya (Central Siberia); not known which race breeds in Canadian Arctic north from Melville and Bathurst Islands, on Svalbard, and on Novosibirskiye Islands. *C.c.rufa* breeds in Canadian low Arctic and *C.c.rogersi* on Wrangle Island (north-eastern Siberia) and Alaska. Map **24**.

Movements. Migratory, with four main breeding areas. In the Nearctic, birds breeding south of 72°N, i.e. south of Queen Elizabeth and Ellesmere Islands, winter in South America (Argentina etc), whilst those breeding even further north on the Canadian high Arctic islands and northern Greenland winter in western Europe. In the Palaearctic, birds breeding in north-central Siberia migrate through western Europe to winter in West Africa, with smaller numbers passing on to winter in South Africa. The breeding populations from north-eastern Siberia and northern Alaska winter mainly in Australasia, with smaller numbers in the East Indies; also occurs in small numbers on the Pacific coast of South America.

Nearctic birds arrive on their breeding grounds from late May to early June, staying till August, and many returning birds breeding in Canada and western Greenland are believed to cross the Greenland icecap, making short stopovers in Iceland (i.e.

July–August), with some autumn birds reaching south-western Norway and Denmark (August–September). Sizeable flocks are present in their moulting areas around Britain and the Dutch Waddenzee to western France (late July–August), with juveniles arriving at least two or three weeks after the adults. After moulting some birds move west from the Waddenzee to the Wash (England), and from the Wash to the Irish Sea. In spring, concentrations of birds build up in some larger estuaries, i.e. Morecambe Bay and the Waddenzee, between March and April, prior to departure. Many birds make stopovers in Iceland (late May to early June) and are believed mainly to be Canadian and west Greenland birds which recross Greenland icecap, while east Greenland breeding birds largely overfly Icelandic staging areas.

North-central Siberian birds which migrate through Europe depart from their breeding areas a little later than Nearctic birds (end-August). The main movement of birds from north-western Russia is overland to the Gulf of Finland and the Baltic. In Finland peak numbers occur from the end of July to early August (adults) and mid-August to September (juveniles). Siberian birds move quickly along the west European coastline to moulting and wintering areas from Morocco southwards, mainly Banc d'Aguin (Mauritania), smaller numbers arriving in South Africa in November. Spring departure from South Africa is via West Africa and western Europe, rather than by the more direct eastern route through the Middle East (only a vagrant in East Africa). Birds leave South Africa from mid-May, stopping to feed and deposit fat reserves in Vendée (France) in mid-May, and on the Wattenmeer (West Germany) late May to early June, or Porsanger (Norwegian Finnmark), with few other staging posts.

Feeding. Feeds gregariously outside breeding season, often in huge flocks, the majority of birds feeding around low tide. Feeds predominantly by touch, probing in soft mud, mostly inserting bill to full length, but also detects prey by sight. May also insert tip of bill and push forward through wet ooze. On the upper shore, forages by pecking at surface of sand. May wade up to its belly, and also immerse head fully. On breeding grounds feeds mainly on insects and plant material. Away from breeding grounds feeds mainly on bivalve and gastropod molluscs, particularly baltic tellin; also cockles, periwinkles, mussels, crustaceans, polychaete worms, as well as adult insects, their larvae and eggs, and vegetable matter.

Social and breeding behaviour. Both sexes arrive together on the breeding grounds, or sometimes paired. Display flights by the male occur from the day of arrival. He flies up slowly and circles (20–200m) with rapidly vibrating wings, then glides down on outstretched wings held above the horizontal, usually singing. Flight to ground is a swift glide with wings held in a V, terminating with wings-high display. Display flights occur less frequently after the eggs hatch. In the early stages of territory occupation, the pair may fly around together in wide circles, male singing, and then both birds suddenly swooping down to land. Prior to copulation, the male was seen to fly up to the female and perform a wings-high display, at the same time uttering a soft courtship note, before mounting the female. Several scrapes are made before one is chosen and the eggs laid, and side-throwing is common while the bird is scraping. Male may relieve female at nest after giving display flight, then diving straight down to nest, and female flying off low and fast. The species has a monogamous mating system. Outside breeding season feeds in densely packed flocks that spread out carpeting the mud-flats and that fly in ever tighter, ever-changing formations.

Nest, eggs and young. Nests solitary, on open ground, usually near water. A shallow scrape, lined with plant material or lichen. Eggs 3–4, pale green-olive with small brown markings. Incubation period 21–22 days, by both sexes, and young cared for by both parents at first, but female leaves before young fledged. Fledging period 18–20 days. Age of first breeding, probably 2 or 3 years.

SANDERLING   *Calidris alba*

Du – Drieteenstrandloper
Fr – Bécasseau sanderling
Ge – Sanderling
Sp – Correlimos tridáctylo
Sw – Sandlöpare

Pl. 10

Identification. Length 7½in. A plump, short-billed fast-running and energetic shorebird – no other compares – which races after retreating waves to snap up some tiny morsel left by the tide, before dashing off again, legs a blur. The summer adult has strikingly rufous-buff upper-parts, head and breast, etched black and white, contrasting with a pure white belly. In winter it is whiter than any of its small beach companions and the only real risk is in flight, when it may be confused with a winter-plumage Grey Phalarope, of very different habits (see that species). The head and under-parts are white, and the upper-parts pale grey, with a diagnostic dark 'shoulder patch' showing in the closed wing. In flight it reveals a very striking white wing-bar which few other small waders can match, and white outer-tail feathers. Juvenile plumage is distinctive – crown is streaked black (forming a small cap), and the rest of the upper-parts are chequered above with cream and white spots on blackish feathers, and the breast is washed buff. Bill and legs black.

Voice. Characteristic call outside breeding season in flight is a soft '*twick-twick*'; when feeding in flock, birds have quiet conversational twittering calls. The song of the male in the breeding season is a short, loud, rather strident, churring '*trrr-trrr-trrr*', which changes in pitch at times. Male has a soft '*chert-chert*' when courting female on ground, and female may regularly utter sharp, high-pitched squeaks, or give buzzing calls near scrape. Alarm calls '*chidik*' or sharp '*wit-wit-wit*', given when young in danger.

Habitat. Nests on barren and stony tundras with scant vegetation, and frequents chiefly sandy beaches on migration or in its winter quarters.

Distribution. Breeds in arctic North America, including Alaska, Greenland, Spitzbergen, Taimyr Peninsula, Severnaya Zemlya, the mouth of the Lena and on the New Siberian Archipelago. Winters in the western hemisphere from British Columbia and Massachusetts to southern South America, and in the east from the British Isles and Indo-China south to South Africa and Australia. Map **25**.

Movements. Western Palaearctic migrants and winter visitors are mainly derived from two distinct populations, Greenland and Russian, but their movements and winter range are only partially understood. In South Africa, winter visitors may include birds from either region, so that at present there is little evidence to suggest that these two populations have separate winter ranges. Birds occur on passage in Norway (probably from both populations), Sweden, Finland and Denmark, from mid-July (adults) to early October (probably juveniles), and further south, reaching Morocco from late July. Passage also occurs inland on the Caspian and Aral Seas and the East African lakes. Northward migration in the spring occurs in southern France in April–May, in the Netherlands from mid-February to late March, with a second peak from mid- to late-May, Britain in May, and Finland – Russia from late May to early June. Birds also arrive in Greenland from late May to early June, staying till mid-August (adults) or early September (juveniles).

Feeding. Feeds mainly by probing, interspersed with short, fast runs and occasional pauses. Sturdy bill enables probing in fairly hard ground. Great dexterity shown in snatching items washed in by tide. Food mainly invertebrates. In breeding season, insects and their larvae, spiders, crustaceans, also plant material and seeds. In winter insects, including flies, beetles, bugs, polychaete worms, shrimps, molluscs and fish.

Social and breeding behaviour. Birds arrive on their breeding grounds in mixed-sex flocks, and ground chases take place soon after arrival. Immediately after pairing the birds become inseparable. The male performs a display flight; its chief function is probably to advertise for a mate, but it is commonly linked with aggression to other males. In the display flight the male flies at 5–10m, vibrating wings rapidly and then giving a brief glide. Throughout the performance he sings. Display flights appear to be little performed once the pair is established. Copulation is initiated by the female, outside the nesting area. She sits in an old scrape with head held low and tail almost vertical, rotates a little and calls. The male runs up to her and gently eases her out of the scrape by placing his bill under her belly. They both then run side by side, bodies pressed close together for about three metres; finally the male stops the female by pressing his lowered bill against her breast. The female stands on straight legs and the male mounts, fluttering his wings for balance, and pulling at the feathers of her nape. A monogamous mating system has been observed in one study of Greenland birds, but other studies in northern Canada suggested the occurrence of simultaneous double-clutching, this being either of the monogamous type or of a successively bigamous type. Gregarious outside breeding season, found in small, loose parties along the tide-line. Flocks are generally larger at roosts than when foraging.

Nest, eggs and young. Nest is a small scrape on ground in open, lined with a few small leaves, but no deliberate attempt is made to line nest. Eggs 3–4, dull green-olive with sparse brown spots. Incubation period 24–27 days, by both sexes, but one or the other leaves the brood. Fledging period about 17 days. Age of first breeding, probably two years.

SEMIPALMATED SANDPIPER   *Calidris pusilla*

Du – Kleine Grijze Strandloper   Fr – Bécasseau semipalmé
Ge – Sandstrandläufer   Sp – Correlimos semipalmeado
Sw – Sandsnäppa

Pl. 11

Identification. Length 5–6in. Very like Little Stint but slightly bulkier, and in all plumages relatively drab and uniformly, but coarsely, marked. Bill typically thick-based, more blunt-tip profile with spatulate end, and shows partly webbed toes, as Western Sandpiper (only two stints with this character). Legs look long due to greater extent of exposed tibia below the body than in Little Stint.

Adult in summer is less chestnut above than either Little Stint or Western, and is also paler than Least Sandpiper. Upper-parts, ochre-brown with scapulars lacking bright chestnut bases of Western, and breast finely streaked rather than spotted, extending on to the flanks. Remainder of under-parts white. Adult in winter, ochre-grey above (recalling winter Dunlin) and the feather pattern is more uniform than Little Stint (except for very dark centres to rear scapulars). Forehead also shows less white, cheek-patch more obvious and has longer white supercilium. Chest marks at bend of wing also more obvious.

Juvenile distinctive, and is dull grey-brown or ochre-brown above, with dark centres and pale buff fringes and tips to the feathers, creating a lace-like pattern on the mantle, and scales over the scapulars. Head pattern stronger than Little Stint – forehead greyer, and grey streaked crown separated from darker dull brown ear-coverts by distinct supercilium which broadens behind eye. The throat is white, extending under the cheeks to form a noticeable half-collar, and there is a necklace of fine, grey-brown streaks on the sides of the neck. Compared with juvenile Little Stint the colouring is generally colder, less rufous and more scaly above, showing less striped pattern, and the lack of the classical white V on the mantle is a consistent plumage difference. Shows a narrow white wing-bar in flight. Bill black (typically shorter than Western, but some overlap), legs dark olive-black. Common call in flight is a rather loud '*cherk*', softer and less reedy than similar call of Pectoral Sandpiper, and quite distinct from Little Stint's '*chit*' notes.

Voice. Distinctive short, clipped, quite low-pitched '*churp*', '*cherk*' or '*krit*' – very different from calls of Western Sandpiper, Little or Red-necked Stints. Calls are more husky, or harsher than Little Stint. Autumn vagrants gave sharp '*chirrik*', '*chirruk*' or '*chirrip*'. The song-flight call given on breeding ground is a prolonged, mechanical, trilling '*ree-ree-ree*', or '*di-jip-di-jip-di-jip*' given in another aerial display.

Habitat. Breeds on grassy or hummocky wet tundra, near marshy pools. In other seasons occurs mostly on mudflats and beaches, also on river bars and lake shores.

Distribution. Breeds from the arctic coasts of Alaska eastward through Mackenzie to coastal Labrador. Winters mainly in coastal South America, north to the West Indies and the Pacific coast of Central America. Accidental in the Azores, British Isles (45), France and West Germany.

Movements. Breeds in three separate areas – Alaska, central and eastern Canada. Migration routes of Alaskan birds mainly lie through the Great Plains region of Canada and the U.S.A. Central Canadian birds have a more elliptical migration route. In autumn birds pass south-east through James Bay, then south in a corridor that intersects the Atlantic coast in a zone between the Gulf of St. Lawrence and Virginia (mixing there with eastern birds). Spring passage takes place through the Gulf of Mexico, and north through central U.S.A. to west of James and Hudson Bays. East Canadian birds pass through the Gulf of St. Lawrence in autumn, where ringing has shown many transoceanic flights direct to the eastern Caribbean. Highest concentrations of birds occur in south-eastern Canada in autumn (especially in the upper Bay of Fundy) and few birds follow the U.S.A. coastline southward. The spring route lies along the Atlantic coast of the U.S.A., probably turning north-west near the Canadian frontier. All three populations probably meet in South America and the Caribbean.

Feeding. Forages for food by performing single, halting pecks, also snatches, as well as probing shallowly in soft mud. On wintering areas, where it overlaps and certainly competes with Western Sandpiper on coastal mudflats, it probes far less, foraging mainly on wet or dry mud, while the longer-billed Western forages mostly by probing in wet mud or water. On breeding grounds takes mostly aquatic insects and their larvae.

Social and breeding behaviour. Arrives later on breeding grounds than other *Calidris* sandpipers (late May to third week in June), appearing in mixed-sex flocks, and territorial advertisement by the males begins almost immediately. Males may re-occupy their old territories, gradually intensifying their display behaviour and aggressive encounters. The display flight is performed over a small area at a height of 8–10m above the tundra, occasionally much higher, reaching 60m or more. Often the bird hovers in mid-air, trilling during much of the flight. Pair formation may occur three to six days after territory established, and another four to six days elapse between pair formation and the laying of the first egg, with the male's territorial display flights occurring less often. The species has a monogamous mating system. Gregarious in winter, often consorting with other small waders. Occurs in large flocks prior to spring migration.

Nest, eggs and young. A nest cavity is lined with bits of dried leaves or grass and is usually placed in a grassy hummock in damp or wet ground. Eggs 4, buff with overlying spots of a brown shade. Incubation period 20 days, by both sexes, although the female may subsequently desert, leaving the male with the eggs and the care of the young. Fledging period about 16 days.

WESTERN SANDPIPER   *Calidris mauri*

Du – Alaskastrandloper   Fr – Bécasseau d'Alaska
Ge – Bergstrandläufer   Sp – Playerito occidental
Sw – Tundrasnäppa

Pl. 11

Identification. Length 5½–6¼in. Largest of stints, looking longer-bodied and standing higher than Little Stint or Semipalmated, with characters of small Dunlin, including unusually long, more droop-tipped, deep-based bill and longer legs (feet partially webbed as Semipalmated). In most plumages, more contrastingly coloured than other stints. However, smaller (shorter-billed) and duller individuals invite confusion with the above-mentioned stints, and even a runt Dunlin can mislead the most experienced.

Summer adult unmistakable: rich rufous-brown above (warmer than Semi-palmated), with conspicuous chestnut edging, especially to the rear of crown, ear-coverts and scapulars. Under-parts whitish, with breast heavily spotted and streaked blackish-brown, with larger black arrow marks on flanks. In flight shows a narrow, whitish wing-bar, rump and tail-pattern as Little Stint. Winter adult, pearly-grey above, head noticeably pale, with forecrown and lores virtually white – unlike any other stint. Many birds in late autumn retain patches of chestnut on mantle and scapulars. Under-parts white, with chest markings reduced to fine grey streaks, strongest at sides, but often stretching right across breast, unlike Semipalmated.

Juvenile distinctive, showing a broad, almost white supercilium (square-ended, only indistinctly forked), the most striking of any stint, with forecrown (whiter than Semipalmated) yielding white face and contrasting with more rufous crown and ear-coverts, and white throat extending to form half-collar. The upper-parts are mixed rufous-brown and dark grey, with rufous feathers much warmer than juvenile Semipalmated. Tips of feathers characteristically bright chestnut and white, giving a more strikingly patterned appearance than in Semipalmated, but lacking the more uniformly warm and evenly scaled appearance, or white V on mantle as Little Stint. Chest-patches buff-grey and streaked more strongly than in Semipalmated or Little Stint. Remainder of under-parts strikingly white. Legs and bill, black. Call '*cheet*' – very different from call of closely related Semipalmated, or short, clipped '*tit*' of Little Stint.

Voice. Gives a short, high-pitched and penetrating '*cheet*' or '*jeet*' (recalling White-rumped Sandpiper), and a harsh, high '*dzee*', approaching usual call of Dunlin. Other short calls range from '*chee-rp*' and '*preet*' to '*pit*'. Flight-song on breeding grounds (shorter than most sandpipers) a few notes on rising pitch, then '*tweer-tweer-tweer*' – trill or purring call.

Habitat. In breeding season nests on heath-covered tundra, especially well drained sites with dwarf willow in a mosaic of sedge marshes. Nests in drier situations than Semipalmated Sandpiper. In winter found on mudflats and sandy beaches, feeding close to the tideline, typically by or in water, rather than on large exposed tracts of sand or mud.

Distribution. Breeds in north-eastern Siberia on the east coast of the Chukotski Peninsula, and the far western tip of Alaska, east to Point Barrow. Winters mainly in southern U.S.A., West Indies, Central America and South America to Peru and Surinam. Accidental, Azores, British Isles (7), France and Denmark.

Movements. Migratory. In North America migrates through the Pacific provinces, including some inland. Rare on the east coast of Canada, but occurs regularly on the Atlantic coast from Massachussetts (late July to early October) southwards, confirming that some east to south-east movement takes place across the U.S.A. Birds depart from their Alaskan breeding grounds from early July and movement in the western U.S.A.

continues to late November (peak numbers mid-September), some birds reaching their winter quarters in August. Migrating east Siberian birds are believed to cross in autumn to Alaska and Canada and migrate with the local birds, as the species is unknown on the coasts of eastern Asia. Return passage through the U.S.A. is from early April into June (peak in third week April), and Alaskan breeding grounds are re-occupied from the third week of May (much less evident on the Atlantic coast of the U.S.A. in spring).

Feeding. Usually probes for prey, with actions recalling Dunlin rather than other stints. Habitually enters water in search of food. In wintering areas co-exists with Dunlin, taking various invertebrates, but competing relatively little with the latter because of their shorter bills, that are less suited to deep probing. In summer feeds mainly on insects, their pupae or larvae and various other invertebrates.

Social and breeding behaviour. Males usually arrive on their breeding grounds in Alaska in mid-May, a few days ahead of the females. In western Alaska breeding dispersion in this species approaches a colonial pattern, like Temminck's Stint, although the breeding density is much lower in the interior of northern Alaska and Siberia. Once the male has established a small territory, he begins to advertise actively by singing and calling. The display flight may be either a slow, patrolling flight (2–30m above ground), or a low, rapid flight, followed by an abrupt upswing, then a steep gliding descent, during which time the male gives a series of ascending notes, followed by a descending buzzing trill. When the female settles on the male's territory he begins to perform courtship displays to her, including a stance in which the tail is vertically cocked, a nest-scraping display, and neck-preening. Copulation is typically preceded by the tail-up courtship stance and trilling call, and the male often raises one wing to the vertical towards the female. If she is receptive, copulation follows, after which they perform neck-preening behaviour. By mid- to late June, when most clutches hatch, nearly all aggressive and territorial display behaviour ceases. The species is characterised by a strong monogamous pair-bond, formed early in the breeding period and lasting until about the time the young are able to fly. Outside the breeding season found in flocks, freely consorting with other small waders.

Nest, eggs and young. Nest is usually placed under dense cover, i.e. dwarf birches, and well concealed. The shallow scrape is lined with lichen fragments and leaves. Eggs 4, buffish, heavily marked with dark reddish-brown. Incubation period 21 days, by both sexes in Alaska, but in Siberia females often abandon their mates during incubation, usually only the males attending the young, and even they depart before the young finally fledge. Fledging period about 19 days.

RED-NECKED STINT   *Calidris ruficollis*

Du – Roodkeelstrandloper   Fr – Bécasseau à col rouge
Ge – Rotkehlstrandläufer   Sp – Correlimos cuellirojo
Sw – Rödhalsad snäppa

Pl. 10

Identification. Length 5–6¼in. Slightly larger, more thickset than Little Stint, with shorter, more stubby bill (but lacking swollen and blunt tip of Semipalmated), also slightly shorter-legged and longer-winged. Breeding adult unmistakable, with uniform rufous head and upper neck, back dark brown with rusty-chestnut edgings. Wing-coverts greyish-brown, with whitish fringes, noticeably paler than back (unlike Little Stint). Winter adult and juvenile resemble Little Stint and Semipalmated, but juvenile lacks rich rufous tones and white V on mantle of similarly aged Little Stint.

Winter adult, upper-parts lighter grey (feathers with finely streaked darker shafts), more uniform that most Little, or Semipalmated. Head pattern more distinctly streaked than Little, with dark-grey line through eye, contrasting with white supercilium and strikingly white forecrown. Tertials noticeably dusky, lacking paler fringes of Little Stint. Under-parts white, like Sanderling, with chest washed grey only at sides. When tail spread, may appear paler than Little (feathers white on inner webs). In flight shows well defined whitish wing-bar.

Juvenile, similar to Little Stint, but head pattern rather plainer (darker through the eye), also has paler wing-coverts and tertial fringes. Colour of upper-parts colder than Little, more blackish-brown, particularly on mantle (feathers with dull buff and whitish fringes), sometimes forming a diffuse and incomplete V, but far less distinct than in Little, and not meeting over back. Later in autumn upper-parts wear quickly, becoming darker and greyer than Little (losing all vestiges of mantle V; drabber than Semipalmated). Wing-coverts pale buff or ochre (not chestnut like Little Stint). Forecrown and supercilium duller than Little, and not forking prominently above eye. Lores and ear-coverts, greyer than Little Stint. In early autumn it is probably the palest of all Stints. Semipalmated should also be eliminated by absence of foot-webs. Has squeaking call notes, unlike commonest calls of Semipalmated or Little Stint.

Distinction from atypically plumaged Little Stint is extremely difficult. Stint identification has never been easy, requiring the sharpest of eyes, the greatest attention to minute detail and the most patient analysis of all characters. If a Red-necked or any other rare Stint is encountered in the autumn, an essential first step is to decide whether it is an adult or a juvenile, and then make comparisons with Little Stint of the same age.

Voice. In flight gives a high, clear, squeaking 'week'. Some calls close to Little Stint, but generally coarser and more typically squeaking 'pip' or 'pit', also thin, squeaky 'twick-twick-twick'. Calls generally weaker and less penetrating than 'chit' of Little Stint. Also uses an abrupt rolled 'chirp' in flight.

Habitat. Breeds on higher ground, away from flat low tundra. Inhabits foothill and mountain landscapes with a complex of tundra vegetation types, where ridges covered with mosses, lichens and cotton-grass, sometimes nesting on dry stony patches. In winter on coasts, resorting to tidal flats and muddy sand, salt marsh and seasonal pools. Also inland in Australia on edges of pools, lakes or swamps.

Distribution. Breeds in eastern Siberia in eastern Taimyr peninsula and Lena delta to Chukotski Peninsula and perhaps further south, also sporadically in western Alaska. Main wintering areas lie from southern China westwards to Burma, southwards through the Philippines, Malaysia and Indonesia to Australia and New Zealand. In Europe confirmed observations are known only from West Germany (August 1968), East Germany (July 1979) and British Isles (July 1986). Difficulties in field identification probably cause this species to be very easily overlooked.

Movements. Some Siberian birds migrate overland (July–September), through Krasnoyarsk, Irkutsk and Buryatskaya regions, crossing Mongolia and Manchuria. Others migrate along the coasts of eastern Asia, some directly crossing Sea of Okhotsk, with others filtering through Micronesia, Bismarck archipelago and Solomons, suggesting a route out over the western Pacific from eastern Asia to Australia (where numerous August–April). A few more westerly orientated birds cross the Bay of Bengal to southern India, with stragglers reaching the west Indian Ocean in the Seychelles and Natal (South

Africa). A few reach western Alaska in autumn, and may winter in the New World. Breeding areas re-occupied late May to early June.

Feeding. Birds forage in dense or loose flocks, obtaining food in typical stint-like fashion, pecking, jabbing and probing. They take small crustaceans and molluscs, polychaete worms and insects. Summer foods diverse, including beetles, weevils, mosquitoes, insect larvae and tiny seeds.

Social and breeding behaviour. Red-necked Stints mate monogamously, but social behaviour not well known. Shortly after arriving on their breeding grounds the males indulge in display flights (20–30m above ground), on rapidly beating wings, with glides, or sometimes flying more slowly on bat-like wings and giving a strongly nasal, rising '*wannh-wannh-wannh*'. At the end of the display the male falls to the ground with wings held in a high V. Outside the breeding season the birds are highly gregarious, often occurring in dense flocks, mixing freely with birds like Curlew Sandpiper and Sharp-tailed Sandpiper.

Nest, eggs and young. Nest in a tussock of grass on tundra. Eggs 4, yellow-tinged, with rufous-cinnamon spots, particularly at the larger end. Incubation is shared by both sexes. Females breeding early in the season often aid in rearing young, while late breeders abandon the nest earlier. Incubation and fledging periods not known.

LITTLE STINT   *Calidris minuta*

Du – Kleine Strandloper   Fr – Bécasseau minute
Ge – Zwergstrandläufer   Sp – Correlimos menudo
Sw – Småsnäppa

Pl. 10

Identification. Length 4¾–5½in. Most birds distinctly smaller than Red-necked Stint, with finer bill (with less obvious base and width), but bulkier than Least Sandpiper. Breeding adult and juvenile markedly chestnut above, the latter with sharply defined white V on mantle, matched only by juvenile Long-toed Stint.

Summer adult, upper-parts foxy, feathers with dark-brown centres and light rufous fringes or tips, creating beautiful pattern, with usually distinctive pale yellowish stripes along edge of mantle, but lacking obvious whitish stripes. Head, suffused with buff, or reddish-brown on ear-coverts, but never as strongly as in Red-necked or Western Sandpiper. Supercilium buffish-white, rather indistinct. Wing-coverts brown with buff-and-white edges. Chest with full or partial gorget, finely spotted and streaked red and brown. Rest of under-parts white. In flight shows a conspicuous white wing-bar. Lower back and rump black with chestnut tone, tail-coverts black, all contrasting with white lateral coverts and grey outer-tail feathers. Adult in winter, upper-parts mousy-grey, and head pale faced with white forehead and whiter supercilium, with pale dusky lores and ear-coverts. Crown patch smallest of all stints in winter. Wing-coverts uniform pale grey-brown, with outer coverts fringed paler, but whitish fringes on inner coverts. Under-parts white with grey smudges at sides of breast.

Juvenile most marked of all stints with classic white V, formed by stripe on edges of mantle and pale margins to scapulars (retained to October, or even November). Upper-parts chestnut-brown, with delicate lace-like pattern of scales, formed by buff-and-white fringes and tips; wing-coverts similar, being mainly brown with chestnut fringes and tips (pale buff or ochre in Red-necked Stint). Head pattern usually diffuse, with off-white supercilium forking above and behind eye (more than any other stint), and dusky lores with paler brown ear-coverts, unlike Red-necked Stint. Legs and bill, black.

Voice. In flight a short '*chit*' – repeated, also '*titti-tit-tit*'. Song on breeding ground (both sexes) a weak, squeaking '*svee-svee-svee*' – on ground and in flight. Also a soft flat trill, or other buzzing and trilling notes recorded in spring and autumn.

Habitat. Breeds on high arctic coastal mainland tundra and islands, on swampy, mossy or dry tundra, nesting especially on sites overgrown with willow scrub. In winter, chiefly on coasts, mudflats, estuaries, tidal creeks and lagoons. In Africa also inland on lakes and marshes and the shores of the Great African lakes.

Distribution. From north-eastern Norway across northern Siberia to about the delta of the Yana river. Winters mainly in Africa, around the Indian Ocean and on the coasts of the Indian subcontinent, with variable numbers in the Mediterranean basin and the Persian Gulf. While the species is abundant on African coasts, it is also widespread inland, especially around the wetlands of the Sahel and savanna zones and on the Rift Valley lakes. Map **26**.

Movements. Migrates on a broad front over much of the western Palaearctic, and wintering areas in relation to breeding range determine S.–S.W. autumn movements. Present on breeding ground from late May to August, with small numbers of adults returning through Finland in July, and large numbers of juveniles in August–September. In Sweden and Britain, passage from July to October, and further south in Morocco from late July (adults) and a month later (juveniles). In spring the species is a relatively scarce migrant on western coasts, suggesting a main return north-east from West Africa across the Sahara and Mediterranean. Birds return to Europe in mid-May and in Finland from late May to early June. Many Siberian birds on spring and autumn migration use more easterly routes through the Caspian area and Kazakhstan lakes, to and from East and South Africa.

Feeding. Picks food items off surface either diligently or with characteristic dashing action, using sight to detect prey some distance ahead. Occasionally recorded probing in sand. In summer feeds mainly on insects – dipterans, beetles and their larvae, particularly mosquitoes and craneflies. Also takes some vegetable matter and seeds. In winter, insects and small molluscs and crustaceans.

Social and breeding behaviour. On spring passage both birds may court and pair soon after arrival in breeding areas. The display flight is distinct from Temminck's Stint and performed by both sexes, singly or in pairs. The Little Stint is not as territorial as Temminck's and it defends no clearly defined areas, so that the display flight is performed for sexual attraction only. The display flight sequence (given a few metres above ground) varies: there may be an exaggerated slow wing-beat with legs dangling, and the bird may also make a brief flight with quivering wings held in a V, and a more gliding flight with wings decurved. An almost vertical flight also occurs, with the bird rising to 20–30 metres before spiralling slowly down. Bird sings during the performances. Wings are raised and fluttered by the male during copulation, which, like scrape-making, is almost identical to Temminck's Stint. Mating system probably involves successive bigamy by both sexes, each female laying two clutches by different males in different areas. Gregarious, usually found in flocks varying from a few birds up to several thousand. Readily consorts with other small waders, e.g. Dunlin and Curlew Sandpiper – more so than Temminck's Stint.

Nest, eggs and young. Nest is a shallow cup lined with leaves and pieces of grass, usually close to water. Eggs 4, pale green to buff, well marked with chestnut or dark brown. Double clutching occasionally occurs, with male incubating first clutch and female second clutch. Incubation period 20 days, probably by both sexes. Fledging period and age of first breeding, not known.

TEMMINCK'S STINT   *Calidris temminckii*

Du – Temmincks Strandloper   Fr – Bécasseau de Temminck
Ge – Temminckstrandläufer   Sp – Correlimos de Temminck
Sw – Mosnäppa

Pl. 10

Identification. Length 5–6in. Much plainer and greyer, and more attenuated (wings cloaking tail at rest) than Little Stint, with grey breast-band, shorter, dull yellowish-brown legs, and in flight white (not grey) sides to the tail, and narrower white wing-bar. Bill short, straight or slightly decurved, and finer than Little Stint.

Adult in summer is grey-brown above, marked blackish and dull rufous, and is much duller than other stints. The breast is strongly marked grey-brown, streaked brown, and the rest of the under-parts are white. Head pattern indistinct, with dull whitish supercilium showing little contrast between grey-brown crown and dusky-brown ear-coverts. Adult in winter, dull grey-brown above and much darker than Little Stint. Indistinct head pattern and clouded dark grey-brown chest-patches remain obvious. Legs duller, grey-green to olive-brown.

Juvenile is brownish-grey above, with fine dark crescents and scaled buff. The breast is brownish-grey, contrasting with white throat-patch – no other stint is as dark-chested in autumn. Head rather dark, with noticeably indistinct supercilium. At long range appears uniform above and dark sides to breast recall Common Sandpiper. Usually towers when flushed, giving a trilled '*trrrrit*' distinct from other stints.

Voice. Gives a distinct, rapid, cricket-like '*trrrrit*', or extending into a longer twitter with rising inflection, '*tirr-it-tit-tit*'. Song is a tinkling trill, rising and falling, sustained sometimes for several minutes.

Habitat. Breeds in the arctic zone, but avoids more extreme situations and exposed coasts. Nests in wet sphagnum bogs, in sides of hummocks close to pools of water, but also recorded on dry ridges with small bushes. On migration tends to move cross-country, stopping on margins of all kinds of inland waters. In winter also favours fresh-water sites, or prefers sheltered inlets, estuaries or salt marshes, avoiding sandy and open beaches.

Distribution. Breeds in Eurasia from Scotland (a few pairs nesting annually since 1969) and northern Scandinavia east through northern Russia and Siberia to the Chukotski peninsular and Anadyrland. Winters from Mediterrranean basin south to Africa, mainly in Sahelian and savanna zones, sparingly in Gulf of Guinea, Arabia, southern Iran to the Indian subcontinent, Malaya and south-eastern China and Japan. Accidental in Atlantic Islands, Portugal and Ireland. Scarce, but regular migrant in Britain – mainly east coast. Map **27**.

Movements. Migrates overland on broad front from breeding areas, with smallest numbers occurring in western maritime countries. In Fenno-Scandia adults leave young before fully fledged, in early July, and at the end of the month in Siberia, with juveniles leaving in early August. Passage through Europe and Turkey is from late July to late September. Adults arrive in Pakistan from mid-August. Also in August in Africa, where mainly present from October to March. Birds depart from winter quarters in March–April, crossing Europe and Turkey mid-April to mid-May. European breeding areas re-occupied from mid-May, and at the end of the month – till early June in Siberia. Probably the majority of western Palaearctic birds winter in the northern tropics of Africa, from Senegal to Chad, penetrating further south in East Africa.

Feeding. Feeding behaviour essentially similar to other *Calidris*, picking prey from sand or mud and from vegetation, rarely ever probing. However, feeds more methodically than Little Stint and less inclined to run about. In breeding season feeds mainly on insects and their larvae, particularly craneflies and midges. In winter, mainly small worms, crustaceans and small molluscs.

Social and breeding behaviour. On arrival on breeding grounds the males quickly establish territory, which they advertise by singing (on ground or in air) and performing display flights. Typically the male flies in a wide circle (1–10m above ground), with tail spread and wings held in a trembling V, song sustained throughout. Wing-raising display also occurs on ground, when male perched on boulder, and also used in aggressive encounters as in many *Calidris* species. Both sexes are successively bigamous. Pairs form short-lived pair-bonds, and it is not until the female has completed her first clutch, and turned it over to the resident male, that she leaves her first mate and pairs with a new one. The courting male runs round the female with one or both wings uplifted, alternately trilling and giving an excited '*tsriuu*' call. Later he makes a scrape, usually in presence of female, leading her through the grass with tail cocked. If the female follows, the male stands up with wings spread, and the female then sits in scrape under male's fanned tail. In successful courtship, the female invites copulation by standing still and stooping. The male dances about close behind her, fluttering his wings held in high V, and then slowly lifts off with dangling legs and alights on the female's back. Moderately gregarious, but occurs in smaller parties then most stints, outside breeding season.

Nest, eggs and young. Nest is a shallow cup on ground, in open or low vegetation. Loose colonial nesting, with some nests fairly near each other. Eggs 4, greenish-grey fading to buff, marked with brown spots. Female lays 1–3 clutches in rapid succession, in different males' territories. Incubation period 21–22 days and young cared for by single parent. Fledging period 15–18 days. Age at first breeding, first year in female and one-three years for male.

LONG-TOED STINT   *Calidris subminuta*

Du – Taigastrandloper   Fr – Bécasseau à longs doigts
Ge – Langzehen-Strandläufer   Sp – Correlimos siberiano
Sw – Långtåsnäppa

Identification. Length 5–5½in. Approaching Little Stint in size, but less compact, slimmer and with slightly longer, paler legs (compare Least Sandpiper and Temminck's Stint) and distinctly longer toes. Bill, short, faintly decurved, tapering to a fine tip. Often shows more upright posture, looking longer-necked, and in some plumages may recall a diminutive Sharp-tailed Sandpiper.

Adult summer, upper-parts brownish-black with extensive bright chestnut fringes. Black-chestnut flecked crown contrasts with creamy supercilium (appearing longer than in other stints), and pale rufous ear-coverts. Scapulars brownish-black with paler chestnut fringes, and wing-coverts dark grey-brown edged paler. Under-parts white with the breast finely streaked buffish-brown. Adult winter, darker above than Least Sandpiper, and much darker above than the rest of the stints. Upper-parts blackish-brown with dark grey-brown fringes. Markings on the forecrown and ear-coverts remain pronounced, so that the head lacks a pale face. Under-parts white, but the breast has dark grey-brown smudges and some fine streaking.

Juvenile is similar to the summer adult, but the mantle has a distinct scaly chestnut pattern and the scapulars are fringed whitish. On some birds there is a creamy-buff stripe on the mantle, forming a bold V, as in Little Stint. Wing-coverts are broadly edged bright buff-brown. The head pattern shows a strong contrast between the dark forecrown and the creamy supercilium and there is also a much longer cap to the head than in any other stint. Breast, suffused buff, lightly streaked brown.

In flight shows a short, indistinct, whitish wing-bar and the lower back and the centre of the rump are black with dark grey-brown outer-tail feathers. Bill, yellowish or olive-brown with dark tip; juvenile has a greenish base to the dark bill. Legs and feet, dull yellow, olive or grey-green, toes noticeably long and extending beyond tail in flight.

Voice. Commonest call a dry purring '*prrp*' or '*chrrup*'; other calls include '*dwit-dwit-dwit*' or '*trit-trit-trit*', '*trrr-trrr-trrr*' and a high-pitched '*twirr*'. Song is a slow, repeated '*kroer*'.

Habitat. Breeding areas are uniquely centred on the taiga zone, on tundra-like or boggy areas where mosses, low sedges and dwarf willow are present; also on mountain tundra and unwooded elevated terrain with small marshy areas. In winter, found both on inland marshes and tidal flats. Has a preference for fresh-water habitats, where soft mud and some scattered low clumps of soft vegetation are present.

Distribution. Breeding area imperfectly known (range markedly disjunct). In the forest zone of Siberia, from the Kamchatka Peninsula and Koryak Highlands along the west side of the Bering Sea westward to western Siberia near the Ob River. Nowhere does it reach the Arctic Ocean. Winters from south-eastern China to Bangladesh and southwards to the Philippines (important wintering area), Malaysia and Indonesia, including the Celebes and a small number recorded annually in Australia. Recent observations suggest a small passage through Iran and Aden to East Africa. Only two confirmed records are known from Europe, Sweden (October/November 1977) and Britain (August/September 1982).

Movements. Migrates overland from its disjunct breeding grounds on a broad front through continental Asia. The more westerly breeding populations cross southern central Siberia and Mongolia and the more eastern birds pass down through the Russian maritime provinces, Manchuria to Japan and Korea. Both these routes eventually converge in China (from mid-July). The main autumn movements through Mongolia, Korea and Japan are from August-September. Birds also arrive in Malaya and Java from August, with a few reaching northern Australia and Victoria (September to April). Spring return starts in March, with the main passage in April-May, when the species is common in China. Breeding grounds re-occupied in late May to early June.

Feeding. Little information, but evidently its long toes enable it to walk and feed over floating vegetation more easily than its congeners. Recorded taking beetles, small gastropods, molluscs and amphiods.

Social and breeding behaviour. Little studied, but in early June the male performs a courtship flight (up to 100m), circling over the tundra, alternately fluttering his wings and gliding, calling all the while. The mating system is uncertain, but thought to be monogamous. Outside the breeding season gregarious and freely consorting with other stints.

Nest, eggs and young. Recorded nesting near pools and in damp areas in low tundra-like vegetation. Eggs 4, grey-green with underlying streaks and spots of light brown and marked with larger, darker spots, mostly at larger end. Little other information and no records confirming incubation by the females, which migrate southward as early as late June and early July, leaving the care of the young to the males.

LEAST SANDPIPER   *Calidris minutilla*

Du Amerikaanse Kleine Strandloper   Fr Bécasseau minuscule
Ge Wiesenstrandläufer   Sp Playerito menudo
Sw Dvärgsnäppa

Pl. 11

Identification. Length 5–5¼in. Smallest stint, with fine, needle-like bill, small square head, shorter wings, shorter and usually greenish or yellowish legs (compare Temminck's and Long-toed Stints). Rather dark plumage at all seasons, i.e. rich dark brown in summer and juvenile dress, more dusky in winter. Adult summer, upper-parts dusky brown with chestnut and grey fringes, appearing more uniform than Long-toed Stint, and darker than all other stints. Head rather dark and strongly streaked, with indistinct whitish supercilium. Chest washed brown and strongly streaked, more so than in Long-toed. Adult winter, upper-parts blackish-brown with broader grey edges, contrasting with darker feather centres, recalling adult Long-toed, and more prominently marked than other stints. Retains much of its finely streaked gorget in winter.

Juvenile as summer adult, but mantle has a scaly chestnut pattern, and scapulars are fringed whitish. Wing-coverts are brown and broadly edged bright buffy-brown, or chestnut on the inner coverts and tertials. Sometimes shows a thin white V on mantle, as in Little Stint. Supercilium buffy white, forking slightly above eye – head pattern recalling Little Stint. Sides of the breast are suffused buff and lightly streaked brown, sometimes forming complete gorget, unlike all other stints, except Long-toed and Temminck's. Rest of under-parts very white. In flight shows a narrow white wing-bar and a tail pattern similar to Little Stint. Distinctive '*kreet*' call.

Voice. Usual call a weak, grating '*threep*', becoming more trilling, a drawn-out '*kreet*' or '*kreep*', quite high in pitch; also '*kree-eet*', '*triip-trip*' and '*trip-rrip-peet-wit*' recorded. The flight song is a protracted thin trill, which does not carry very far.

Habitat. Breeds in subarctic, mainly within the coastal belt altitudes. Found on wet tundra, where tussock grasses and heath, mossy hummocks or wet sedge-meadows near the tree line. Outside breeding season, beaches and tidal flats, sandy lake shores and margins of fresh-water marshes.

Distribution. Breeds from Alaska through northern Canada eastwards to Labrador and Newfoundland. Winters mainly on the Gulf coasts of the U.S.A., Central America, the West Indies, and northern South America. Accidental in Iceland, Azores, British Isles (29), France, West Germany, Finland and Austria.

Movements. Migrates from its subarctic breeding areas on a wide front across the North American interior, as well as along the coast. Movements start in mid-July, with large numbers passing in August–September, trailing off in October. The first peak, July to mid-August (adults), and juveniles predominate in the second, larger, peak from mid-August. Ringing recoveries confirm the major use of a transoceanic route from the Maritime provinces and New England to the Lesser Antilles and probably north-eastern South America. Birds using other interior routes through North America probably arrive further west in South America or winter in the Gulf of Mexico or the Caribbean. Spring passage is rather late, with the peak passage through the U.S.A. during the first three weeks of May, and crossing Canada mainly in the second half of May. Breeding areas are re-occupied during the first half of June. Large numbers follow the Atlantic coast in spring, but there is no evidence for transoceanic movement then.

Feeding. Forages mainly by making pecking rather than probing movements, either singly or in multiple series. Its food includes amphipods, the larvae and pupae of midges, small beetles and vegetable matter.

Social and breeding behaviour. Shortly after arriving on breeding grounds, males occupy territory and advertise with display flights to attract mates. In the display flight the male flies steeply up to 15–20m and then hovers, or continues with an alternating fluttering flight, holding wings outstretched but motionless, and singing. The flight is ended in a dive, or by slowly parachuting down. The song may also be given on the ground during courtship. The male plays a major role in incubation, typically incubating during most of the daylight hours, and is also primarily responsible for raising the young. The species has a monogamous mating system. Gregarious outside breeding season.

Nest, eggs and young. Nest is a cavity in a clump of grass or moss, scantily lined with pieces of grass or leaves. Eggs 4, buff with ashy spots and blotches of chestnut. Incubation period, 19–23 days. Fledging period, not established.

WHITE-RUMPED SANDPIPER   *Calidris fuscicollis*

Du – Bonaparte's Strandloper   Fr – Bécasseau de Bonaparte
Ge – Weissbürzelstrandläufer   Sp – Correlimos de Bonaparte
Sw – Vitgumpsnäppa   **Pl. 11**

Identification. Length 6½–7in. Slightly smaller than Dunlin, with more attenuated body, short straight bill and long wings, extending beyond tail at rest. Has a conspicuous white patch above the tail like Curlew Sandpiper.
   Adult summer, upper-parts blackish-brown edged chestnut and buff, more whitish streaking on hind-neck. Under-parts white, with flanks spotted and streaked brown. Indistinct whitish supercilium. Has a U-shaped white band over blackish-brown tail, which is positioned lower than in Curlew Sandpiper — giving longer-tailed effect. Adult winter, ashy-brown above, with very pale buff fringes to wing-coverts. Breast pale ashy-brown with soft streaking. Throat and rest of under-parts white.
   Juvenile resembles breeding adult, but upper-parts more intensely coloured, blackish and grey-brown with extensive whitish-buff fringes, forming a scaly pattern. Wing-coverts greyish-brown edged cinnamon-buff or chestnut-buff. Scapulars show noticeably rusty-chestnut fringes. Under-parts white with buff breast softly streaked. In flight shows a white wing-bar, but less noticeable than in Curlew Sandpiper, with which it also shares a white patch above the tail. Bill black, occasionally showing yellowish-brown tinge to base. Legs black, with slight olive tinge.

Voice. Commonest call is a high-pitched, quiet, thin *'jeet'*, which may be a single note or repeated in series. In the display flight the male gives a rattling sound like a typewriter carriage, interspersed with a few pig-like *'ng-oik'* notes.

Habitat. Breeds on lowland and upland tundra. Ideal habitat consists of hummocky, well vegetated tundra that remains wet, and often occurs around the edges of pools and lakes. In winter forages on mudflats at low tide. On passage, visits inland lagoons and muddy edges of lakes or sand bars on rivers.

Distribution. Breeds on the mainland and islands of arctic Canada, from northern Mackenzie east to southern Baffin Island, irregularly in northern Alaska. Winters mainly in eastern South America, from Paraguay south to Tierra del Fuego and the Falkland Islands. Accidental in Iceland, Spitsbergen, Azores and in several European countries, including the British Isles (279).

Movements. Migratory, wintering in South America. Some passage is evident in July. i.e. males leave territories while females are still incubating. However, the main passage through the U.S.A. occurs in September, and later at Lake Ontario (October to early November). Rare on passage on the Pacific side and autumn passage is partly through the North American interior and across the West Indies. Largest numbers use the Atlantic coast, in contrast to the spring. It is believed that some birds are capable of making a non-stop flight over the sea from the Gulf of St. Lawrence to north-eastern South America. The first autumn migrants reach the West Indies in July, and arrivals occur in Surinam from mid-August (continuing to late November), and some birds reach Buenos Aires by early September (where common till April). The spring movement in South America is from March to mid-May, and route lies over the Greater Antilles and the Gulf of Mexico to southern U.S.A., continuing north through the interior. Birds are very rare on the Atlantic coast in spring, hence an elliptical migration for many birds. Passage through the U.S.A. is from late April to May, and breeding areas are re-occupied by early June.

Feeding. Feeds by picking and probing. On the breeding grounds feeds by deeply probing into moss and wet vegetation. Takes a variety of insects, adult and larval craneflies, beetles, tiny molluscs, various aquatic worms and some seeds.

Social and breeding behaviour. Shortly after arrival on their breeding grounds the males take up territory and begin to display. Ground and aerial displays include pursuit flights of the female and attempted copulation on the ground. In dense breeding populations the territorial display of males is a low flight of 5 to 10m, a song, and then a glide back to the ground on out-stretched wings. At lower breeding densities, the males rise to heights of 15 or 30m and give repeated trilled calls during long, hovering flights. In typical display posture the wings are held stiffly outward, rump exposed and tail slightly raised, exposing the under-tail coverts. The male runs about in this posture giving a low buzzing or growling sound. Nesting of the female is done without regard to the male's territory, so that his territory is used purely for sexual advertisement. The species has a polygynous mating system. Gregarious outside the breeding season, freely consorting with other small waders.

Nest, eggs and young. Nest well concealed in deep depression in hummock and lined with willow leaves, mosses and lichens. Eggs 4, buff, spotted and blotched with medium to dark reddish-brown, mainly concentrated at larger end. Incubation period 22 days, by female only. Fledging period 16—17 days, young tended by female only.

BAIRD'S SANDPIPER *Calidris bairdii*

Du – Baird's Strandloper	Fr – Bécasseau de Baird
Ge – Bairdstrandläufer	Sp – Correlimos de Baird
Sw – Gulbröstad snäppa	

Pl. 11

Identification. Length 7¼in. A large American 'Stint' only slightly smaller than Sanderling, but with more horizontal carriage, and longer wings extending beyond the tail at rest combine with short straight bill and short legs to give distinctive silhouette, only shared by White-rumped Sandpiper. Juvenile readily separable by noticeable scaled appearance above.

Adult summer, upper-parts blackish-brown, broadly scaled with warm or light buff and brown margins. Buffish-white supercilium extending to rear of ear-coverts and paler hind neck contrast with very dark crown to give capped appearance. Chin and throat white and chest-band warm buff, finely streaked sepia. Rest of under-parts pure white. Adult winter, like breeding adult but head and upper-parts become greyer brown, and wing-coverts greyish-brown with very pale buff fringes. Under-parts as summer, with more buffy breast-band, faintly streaked. Browner on upper-parts and buffier on chest than most other non-breeding *Calidris*.

Juvenile, distinct scaly appearance to back. Upper-parts buffy-brown, with prominent scaly pattern formed by whitish tips to feathers, and scapulars edged bright cinnamon-buff. Creamy eye-stripe meets in a V over bill and ends rather squarely at rear of the crown. Crown and sides of head finely streaked sepia, and buffy breast-band contrasts with pure white under-parts. Bill and legs black.

In flight shows a short, indistinct, palish wing-bar (least striking of most *Calidris*), whilst the blackish rump and upper tail-coverts lack contrasting white lateral coverts, which is diagnositic; tail ash-brown and outer tail feathers greyish-brown.

Voice. Commonest call, '*kreep*' or '*p-r-r-reet*'. In the display flight the male utters a frog-like trilled song.

Habitat. A high-arctic breeding species found on upland, well drained, exposed tundra and dry elevated sites, even occurring on boulder-strewn mountain sides. In Siberia, on dry, elevated, stony ground and on dry lichen or moss-lichen tundra. Occasionally feeds on beaches or on shallow pools of coastal marshes, but generally prefers inland to coastal habitats on migration, i.e. margins of lakes and ponds, or river bars. Will also feed in short grassy areas.

Distribution. Breeds from north-eastern Siberia to St. Lawrence Island, northern Alaska and northern Canada east to Baffin Island and north-western Greenland. Winters in South America from the high Andes of southern Ecuador southwards to Patagonia, where also plentiful at sea level. Accidental, Azores and in several European countries, including the British Isles (121).

Movements. Migratory, with adults leaving breeding areas in late July (females slightly earlier), mostly funnelling through Canada west of Hudson Bay and then travelling over the prairies of southern Canada and northern U.S.A. The prairies are an important staging and fattening area, preparatory to direct non-stop flight to the South American Andes and further south. Main migration routes lie inland along the mountainous ranges of the Rockies and the Andes. Most adults have left the U.S.A. by mid-August and use the great circle route to northern South America, which involves a long sea-crossing over the eastern Pacific. Juveniles migrate more leisurely, leaving their breeding areas from late July, with a peak passage in U.S.A. during the second half of August, moving on a broader front than the adults; but still a scarce migrant in Canada east of Hudson Bay (where extremely rare in spring despite breeding in western Greenland). Unlike the adults, many juveniles move into S.W. U.S.A. (Texas, Arizona), but still bypass or overfly Central America on their way to their southern wintering areas. In spring birds leave their wintering areas by very early March, again by largely bypassing or overflying Central America, and passing through the interior of the U.S.A. and Canada (April–early May). Breeding grounds are reoccupied in late May and early June. Those birds breeding in north-eastern Siberia cross to Alaska and Canada in autumn and join Nearctic population which winters entirely in South America, south of the Equator.

Feeding. Feeding actions less varied than its congeners, picking up or pecking at food and moving forward at a rather even pace, diligently seeking food. Little probing seems to be performed. In summer forages for beetles, spiders and adult dipterans, and especially cranefly and midge larvae.

Social and breeding behaviour. Birds arrive near their breeding grounds at Barrow

(Alaska) in early June, as the adjacent tundra is still covered by snow. Immediately there is a flurry of concentrated male display, which is almost lek-like, on exposed sites right on the coast. It involves much territorial display and aerial song, which only ceases as the snow melts on the adjacent tundra, thereby allowing the males to occupy their nesting territories. Whether pairing occurs on these temporary display areas is unknown. The species has a seasonally monogamous mating system. The displaying male flies higher than other *Calidridines* (except Knot), and while flying with a continuous wing-beat, gives a frog-like trilled song similar to Dunlin near the peak of the ascent, which continues during a downward glide back to earth with the wings held in a V. Sometimes the male will remain aloft for two to three minutes, circling and trilling, and shorter flight notes sounding like '*cree*' or '*dree*' are also sometimes given. Outside the breeding season, gregarious, and freely mixing with other small waders on passage.

Nest, eggs and young. Nest is a shallow depression on bare or amongst mat vegetation, with a lining of lichen and bits of other plants. Nests are more exposed, like plovers or Turnstones. Eggs 4, creamy-buff, profusely speckled with reddish-brown and pale purple. Incubation period 21 days, by both sexes, and young initially cared for by both. Fledging period 20 days.

PECTORAL SANDPIPER   *Calidris melanotos*

Du – Amerikaanse Gestreepte Strandloper
Fr – Bécasseau tacheté
Ge – Graubruststrandläufer
Sp – Correlimos pectoral
Sw – Tuvsnäppa

                                                                        Pl. 12

Identification. Length 7½–9in. Variable in size, between Dunlin and a very small Reeve. A rather erect sandpiper with small head, straight and slightly tapering bill and deep pectoral band ending sharply against white of lower breast (compare Sharp-tailed Sandpiper). Breeding adult and juvenile show distinct white V's on mantle, have elongated central tail feathers and pale yellowish-green legs.

Adult summer, upper-parts blackish-brown with variable chestnut and buffish fringes; wing-coverts greyish-brown. Crown blackish-brown streaked tawny, contrasting with buffy-white eye-stripe. Deep pectoral band, with dusky streaks in lines on buff ground, contrasts sharply with white under-parts, including white chin and throat. Adult winter, upper-parts more greyish-brown, drabber, but still retaining well marked pectoral band.

Juvenile closely resembles breeding adult, but brighter, with more whitish-buff fringes, especially on the scapulars, forming strong white lines, creating two white V's on the back. Under-parts white with buffish breast streaked in dark brown lines. A few juveniles may very occasionally lack full gorget and can be confused with Sharp-tailed Sandpiper.

In flight wings look uniformly dark, although at close range a thin pale line does show. Lower back, rump and upper tail solidly black, contrasting with grey outer tail feathers and strikingly white lateral tail-coverts. Bill brownish-black, with the basal third often tinged olive-green. Legs variable in colour, but generally dull brownish-yellow or dull yellowish-green.

Voice. When rising gives a hoarse, reedy '*krrik*' or grating '*trrip-trrip*' or '*prrp*', and in greater alarm a loud, harsh '*trrrerp-trrrerp*'. In display flight the male expands his chest into a prehensile 'balloon' and gives a hooting '*who-u*' call 10–20 times in series, at a rate of about four a second. A coughing '*craw-craw ki-li-li*' is given in ground display.

Habitat. Nests in all kinds of tundra vegetation that provide continuous cover of grasses or sedges and well drained nest sites. Males prefer to establish territories where the wet tundra has promontories, i.e. mounds or hummocks, or along ridges adjoining ponds or marshy basins. In winter occupies many wet, grassy habitats, such as coastal marshes, temporary pools in grasslands and freshwater ponds.

Distribution. Breeds in coastal tundras of Siberia from the Taimyr peninsular, east to the western and northern coasts of Alaska, the northern coasts of Canada (including some islands) and the western shores of Hudson Bay. Winters mainly in South America from southern Bolivia and northern Argentina to Paraguay, but also in smaller numbers in the Pacific to Australia and New Zealand. Accidental, Spitsbergen, Bear Island, Iceland and in most European countries. Recorded annually in recent years in Azores, Ireland and Britain (25 + per year).

Movements. The male leaves while the female is still incubating in July. Autumn migration is prolonged, though individual flocks may cover great distances rapidly. The main passage through North America is mostly overland and primarily in the interior, with passage in the U.S.A. from late July to September. Large numbers also occur in autumn in the Canadian maritime provinces and in New England, though small numbers are present in the south-eastern U.S.A. Some eastern birds may make a long direct flight over the west Atlantic to northern South America, as occasionally large falls occur in Bermuda and the species commonly occurs in autumn in the West Indies. Birds arrive over an extended period in South America, from early August into November, leaving their winter quarters in late February through March. In spring it is rare in the West Indies, indicating extensive overflying of the Caribbean, and then the main passage is through the interior and west of Hudson Bay (April to early May). Breeding grounds are reoccupied from the end of May or early June. The Siberian population is believed to cross to Alaska and Canada in the autumn, before flying south. There is also a small regular migration through eastern Asia, south to Japan and Korea, with birds wintering sparingly in Australia and New Zealand. Small numbers also winter on islands in the central Pacific.

The Pectoral Sandpiper is the commonest Nearctic vagrant to Europe and is annual in autumn in the British Isles (late August to mid-October). Autumn arrivals are normally associated with Atlantic depressions.

Feeding. Feeding action combines picking and fast probing. Walks and stands for long periods, wading occasionally. Takes chiefly insects, crustaceans, earthworms and some vegetable matter.

Social and breeding behaviour. Pairing and territorial flights begin within a few days of the birds' arriving on their breeding grounds. Males disperse to territories and perform display flights that are only a few feet above the ground, for a distance of some 120–150m. The flight is slow, with shallow or deep wing-beats, and the bird has a swollen, 'balloon-like' chest, with the streaked gorget extending below the white underparts. He gives a rapid, pumping hoot, which is often synchronised with the beats. The flight may end with a direct drop to the ground, or with a soaring-upward and gliding descent. In the ground display the male extends his chest into a 'balloon', droops his wings, raises his tail and follows the female in short runs, calling. This is doubtless a courtship display, but the male has also been seen to give a vertical wing-raising display prior to copulation. This species has a short pair-bond and mating is polygynous or promiscuous. In winter occurs in small parties or singly.

Nests, eggs and young. Nests are typically well hidden in grassy hummocks over wet ground and lined with dried leaves or grasses. Eggs 4, pale olive heavily marked with small dark blotches and spots in dark brown or purplish-brown. Incubation period 21–23 days, by female only, and young cared for by female. Fledging period about 21 days.

SHARP-TAILED SANDPIPER   *Calidris acuminata*

Du – Siberische Gestreepte Strandloper
Fr – Bécasseau à queue pointue
Ge – Spitzschwanzstrandläufer
Sp – Correlimos acuminado
Sw – Spetsstjärtad snäppa

Pl. 12

Identification. Length 6¾–8in. Similar to Pectoral Sandpiper but rather stockier, with shorter neck, flatter crown, slightly shorter straight bill and wedge-shaped tail. Also has a dark rufous cap (more rufous than mantle), which contrasts with a long creamy supercilium. Under-parts show no sharp divide on lower breast, lacking vertical streaked gorget, ruling out all but a few juvenile Pectorals.

Adult summer, differs from Pectoral in having darker, richer tawny crown, forming a more distinct cap, and more prominent white supercilium behind the eye. More chestnut upper-parts and darker buff ear-coverts, with spotted chin and throat. Chest and flanks pinky-buff, heavily spotted and barred with small Vs, and marked arrowheads on the flanks to under-tail coverts. Legs duller, green-slate. Adult winter, more greyish-brown above with grey-buff breast-band lightly streaked at sides, merging into white belly. Again shows more contrasting head pattern than Pectoral.

Juvenile has bolder rufous cap and broader creamy supercilium extending to rear of crown, with whitish face. Upper-parts have the feathers black, narrowly fringed pale cinnamon or buff, scapulars fringed whitish (showing distinct white V on mantle), and tertials fringed brighter rufous-cinnamon. Has warm-buff chest streaked brown forming collar, but not a complete gorget as in most Pectoral Sandpipers. Legs duller, grey-olive tinged yellow. In flight rump and tail pattern similar to Pectoral, and also lacks obvious wing-bar.

Voice. Readily distinguished from Pectoral Sandpiper's more reedy call, being higher-pitched and more metallic. Call note when flushed is a repeated short, soft, metallic *'pleep'*. On the ground a repeated *'whit'* or *'wheep'*, and in flight a more swallow-like *'trrrt'* or *'tree-trit'* or combining *'pleep'* call to give *'plee-plee-plee-trrrt-trrrt'*. In the display flight the male utters a short, trilling, crackling warble, unlike any other Calidridine vocalisation.

Habitat. Although it often nests in the same area as the Pectoral Sandpiper, and their breeding habitats overlap, it seems to prefer areas where shrubby tundra alternates with sedge bogs, whilst the Pectoral prefers somewhat drier areas. On passage found by fresh-water lakes and in other especially grassy areas, similar to Pectoral; also on brackish lagoons and river mouths on coasts. In winter will forage on open mudflats, but prefers shallow, brackish lagoons and coastal swamps, frequently hidden among vegetation.

Distribution. Breeds on the northern Siberian tundra from the Lena River delta to the Kolyma and Chaun Gulf, wintering in the Pacific south to the Equator, from New Guinea and Tonga, south to New Caledonia, Australia and New Zealand. Accidental, British Isles (19), France, Norway and Sweden.

Movements. Migratory, with birds leaving their northern Siberian breeding areas in July (males first), on a broad front probably stretching at least between Lake Baikal and the Bering Sea, and continuing overland through Mongolia and Manchuria and coastally to Japan and southern China, only straggling as far west as Malaya and the Indian region. Birds continue south over the sea, crossing to Micronesia and the Philippines to winter in Melanesia and Australasia. A few cross the Bering Strait from Siberia to Alaska, occuring as a migrant on the Pacific coast of North America. Some migrants appear in Japan in late July, but the main passage through south-east Asia is in August–

September, with birds arriving in their winter quarters in Australia (where numerous in winter) from the end of August. Return movement through south-east Asia is from mid-April to early June (peak early May), and breeding areas are reoccupied in late May-early June.

Feeding. Feeding actions combine picking and probing. Early in the breeding season its major foods are cranefly larvae. In winter it feeds on small crustaceans, molluscs, kelp flies, small insects and small amounts of vegetable matter.

Social and breeding behaviour. Breeding behaviour only partially studied, although mating resembles the behaviour of the Pectoral Sandpiper and is either polygynous or promiscuous. Shortly after their arrival on the breeding grounds the males perform display flights over their territories and, like the Pectoral Sandpiper, have a large breast sac which is important in their flight displays. However, unlike the Pectoral, the male rises steeply over the tundra to 30–40m, sets its wings and starts to glide, giving its unusual dry, cackling warble until about halfway through the descent, when it ceases, and then glides silently down. In precopulatory behaviour the male approaches the female with bent legs, bill resting on inflated throat whilst ruffling the back feathers and tail coverts. The wings are slightly spread and the tail is spread downward and then raised almost vertically and quivered. The male then gives two distinctive calls, a series of '*khruk-khruk-khruk*' notes followed by a ringing series of clicking '*pot-pot-pot*' notes. Outside the breeding season the species is gregarious, occurring in small parties to large flocks and mixing freely with other waders such as Red-necked Stint and Curlew Sandpiper.

Nests, eggs and young. Nests in wet tundra, placing nests in dense sedges, selecting the wettest habitats of all the Calidridines. Eggs 4, olive-brown or green, finely peppered with dark brown spots and larger end sometimes covered with patch of dark brown. The females bear all responsibility for incubating the eggs and brooding the young. Incubation and fledging periods not known.

CURLEW SANDPIPER   *Calidris ferruginea*

Du – Krombekstrandloper
Fr – Bécasseau cocorli
Ge – Sichelstrandläufer
Sp – Correlimos zarapatín
Sw – Spovsnäppa

Pl. 9

Identification. Length 7–7½in. Similar to Dunlin, but more attenuated, with longer neck, bill and legs, standing higher, with distinctive broad white band above tail (compare White-rumped Sandpiper).

Adult summer, upper-parts dark brown broadly edged bright chestnut and tipped whitish. Wing-coverts greyish-brown. Some white around the bill and the remaining under-parts are deep chestnut-red with a few brown bars on the flanks. Vent and under tail-coverts white, and the 'rump' is white, obscured by dark bars. Adult winter, dusky-grey above, contrasting with blackish primaries, and almost completely white below. Prominent whitish supercilium and absence of markings on upper tail-coverts make the white band over the tail more prominent. Sparse grey-brown streaking on upper breast.

Juvenile resembles non-breeding adult, but is dusky-grey above, with white margins creating a beautiful scaly pattern, particularly on the scapulars and wing-coverts. Under-parts white, suffused pinkish-buff, with faint streaking on the upper breast. Has a cleaner, longer, white supercilium than Dunlin.

In flight shows obvious white wing-bar and white band over tail. Bill black, long, narrow and evenly decurved over the distal two-thirds of its length. Legs black.

Voice. A soft, rippling '*chirrup*', lacking Dunlin's grating quality. Flocks on the wing have pleasing twittering sounds. On the breeding ground the male has a varied repertoire, quite unlike other *Calidris*, which tend to have rather monotonous trilled songs. The song flight, in its complete form (lasts 10–15 seconds), includes an initial series of chattering notes, a number of trilled doublets and a complex four-part phrase, ending with a number of drawn-out whining notes.

Habitat. Breeds along the high arctic lowland coastal belt of northern Siberia. Nests often sited on gentle slopes of hummocky tundra, or on rough grassy slopes of drier ridges near extensive bogs and pools. Winters on extensive mudflats, sandy beaches and salt marshes, or on lagoons and lakes, or river sandbanks.

Distribution. Breeds in Siberia, mainly in the Taimyr peninsular and very locally east to the region east of the Kolyma, breeding rarely in western Alaska. Winters in Africa, Arabia and the Persian Gulf, India and the Indo-Chinese countries south to the Sundas, Australia and New Zealand. Straggler to North America.

Movements. Migratory, males leaving arctic breeding areas in Siberia before females and juveniles. Chiefly a coastal species in western Europe, but many migrants travel exclusively overland across eastern Europe and Siberia. Ringing evidence indicates three main routes through the western Palaearctic – 1. White Sea to coasts of western Europe (via Norwegian coast or overland to the Baltic), then continuing to West Africa; 2. overland across eastern Europe to the Mediterranean, and on to West Africa with some following the coast and others making a direct flight over the desert to the Gulf of Guinea; 3. overland across Russia to the Black and Caspian Seas, then on to the Middle East and south to East and South Africa (and including Siberian birds originating at least as far east as the Lena). Birds wintering in West Africa return through the Middle East and eastern Europe, so that very few occur on the Atlantic and North Sea coasts in spring. Autumn birds migrate rapidly, with adults reaching western Europe from mid- to late July, and juveniles following in August–September. Spring migration occurs in late April–May in the Mediterranean basin, and breeding grounds are reoccupied in early June. Many, mostly young, birds remain in their winter quarters during the summer. Passage numbers in autumn in north-western Europe show fluctuations, with regular peaks every three to four years.

Feeding. Has the longest and most decurved bill of any *Calidris* and forages by jabbing and probing or by 'stitching' – making a series of closely spaced probes while often standing still. Its longer legs also enable it to feed in deeper water than Dunlin, and on a rising tide it will continue to feed, submerging its head. In summer feeds chiefly on insects, especially the larvae and pupae of midges and craneflies, also vegetable matter and seeds. In winter takes many polychaete worms, also dipteran larvae and pupae, molluscs and some ostracod and amphipod crustaceans.

Social and breeding behaviour. Males become territorial shortly after arriving on their breeding grounds and indulge in low display flights. The song is often given near the end of the flight with full and rapid wing-beats, sometimes interrupted with slower wing-beats and glides. During the gliding part the male raises his head and gives the doublet or whine notes. An elaborate ground display may precede copulation, with the male raising both wings and fanning his tail, moving back and forth, exposing the white patch over the tail. The species maintains a short-lived pair-bond and presumably has a polygynous mating system as some males may pair with two or three females. Gregarious outside the breeding season, forming large flocks and freely mixing with other waders.

Nest, eggs and young. Nest is a shallow scrape amongst low herbage, or often in an exposed site, with little or no lining. Eggs 4, light olive-green, blotched and spotted with olive-brown. Incubation by female alone, male leaving after egg-laying (period not recorded). Young tended by female only. Fledging period and age of first breeding not known.

PURPLE SANDPIPER *Calidris maritima*

Du – Paarse Strandloper   Fr – Bécasseau violet
Ge – Meerstrandläufer   Sp – Correlimos oscuro
Sw – Skärsnäppa

Pl. 9

Identification. Length 8–8½in. Distinctly larger than Dunlin and more robust, with short legs; met chiefly on rocks. It has a distinct sooty appearance, and at all ages shows dull yellow legs and dull yellow base to slightly decurved bill.

Adult summer, has the head and upper-parts blackish-brown, with whitish-buff and chestnut fringes. The neck and throat are streaked dark brown and the breast is variably spotted blackish-brown, extending in larger spots along the flanks and smaller markings on under tail-coverts. Rest of under-parts white. Adult winter, head and neck uniform slate grey and mantle and scapulars blackish-brown, fringed grey and faintly glossed purple. Small whitish throat; upper breast, slate-grey and lower breast mottled slate-grey-white, with brown streaks along flanks. Shows a small whitish spot in front of eye.

Juvenile has mantle and scapulars blackish-brown fringed chestnut and whitish, and the grey-brown wing-coverts have broad, pale buff fringes. The cap is brownish edged chestnut, and the neck is grey-brown, faintly streaked. Breast, streaked brown and mottled dark grey-brown and white.

In flight shows a wide dark tail with conspicuous white lateral tail-coverts, contrasting with dark centre, also a white wing-bar and trailing edge to secondaries (one or two inner secondaries almost all white). The under-wing is mostly white, contrasting with the very dark breast and flanks.

Voice. In flight a '*weet-wit*' and twittering flocks in spring recall Swallow. Has a wide vocabulary on breeding grounds. The typical song begins with a rapidly accelerating, but variable, '*ter-ter-ter-pree-pree-pree*', followed by '*bi-bi-bi-bi …*' calls, then, in the final descent to the ground, the bird gives a wheezy trilling, moaning call, '*pier-r-r-r-r*'.

Habitat. Breeds on mossy arctic tundra, heaths and moors, not far from coast, or on coastal barren flats, or rocky coasts. Also on higher inland fells or mountain tundra in Scandinavia. In winter it frequents rocky coasts, but is also attracted to breakwaters, jetties or piers.

Distribution. Breeds in the islands of the Canadian high arctic, also in Greenland, Iceland, the Faeroes, Norway, Sweden, Spitsbergen and Severnaya Zemlya – as far east as the Taimyr peninsula. Nested Scotland 1978–82. Winters on the Atlantic coast of North America, in south-west Greenland, Iceland, Norway and the Murmansk coast, also in the British Isles, the southern North Sea and on the Atlantic coasts of France and northern Spain. Map **28**.

Movements. Partially migratory, but wholly migratory in high latitudes, i.e. Canadian arctic islands, most Greenland and Taimyr areas, but winters as far north as south-west Greenland or Murmansk, where coasts ice-free. The most easterly breeding birds of the Taimyr and Severnaya Zemlya migrate west through the Barents Sea, since no known wintering areas in Asia. West European wintering flocks include some birds originating from north-western populations. From the end of June females leave their breeding grounds, and males and fledged young follow later in July, all congregating on nearby coasts (rapid moult of adults completed by late August), before migrating. Main autumn passage later than other *Calidris*, e.g. departing from Severnaya Zemlya from late August to mid-September. Main influx into the North Sea wintering areas October–November, coinciding with the main arrival of east Greenland birds in Iceland. In Scotland July–November, and juveniles appearing from mid-September with the main influx of wintering birds. Spring departures from southern wintering areas April–May, with the most northerly breeding areas, i.e. Taimyr peninsula re-occupied in late May to early June.

Feeding. Unlike most *Calidris*, the birds' winter habitats are rocky rather than muddy substrates, so that it is mainly limited to pecking rather than probing in soft substrates. Birds feed close to the water's edge, pecking and probing over crevices, or turning over seaweed to expose prey underneath. They rest during periods of high tide, when their foraging areas are covered. In breeding areas take a variety of insects, spiders, crustaceans, gastropod molluscs, annelid worms and some vegetable matter and seeds. On migration and in winter, molluscs, especially *Littorina* species, are particularly important.

Social and breeding behaviour. Pair formation may occur before, or soon after, the birds arrive on their breeding grounds. Males claim territory which they advertise with song flights, and by chasing off intruders. In the display flight (up to 30m above ground) the male flies in wide circles for some time before descending quickly, calling all the time, and the wings are held in a V over the back like Temminck's Stint. Courtship chases (usually low) may cover some distance, and when the male catches the female, he usually glides on V wings a short distance in front of her, giving part of his flight song. Males chasing females on the ground often perform 'wing-lift' displays, whilst giving the moaning song-call. Copulation is preceded by ground chases, and by the presentation display, in which the tail is cocked and the male assumes a rigid posture (also given in scrape ceremony). He may prepare several nest cups within his territory, one of which the female eventually chooses. The species has a monogamous mating system. Gregarious throughout the year.

Nest, eggs and young. Nest is a small cup, often part-filled with small willow leaves. Eggs 4, creamy-buff, blotched and spotted with brown. Incubation period 21–22 days with male taking greater share, and female finally deserting male near hatching time. Care of young almost exclusively by male. Fledging period not recorded. Some birds breed in their first year.

Disturbed at the nest, Purple Sandpipers perform the "rodent run", in which their hunched posture and creeping gait suggests a vole or lemming rather than a bird. Several sandpipers show similar behaviour, but the display is especially well-developed in this species.

DUNLIN   *Calidris alpina*

Du – Bonte Strandloper
Fr – Bécasseau variable   Ge – Alpenstrandläufer
Sp – Correlimos común   Sw – Kärrsnäppa

Pl. 9

Identification. Length 6¼–7¾in. Smaller than Curlew Sandpiper and more round-shouldered, or shorter-necked, with usually decurved bill, dumpy body and medium-length legs. Variable in size, with the smallest birds often short-legged, with short or almost straight bills, and the larger-bodied birds with long curving bills. Variation in size and plumage can cause confusion with several other small *Calidris*, so that a full study of the Dunlin is fundamental to understanding the identification problems in the genus.

Adult summer, large black patch on lower belly, and upper-parts and crown rich chestnut, streaked and blotched black. Under-parts white, with the throat and breast heavily streaked black-brown. Dusky-white supercilium separates black-streaked chestnut cap from paler grey streaked face and hind neck. Adult winter, greyish-brown above (as Curlew Sandpiper), with wing-coverts greyer, fringed whitish. Under-parts white with the breast streaked grey-brown. Head pattern indistinct, showing a faint whitish supercilium, white chin and throat.

Juvenile more closely resembles breeding adult, but bill shorter and straighter (closely matching Pectoral Sandpiper in shape). Upper-parts blackish-brown with chestnut and whitish-buff fringes, and wing-coverts brownish, with broad buff/chestnut fringes. Under-parts white, with breast streaked brownish and large blackish-brown spots on flanks. Appearance of head rather swarthy, and lack of any distinct supercilium may suggest Purple Sandpiper. Light whitish margins to scapulars form faint V on back, but never as prominent as in Little Stint. In flight shows distinct white wing-bar and white sides to dark tail and rump. Bill and legs, black.

Voice. A short, shrill, rasping '*tree*', '*cheerp*', or a slurred '*treer*' or '*treep*'. The song consists of a regularly repeated series of harsh, frog-like wheezes – '*wrrrrrah-wrrrrrah*' etc, and longer trills consisting of a twittering, whinnying '*chrri-i-i-i-i-ri-ri-ri-ri ...*', accelerating and slightly rising, then slowing and falling slightly. When uneasy, '*quoi-quoi*'.

Habitat. On breeding grounds, habitat similar to Curlew Sandpiper and Little Stint, primarily breeding in tussock tundra and peat-hummock tundra, preferring moist, boggy ground, often interspersed with pools. On upland moors in Britain shares same habitat with Golden Plover. In winter occurs mainly on mud-flats and coastal beaches, estuaries, tidal rivers; also on lagoons and margins of lakes or sewage farms.

Distribution. Nearly circumpolar, breeding in Alaska and arctic North America and from eastern Greenland to north-eastern Siberia, and south in Europe to the British Isles, the Baltic and the coasts of West Germany. Winters south to Baja California, the Gulf of Mexico and Florida, western Europe and the Middle East, Africa south to about Sierra Leone (in west) and Somalia (in east), Arabia and north-western India. *C.a. sakhalina* (breeding eastern Siberia) winters from Sea of Japan to South China Sea. Map **29**.

Movements. Migratory, with three races occurring regularly in western Palaearctic. Most European populations tend to be faithful in successive years to their breeding sites, migration staging-points and winter quarters.

C.a.arctica (N.E. Greenland) present on breeding grounds from late May to mid-August (adults), or early September (juveniles), occurring on passage through Iceland (August) and in Britain and western France (August–September), presumably mainly wintering in north-west Africa. Return migration through Europe, mainly western Britain, in (mainly late) May. Iceland probably overflown, as few identifications in spring.

C.a.schinzii (S.E. Greenland, Iceland, S. Norway, southwards). Passage through Britain July–August (adults) and August–September (juveniles). The majority winter in north-west Africa (especially Morocco and Mauritania), with a few inland in Mali. Icelandic birds return through Britain (mainly west coasts) mid-April to early May. British and continental *schinzii* arrive on their breeding grounds from early to mid-April (late April in Finland), rather earlier than Icelandic birds.

Nominate *alpina* (Fenno-Scandia, east to Kolyma river, USSR) winters in the western Indian subcontinent, coastal Arabia and north-east Africa, the Mediterranean coasts, and western Europe north to Britain, The Netherlands and West Germany. Birds are present in breeding areas from late May to early September, with passage through Scandinavia, Denmark and East Germany July to mid-August (adults) and early August to October (juveniles). Migrants from the White Sea region either follow the Norwegian coast or fly overland to the Gulf of Bothnia. Those wintering in the eastern Mediterranean make long overland journeys across eastern Europe. In western Europe, the most important moulting grounds are on the Waddenzee and the Wash, though smaller numbers use many other North Sea estuaries. After moulting many birds move westwards (i.e. inland peaks in Britain, October–November). Spring return occurs from March to May.

Feeding. Prey located by sight and touch, obtaining food by picking and probing (breeding areas), and by deeper probing on coastal mudflats. Pecks from surface either while walking slowly forward or, especially in shallow water, preceded by a short run. Probes to varying depths (jabbing when bill below half length) with slightly open bill, head usually vibrating up and down. Also feeds by 'stitching', involving very rapid series of shallow probes together, very close – leaving characteristic tracks. Majority of prey swallowed as bill extracted from mud – worms grabbed until whole length pulled out, and often washed before swallowing.

Social and breeding behaviour. Almost without exception males return to the same territory each year, and the females likewise. Pairing takes place in the male's territory, with display flights and ground singing serving to advertise for a mate. In the display flight the male rises steeply from the ground (to 10–50m) and hovers against the wind, to perform a switchback flight, alternating with arched-wings-glide and arched-wings-quiver every five to ten seconds, uttering a series of trills (may last from a few seconds to several minutes). The male slowly moves in wide circles over his territory. When coming down he holds his wings in a V, giving a long trill, and the wings continue to be held up for a few seconds on alighting, before he assumes the upright posture and folds wings. Wing-raising displays are also performed on the ground. Courtship activities include long aerial chases and nest-scraping ceremonies. In this display the male settles into a depression and performs nest-building movements. The female then often moves into the hollow, eventually choosing one in which to lay her eggs. Copulation is preceded by the male closely following the female, raising one or both wings, tilting his tail and trilling. He then takes off and hovers over the female's back before mounting. The species has a monogamous mating system, rarely polyandrous. Gregarious outside the breeding season, often forming very large flocks, like Knot.

Nest, eggs and young. Nest is a shallow scrape, or cup-like hollow, in a grass-tussock, lined with grass or leaves. Eggs 4, pale olive, marked with dark-brown spots or blotches. Incubation period 21–22 days, by both sexes, with the female leaving before the male. Fledging period 19–21 days. Majority of birds breed in their second year, a small proportion in their first.

During the "arched-wings glide" or "quiver", the feathers of the head and neck are raised, and a sequence of courting-trills delivered.

The colour plates

Plate 1   **CRAB PLOVER, OYSTERCATCHER etc.**

CRAB PLOVER *Dromas ardeola*   14″   p 28

Adult: large, mainly white wader restricted to tidal zones; thick, short, black bill and all-white heavy head.

Juvenile: lacks striking pattern of adult, but huge bill still obvious and large head out of proportion to body.

Flight: neck and legs extended – flocks fly low, fast, and in straight lines; easily distinguished by black back and flight-feathers.

OYSTERCATCHER *Haematopus ostralegus*   17″   p 21

Adult (breeding): all black head and neck, long orange-pink bill, stout red-pink legs are diagnostic.

Adult (winter): shows pure white throat-band.

Juvenile: whitish on throat, upper parts fringed paler, legs dull greyish.

Flight: direct, level, strong with shallow wing-beats – travels in lines or V formations. Shows wide, white wing-bar and obvious white rump.

PAINTED SNIPE *Rostratula benghalensis*   9½″   p 19

Adult female (breeding): rufous-chestnut breast with broad white 'shoulder-strap' extending down sides, white 'spectacles' round eyes, buff crown-stripe.

Adult male (breeding): duller than female, shows broad buff barring on wing-coverts and scapulars.

Flight: weak, rail-like, rounded wings show rows of large buff spots, creamy V on back, long dangling greenish legs.

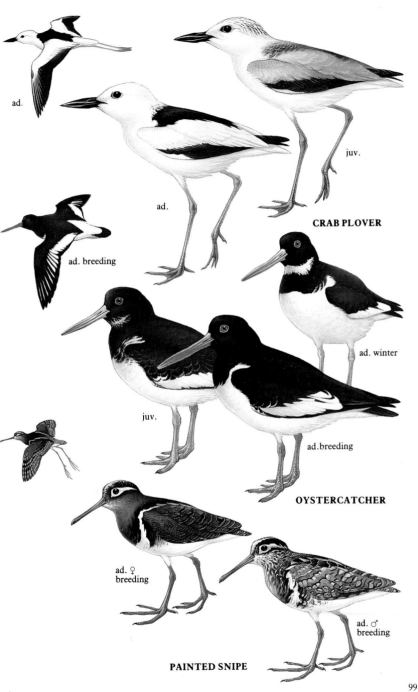

ad.

juv.

CRAB PLOVER

ad.

ad. breeding

ad. winter

juv.

ad.breeding

OYSTERCATCHER

ad. ♀
breeding

ad. ♂
breeding

PAINTED SNIPE

Plate 2   BLACK-WINGED STILT, AVOCET etc.

BLACK-WINGED STILT *Himantopus himantopus*   15″   p 24

Slender, long-necked wader with needle-bill, extraordinarily long, pink legs. Walks delicately with long strides, wades deeply.

Adult male (breeding): mantle glossy black, back of head often black.

Winter: crown/nape white or grey-brown.

Adult female (breeding): mantle browner, wings glossy black; nape mottled dusky.

Immature: mantle browner, legs pinkish-grey.

Flight: direct, usually low – often glides before alighting, when dangles legs to act as rudders or brakes. Silhouette rakish – enormously long trailing pink legs, thin triangular wings (black above and below).

AVOCET *Recurvirostra avosetta*   17″   p 26

Elegant, walks gracefully with neck curved; feeds in shallows with side-to-side sweeps of thin, upcurved bill.

Adult (breeding): mainly snow-white, patterned with black on head/nape and wings; long, lead-blue legs.

Immature: more brownish-black above.

Flight: fairly fast, legs projecting. Above, boldly patterned; below, mainly white with black wing-tips.

STONE CURLEW *Burhinus oedicnemus*   16½″   p 29

Adult: cryptically marked – mostly streaked sandy-brown, shows whitish wing-bar on closed wing. Large, staring yellow eyes, stout yellow-and-black bill, pale yellow legs.

Flight: direct, usually low with deliberate wing-beats, also glides. Wings show two bold whitish bars and a small white patch at base of primaries.

SENEGAL THICK-KNEE *Burhinus senegalensis*   14″   p 31

Adult: slightly smaller than Stone Curlew. Bill longer, shows less yellow. Paler faced, back greyer, shoulders more uniform pale grey – lacks whitish wing-bar.

Flight: wing-pattern differs from Stone Curlew's – shows a single, wide grey wing-panel.

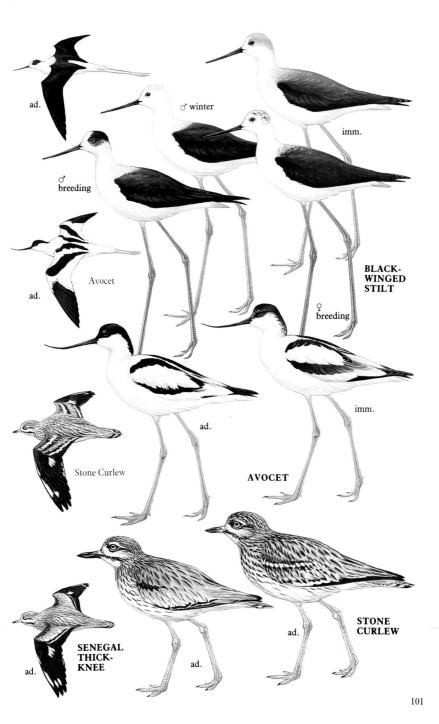

ad.

♂ winter

imm.

♂
breeding

Avocet

ad.

**BLACK-
WINGED
STILT**

♀
breeding

Stone Curlew

ad.

imm.

AVOCET

**SENEGAL
THICK-
KNEE**

ad.

ad.

ad.

**STONE
CURLEW**

ad.

Plate 3   COURSERS, PRATINCOLES

CREAM-COLOURED COURSER *Cursorius cursor*   9″   p 33
Adult: a graceful, sandy-isabelline plover-like bird with contrasting head pattern; long creamy-white legs, short curved bill.

Juvenile: upper-parts show dark feather edgings, head-pattern less well marked.

Flight: direct, fast, legs extending beyond short white-tipped tail. Wings surprisingly large-black below, secondaries tipped white. Above, black primaries contrast with sandy coverts.

EGYPTIAN PLOVER *Pluvianus aegyptius*   8″   p 32

Adult: strikingly patterned – black crown and cheeks divided by long white supercilium to nape; black necklace. Short black bill, legs blue-grey.

Flight: low, on fast flickering wing-beats; has strikingly patterned black- and-white cape-like wings. Tail grey, broadly tipped white.

BLACK-WINGED PRATINCOLE *Glareola nordmanni*   9½″   p 36

Adult male (breeding): differs from Collared in being darker above (little contrast between coverts and flight feathers), shows less red at gape, has black lores, also tail shorter, legs longer.

Adult female (breeding): similar to male – shows narrow black border to creamy throat, both lose sharp outline to throat in winter.

Flight: differs from Collared in having black underwings. Above, wings are darker, more uniform than Collared; also lacks white trailing edge to secondaries.

COLLARED PRATINCOLE *Glareola pratincola*   9¾″   p 35

Adult female (breeding): upper-parts paler than Black-winged, larger area of red at base of bill, eye-ring white. Tail more deeply forked, streamers longer; shorter legged.

Adult male (winter): throat streaked and spotted dusky.

Juvenile: streaked throat; paler fringes to upper parts, short tail streamers.

Flight: differs from Black-winged in having chestnut under-wings and shows white trailing edge to secondaries. Blacker primaries contrast with paler inner-wing and mantle (Black-winged is more uniformly dark above).

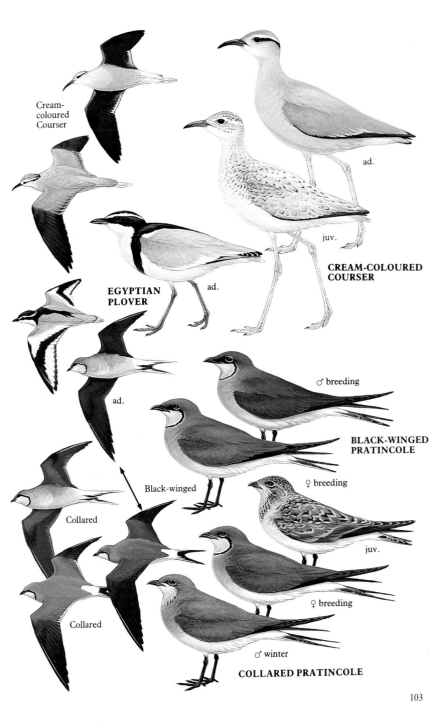

Cream-coloured Courser

CREAM-COLOURED COURSER

ad.

juv.

ad.

EGYPTIAN PLOVER

ad.

♂ breeding

BLACK-WINGED PRATINCOLE

♀ breeding

Black-winged

juv.

Collared

♀ breeding

Collared

♂ winter

COLLARED PRATINCOLE

103

Plate 4   **RINGED PLOVERS**

RINGED PLOVER *Charadrius hiaticula* 7½″   p 40

Adult (breeding): larger more robust than Little Ringed with brighter legs (orange-yellow) and two-toned bill (orange, tipped black), eye-ring dark. Sexes similar.

Juvenile: brown breast-band, legs duller orange-yellow.

Flight: differs from Little Ringed in showing striking white wing-bar and more obvious white side to tail.

LITTLE RINGED PLOVER *Charadrius dubius* 5¾″   p 38

Adult (breeding): smaller, trimmer than Ringed Plover, differing in having yellow eye-ring, flesh-coloured legs, black bill and white line above black on forehead. Sexes similar.

Juvenile: duller yellow eye-ring present (unlike juvenile Ringed) and browner, more hooded head.

Flight: lack of wing-bar diagnostic.

KENTISH PLOVER *Charadrius alexandrinus* 6½″   p 45

Adult male (breeding): smaller, paler above than Ringed Plover with rufous crown, black on sides of breast only and longer, black legs.

Adult female (breeding): unlike Ringed Plover, lacks black mark on forehead, breast patches and band through eye dusky-brown.

Juvenile: paler scaled above, breast patches less extensive than juvenile Ringed, and black not dull yellow legs.

Flight: wing-bar thinner, white tail-sides wider than in Ringed Plover.

KILLDEER *Charadrius vociferus* 9½″   p 43

Adult (breeding): large size, double black-breast bands, red eye-ring, long pale legs and long wedge-tail diagnostic. Sexes similar.

Flight: much larger than Ringed Plover, broad white wing-bar, long wedge-shaped tail, rufous rump.

KITTLITZ'S PLOVER *Charadrius pecuarius* 5″   p 44

Adult (breeding): smaller than Kentish, differs from other ringed plovers in absence of black chest-rings or patches. Throat white, orange-buff below, legs grey-green. Sexes similar.

Juvenile: lacks distinct facial markings or white nape.

Flight: wing-bar ill-defined, tail broadly tipped/edged white. Toes project well beyond tail-tip (not shown).

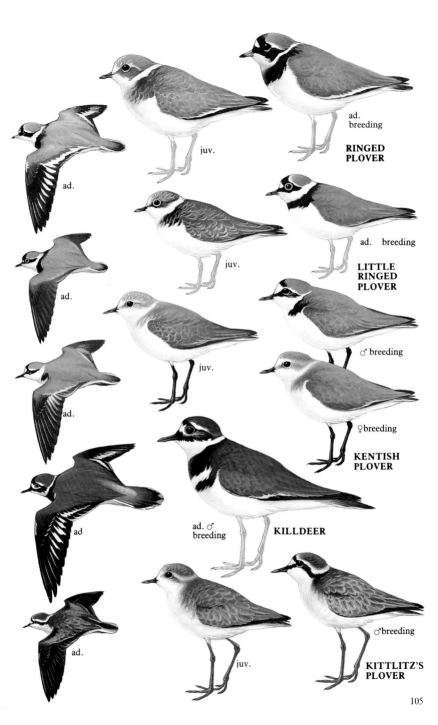

ad.

juv.

ad.
breeding

**RINGED
PLOVER**

ad.

juv.

ad.   breeding

**LITTLE
RINGED
PLOVER**

ad.

juv.

♂ breeding

♀breeding

**KENTISH
PLOVER**

ad

ad. ♂
breeding   **KILLDEER**

ad.

juv.

♂breeding

**KITTLITZ'S
PLOVER**

Plate 5   **SANDPLOVERS etc., TURNSTONE**

LESSER SAND PLOVER *Charadrius mongolus*   7¾"   p 46
Adult (breeding): smaller than Greater. Smaller, less bulbous bill, never with pronounced gonys, length roughly equal to distance from base of bill to rear of eye. Broader rufous-cinnamon breast-band; shorter legs, lead-grey to blackish.

GREATER SAND PLOVER *Charadrius leschenaultii*   9¼"   p 48
Adult male (breeding): larger, longer legged with heavier bill (more bulbous tip) than Lesser, rufous breast-band narrower but shows more white on forehead.

Adult female: resembles a dull breeding male.

Adult (winter): breast shows lateral patches, no hindneck collar, legs typically dark grey.

Juvenile: drab brown and white – very similar to Lesser, but legs noticeably longer and paler.

Flight: prominent white wing-bar and sides to tail – white generally more extensive than shown by Lesser. Toes project beyond tail tip.

CASPIAN PLOVER *Charadrius asiaticus*   7¾"   p 49
Adult male (breeding): more slender build than Greater, deep rusty-rufous breast-band broader, bill finer, whiter face and supercilium.

Adult male (winter): dusky wash across breast unlike both Sand Plovers.

Adult female (breeding): chest-band duller/grey-brown.

Juvenile: upper-parts scaled pinkish-buff, legs often more yellowish.

Flight: wing-bar poorly defined, tail sides narrowly edged white.

DOTTEREL *Charadrius morinellus*   8½"   p 51
Adult male (breeding): blackish crown, broad white supercilia form V on nape, white line across lower breast diagnostic.

Adult male (winter): breast-line dull whitish, belly white, legs dull yellow.

Juvenile: darker-brown above fringed golden-buff, dark cap to head, broad creamy supercilia, breast-line whitish or indistinct.

Flight: lacks wing-bar, tail bordered white.

TURNSTONE *Arenaria interpres*   9"   p 201
Adult male (breeding): portly build, stubby bill, orange legs; pied plumage with orange-chestnut back.

Adult male (winter): upper-parts and breast blackish.

Flight: unmistakable – white wing-bar, shoulder patches and rump.

ad.

♂ breeding

ad. ♂ winter

juv.

♂ breeding

GREATER SAND PLOVER

ad.

juv.

ad. ♂ winter

♂ breeding

♀ breeding

CASPIAN PLOVER

ad.

juv.

♂ breeding

ad. ♂ winter

DOTTEREL

ad.

♂ breeding

ad. ♂ winter

TURNSTONE

Plate 6   GREY and GOLDEN PLOVERS

GREY PLOVER *Pluvialis squatarola*   11″   p 57

Adult male (breeding): stouter than Golden, thicker bill, longer legs; silvery-grey above, whitish top to head, black face/belly.

Adult (winter): brownish-grey, fringed whitish above; under-wings show black axillaries, diagnostic.

Juvenile: grey-brown above, spotted yellow and cream; on the ground larger build separates it from Golden.

Flight: black 'arm-pits', stronger wing-bar, white rump, readily distinguish it from Golden all seasons.

GOLDEN PLOVER *Pluvialis apricaria*   10¾″   p 55

Adult male (breeding): northern form – black face and under-parts, broadly bordered white; southern form – breast and belly black, face dusky, indistinct whitish or yellowish edge to flanks. Both races show white under tail-coverts (mostly black in Lesser Golden).

Adult (winter): golden spangled upper-parts, brighter than juvenile Grey or Lesser Golden.

Flight: 'arm-pits' white, under-wings whitish (dusky-grey in Lesser), no pale rump, narrow white wing-bar most obvious across primaries.

AMERICAN/PACIFIC GOLDEN PLOVERS (LESSER GOLDEN PLOVER)
Pluvialis dominica/fulva   10″   p 53

Recently separated and now considered to form two species – see text for differences between American and Pacific Golden Plovers.

Adult male (breeding): smaller, slighter than Golden, longer legs, narrower wings extend beyond tail. Black below to flanks and under-tail (Golden shows white borders to flanks and under tail-coverts).

Adult (winter): mostly less yellow, more brownish-grey above than Golden, supercilium whiter.

Flight: 'arm-pits', under-wings dusky-grey (white in Golden) dark rump, indistinct wing-bar, less obvious than in Golden.

♂ breeding

♂ breeding

ad. winter

GREY PLOVER

ad. winter

juv.

Grey Plover

southern race
ad. ♂ breeding

ad. winter

ad. winter

northern race
ad.♂ breeding

**GOLDEN
PLOVER**

ad. winter

♂breeding

ad. winter

LESSER GOLDEN PLOVER

Plate 7   **LAPWINGS**

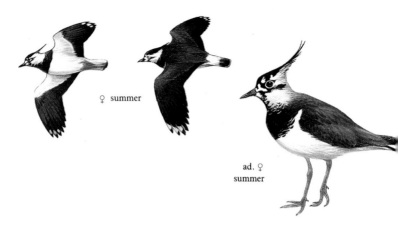

♀ summer

ad. ♀
summer

LAPWING *Vanellus vanellus*   11½″   p 66

Adult male (breeding): Unmistakable – long wispy crest, black breast-band, iridescent greenish-black plumage, cinnamon under-tail coverts unique in the waders of our region.

Adult male (winter): white throat, cheeks buff; whitish margins to chest and scapulars.

Juvenile: shorter crest, less patterned buffy face, brown tone on chest, paler margins to back and wing-coverts.

Flight: broad, rounded black-and-white wings, black tail-band; flocks travel in loosely bunched parties on rather slow, sometimes erratic wing-beats.

SPUR-WINGED PLOVER *Hoplopterus spinosus*   10½″   p 59

Adult male (breeding): slightly smaller than Lapwing with longer legs; black crown/nape with loose crest contrasts with white cheeks/sides of neck, small spur on wing. Sexes similar, no seasonal variation.

Juvenile: more blackish-brown, buff fringes to coverts.

Flight: broad wings show prominent diagonal white panel, rump white and all-black tail unique among large waders of region. Below, all black flight feathers contrast with white underwings, legs extend beyond tail. Flight rather slow.

ad. breeding

♂breeding

ad.breeding

LAPWING

ad. ♂ winter

juv.

ad.

ad.

♂breeding

SPUR-WINGED PLOVER

juv.

111

Plate 8   **LAPWINGS**

WHITE-TAILED PLOVER *Chettusia leucura*   10¾″   p 65

Adult (breeding): unmistakable with pale face, long yellow legs, rosy-buff belly and all-white tail.

Juvenile: upper-parts show dark centres to feathers and paler margins; white in wings/tail as adult.

Flight: action Lapwing-like on well rounded wings, flight often more powerful. Conspicuous broad white band across wings, legs project well beyond all-white tail. Below, black primaries contrast with remainder of white under-wings.

SOCIABLE PLOVER *Chettusia gregaria*   11″   p 63

Adult (breeding): black crown, broad white supercilia meet in V on nape; belly black, shading to chestnut.

Adult (winter): dark cap to head, long creamy supercilium, sides of breast streaked brown, remainder of under-parts white, legs black.

Flight: wings narrower, longer, less rounded than Lapwing. Action free and graceful, recalling latter. Above, pattern of wings reminiscent of Sabine's Gull, tail white with partial black band. Below, black primaries contrast with remainder of white under-wing.

RED-WATTLED PLOVER *Hoplopterus indicus*   13½″   p 62

Adult (breeding): large black-and-white Lapwing with brown back, red wattle, long yellow legs.

Juvenile: white on lower face and throat.

Flight: action recalls Lapwing, wing-beats stronger and more rapid. White diagonal band across wings, tail white with broad black band.

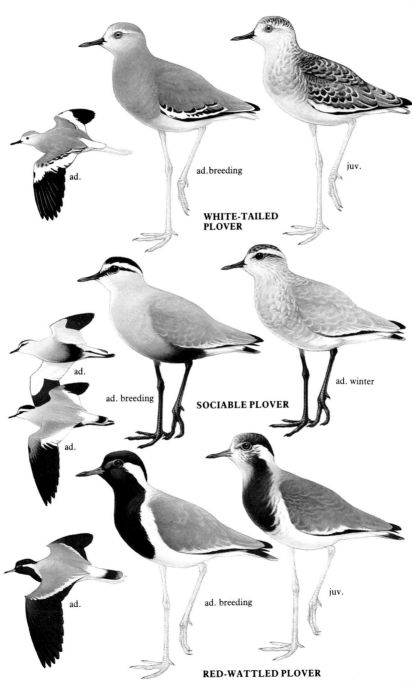

WHITE-TAILED PLOVER

ad.

ad. breeding

juv.

SOCIABLE PLOVER

ad.

ad.

ad. breeding

ad. winter

RED-WATTLED PLOVER

ad.

ad. breeding

juv.

Plate 9 SANDPIPERS

KNOT *Calidris canutus* 9½″ p 71

Adult (breeding): robust, relatively short-billed, much larger than Dunlin; under-parts pink-cinnamon, rump buff-white closely barred black.

Adult (winter): grey, light feather edgings, short greenish legs.

Juvenile: distinctive – browner grey above with clear dark and creamy scaling, tinged pink-buff below.

Flight: stocky appearance – often flies in densely packed flocks. Thin white wing-bar, pale barred (not white) rump, tail uniform grey – lacks obvious dark centre to rump.

PURPLE SANDPIPER *Calidris maritima* 8″ p 93

Adult (breeding): larger than Dunlin, stockier, slightly decurved bill, legs dull yellow. Wide rufous and whitish fringes above, blackish streaks/spots below (lacks Dunlin's black belly patch).

Adult (winter): slate-grey, small white spot in front of eye, yellow legs and base of bill.

Flight: white wing-bar extends onto inner secondaries; lateral tail-coverts white; upper-parts appear very dark, while Dunlin looks paler and greyer on wing.

DUNLIN *Calidris alpina* 7″ p 95

Adult (breeding): rusty back, black patch on belly, long decurved bill (length/curvature variable).

Adult (winter): greyish-brown above, breast streaked.

Juvenile: shorter bill, faint V on back, large blackish-brown spots on flanks.

Flight: distinct white wing-bar, white sides to dark tail and rump.

CURLEW SANDPIPER *Calidris ferruginea* 7½″ p 91

Adult (breeding): longer decurved bill and longer legs than Dunlin; deep chestnut-red below, brown barred flanks. Whiter rump partly obscured by brown bars.

Adult (winter): dusky-grey above, breast sparsely streaked, prominent white supercilium, white rump diagnostic.

Juvenile: distinctive – scaly pattern to back, longer whiter supercilium than Dunlin.

Flight: white wing-bar, conspicuous white band over tail.

winter

ad. breeding

breeding

KNOT

ad. winter

juv.

winter

ad.breeding

**PURPLE
SANDPIPER**

breeding

juv.

winter

winter

ad. breeding

DUNLIN

breeding

winter

winter

juv.

breeding

ad.breeding

**CURLEW
SANDPIPER**

winter

Plate 10 STINTS and SANDPIPERS

LITTLE STINT *Calidris minuta* 5″ p 79

Adult (breeding): short fine bill, rufous-buff above with distinctive yellow stripes along mantle. Wing-coverts and tertials mostly edged bright rufous. Legs black.

Adult (winter): mousy-grey above, white forehead and supercilium.

Juvenile: most marked of all stints – classic white V on back, supercilium forking over eye.

Flight: narrow white wing-bar, white sides to rump, outer tail feathers grey.

RED-NECKED STINT *Calidris ruficollis* 5¾″ p 77

Adult (breeding): slightly larger, more thick-set, stubbier bill, shorter legged and longer winged than Little Stint; distinctive rufous head/neck. Wing-coverts greyish-brown (bright rufous in Little Stint).

Flight: pattern of wings/tail similar to adult Little Stint.

TEMMINCK'S STINT *Calidris temminckii* 5½″ p 81

Adult (breeding): fine bill, grey-brown above marked blackish and dull rufous – dullest stint. Legs yellowish-brown (Little Stint's black).

Adult (winter): dull grey-brown above, much darker than Little Stint, head pattern indistinct, clouded dark grey-brown chest-patches.

Juvenile: upper-parts show fine dark crescents, scaled buff – very different appearance from Little Stint.

Flight: usually towers when flushed, shows white (not grey) sides to tail, narrower white wing-bar than Little Stint.

SANDERLING *Calidris alba* 8″ p 73

Adult (breeding): plump, short-billed, larger than stints; mainly rufous-buff above with pure white belly. Bill and legs black.

Adult (winter): pale grey-and-white with blackish 'shoulders' are diagnostic.

Juvenile: pale grey, etched black above, white below.

Flight: boldest white wing-bar, white sides to tail, very pale appearance on wing.

BROAD-BILLED SANDPIPER Limicola falcinellus 6¾″ p 145

Adult (breeding): slightly smaller than Dunlin, long kink-tipped bill, dark snipe-like plumage, distinct forked supercilium, short legs.

Adult (winter): distinct head pattern retained, black 'Sanderling-like' shoulder-patch present.

Flight: dark upper-parts show thin wing-bar, black centre to tail, sides white.

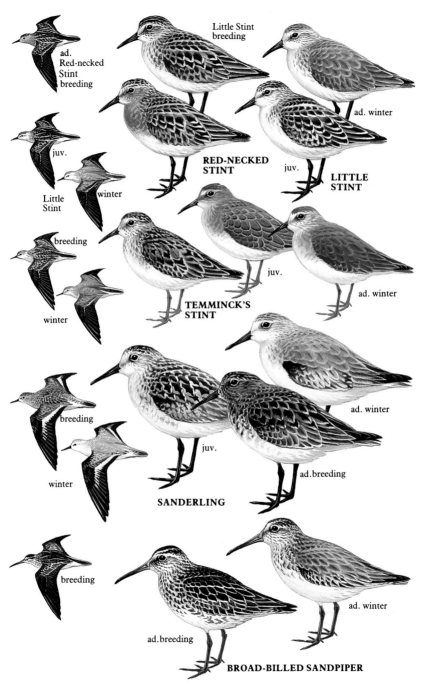

ad.
Red-necked
Stint
breeding

juv.

Little
Stint

winter

breeding

winter

Little Stint
breeding

ad. winter

juv.

**RED-NECKED
STINT**

**LITTLE
STINT**

juv.

ad. winter

**TEMMINCK'S
STINT**

juv.

ad. winter

breeding

winter

ad. winter

juv.

ad.breeding

SANDERLING

breeding

ad. winter

ad.breeding

BROAD-BILLED SANDPIPER

Plate 11   AMERICAN STINTS etc.

LEAST SANDPIPER *Calidris minutilla*   5″   p 84

Adult (breeding): smallest, darkest stint, fine needle-like bill, legs greenish or yellowish.

Adult (winter): blackish-brown above, retains much of its finely streaked gorget.

Flight: thin white wing-bar, tail pattern like Little Stint; juvenile, sometimes shows thin white V on back.

SEMIPALMATED SANDPIPER *Calidris pusilla*   5½″   p 74

Adult (breeding): slightly bulkier than Little Stint; ochre-brown – less chestnut above, breast finely streaked. Bill thicker with spatulate end, toes partly webbed.

Adult (winter): ochre-grey above, chest marks restricted to sides of breast (unlike some Westerns), long white supercilium.

Flight: narrow white wing-bar, tail pattern like Little Stint.

WESTERN SANDPIPER *Calidris mauri*   6″   p 76

Adult (breeding): larger than Little Stint; longer, droop-tipped bill, longer legs; chestnut on head, and scapulars – warmer above than Semipalmated, breast/flanks heavily marked, toes partly webbed.

Adult (winter): pearl grey above, pale headed; fine streaking on side of chest often extends right across breast in a fine bank (unlike Semipalmated).

Flight: narrow whitish wing-bar, tail pattern like Little Stint.

WHITE-RUMPED SANDPIPER *Calidris fuscicollis*   6½″   p 85

Adult (breeding): slightly smaller and body more attenuated than Dunlin, short straight bill, long wings extend beyond tail, white rump.

Adult (winter): ashy-brown above, pale buff fringes to wing-coverts, breast grey-brown and streaked.

Flight: very faint wing-bar (cf. Curlew Sandpiper), U-shaped white band over tail diagnostic.

BAIRD'S SANDPIPER *Calidris bairdii*   6″   p 86

Adult (breeding): stance and shape as White-Rumped (only similar wader with wings projecting well beyond tail); buffish head/breast, blotched or scaled mantle. Juvenile shows a distinctly more scaly appearance to upper parts.

Flight. shows least striking of *Calidris* wing-bars, dark rump, tail and outer tail feathers greyish-brown.

ad. breeding

♂ winter

LEAST SANDPIPER

ad. breeding

SEMIPALMATED SANDPIPER

♂ winter

ad. breeding

WESTERN SANDPIPER

♂ winter

ad. breeding

♂ winter

WHITE-RUMPED SANDPIPER

ad. breeding

BAIRD'S SANDPIPER

119

Plate 12   AMERICAN/SIBERIAN SANDPIPERS

PECTORAL SANDPIPER *Calidris melanotus* 8½″   p 88

Adult (breeding): prominently streaked pectoral band ends sharply on lower breast, white V's on mantle (also present on juvenile), yellowish-green legs.

Adult (winter): more greyish-brown above – still retains well-marked pectoral band.

Flight: dark wings, rump/tail black, outer tail feathers grey, lateral tail-coverts white.

SHARP-TAILED SANDPIPER *Calidris acuminata* 7½″   p 90

Adult (breeding): like Pectoral but shows richer, tawny crown; chest/flanks heavily spotted/marked with V's (reaching under tail-coverts); legs duller green-slate.

Adult (winter): lacks complete streaked gorget of Pectoral, shows more contrasting head pattern, crown more rufous than mantle.

Flight: wings/tail pattern as Pectoral.

BUFF-BREASTED SANDPIPER *Tryngites subruficollis* 7½″   p 148

Adult (breeding): short bill, small head, longish neck; buff-face and under-parts, scaly above, yellow legs (cf. juvenile Ruff).

Flight: underwing white, tips of primaries show delicate blackish pencil marks. Above, no wing-bar, plain rump.

UPLAND SANDPIPER *Bartramia longicauda* 11″   p 179

Adult (breeding): short thin bill, small head, long neck, head/body pattern reminiscent of tiny Whimbrel; long wings, long wedge-tail, legs yellow.

Flight: lacks wing-bar, rump/tail-centre dark; whitish underwings boldly barred black.

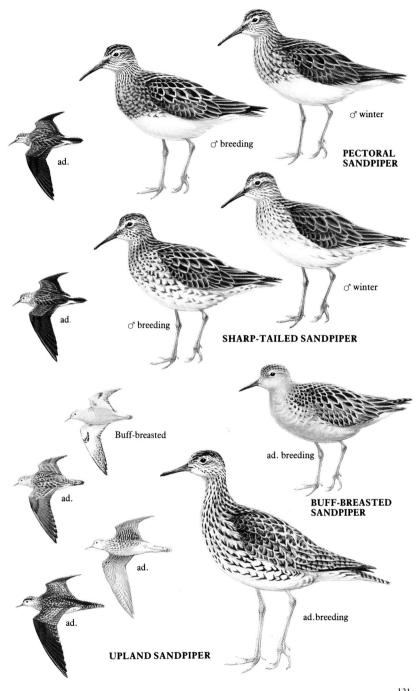

ad.

ø breeding

ø winter

PECTORAL SANDPIPER

ad.

ø breeding

ø winter

SHARP-TAILED SANDPIPER

Buff-breasted

ad.

ad.

ad.

ad. breeding

BUFF-BREASTED SANDPIPER

ad.breeding

UPLAND SANDPIPER

Plate 13   **RUFF**

RUFF (Reeve) *Philomachus pugnax*   8½″ – 11½″   p 149

a-h **Adult males** displaying in their highly variable breeding plumages showing huge, differently coloured loose ruff and long ear-tufts – in various combinations of black, white, purple, chestnut or buff, unique among waders.

i **Juvenile male**: distinctive, boldly scaled pattern above, edged warm buff, breast richly marked golden-buff, legs yellow-brown or greenish.

j **Adult male** (breeding): head-tufts and ruff in relaxed position, grown (April) and lost (June-July) rapidly.

k **Adult male** (winter): grey-brown above edged paler, larger than Reeve, legs variable – orange-red, through yellow to green-brown.

l **Adult female** (breeding): smaller Reeve lacks male's ruff/head tufts, breast/mantle mottled blackish-brown.

m **Adult female** (winter): similar to winter male but smaller size obvious.

Flight: thin white wing-bar, conspicuous white lateral tail-coverts. Males's ruff gives thick-necked appearance in flight.

e

f

g

h

♂♂ in breeding plumage

Ruff

ad. ♂ winter

k

juv. ♂

i

ad. ♂

j

♀ winter

m

Reeve

Ruff

♀ breeding

l

RUFF

123

Plate 14   SNIPES, WOODCOCKS

SNIPE *Gallinago gallinago*   10″   p 153

Adult: very long straight bill, creamy stripes on head/back, centre of belly white.

Flight: shows clear white trailing-edge to secondaries, some white visible on edges of tail when flushed (zigzags, then towers up – fast flight)
Voice: flushed birds give a long harsh 'scaap'.

PINTAIL SNIPE *Gallinago stenura*   10″   p 158

Adult: size close to Snipe but shorter-tailed and relatively shorter-billed. Face pattern differs from Snipe in that the pale supercilium is always broader than the dark eye-stripe at the base of the bill.

Flight: wings appear blunter, upper-wings duller with obscure rear edge to secondaries (white in Snipe). Tail has eight outer pairs of feathers pin-like. Flight, slower, heavier than Snipe, lacks zigzag or towering escape pattern.

Voice: flushed birds give a short rasping 'squik', 'etch' or 'chet', rather weaker and lower-pitched than Common Snipe.

GREAT SNIPE *Gallinago media*   11″   p 156

Adult: bulkier than Snipe; shorter, stout-bill; wing-coverts broadly tipped white; largely barred below, including belly.

Flight: broader winged than Snipe, shows diagnostic white-edged dark central wing-panel, lacks Snipe's white trailing edge, more conspicuous white corners to tail. Flight, slower, straighter, usually brief – like a small Woodcock.

Voice: flushed birds give a low single or double croak: 'etch etch'.

JACK SNIPE *Lymnocryptes minimus*   7″   p 152

Adult: small size, shorter bill, upper-parts glossed purple-and-green with brighter pale buff stripes.

Flight: has silent escape flight – slower more direct than Snipe (no real zigzag or towering), usually for short distance only. Wedge-shaped tail of twelve pointed feathers.

Voice: normally silent when flushed, rarely a barely audible 'gah'.

WOODCOCK *Scolopax rusticola*   13½″   p 164

Adult: much larger than Snipe; stout, long bill, black bars on crown, under-parts barred. Its plumage of mottled chestnuts, browns, buffs and grey provide superb camouflage among leaf-litter on the woodland floor.

Flight: broad rounded wings; flight fast and straight or slow and wavering; roding display at dusk more owl-like.

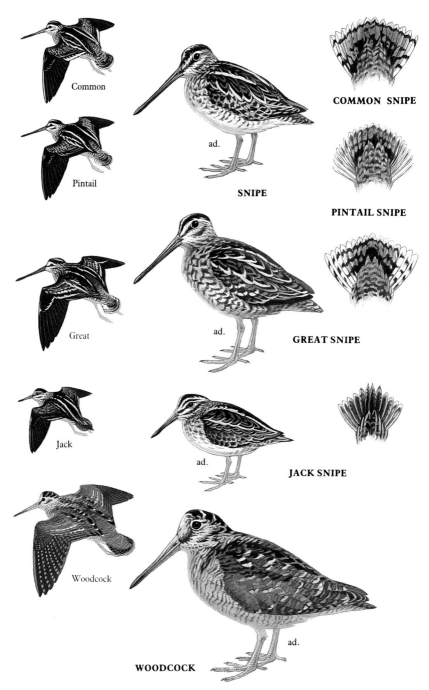

Common

Pintail

ad.

SNIPE

COMMON SNIPE

PINTAIL SNIPE

Great

ad.

GREAT SNIPE

Jack

ad.

JACK SNIPE

Woodcock

ad.

WOODCOCK

Plate 15   AMERICAN DOWITCHERS

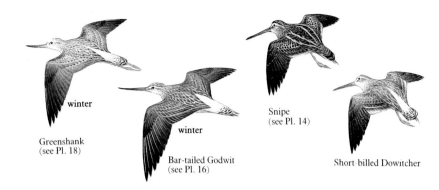

winter

Greenshank
(see Pl. 18)

winter

Bar-tailed Godwit
(see Pl. 16)

Snipe
(see Pl. 14)

Short-billed Dowitcher

LONG-BILLED DOWITCHER *Limnodromus scolopaceus*   11¼"   p 162

Adult (breeding): often longer billed; darker all brick-red below, barring stronger on sides, V's on under tail-coverts, tail may appear darker, as tail bars blackish, wider than white areas between (opposite of Short-billed).

Adult (winter): dusky-grey above, white below, with grey breast – almost identical to Short-billed, except for stronger marks on vent and under tail-coverts.

Juvenile: darker above, greyer below than juvenile Short-billed, back and scapulars have thin reddish edges; tertials usually plain, with narrow reddish edges (Short-billed's tertials show reddish-buff internal markings, giving 'tiger-striped' appearance).

Flight: chunky, snipe-like appearance on wing – both dowitchers show white trailing edge to secondaries, white wedge on back.

SHORT-BILLED DOWITCHER *Limnodromus griseus*   10½"   p 160

Adult (breeding): very like Long-billed, shorter bill (some overlap), under-parts paler orange-red, fine spotting on neck/breast, flanks less barred, whiter belly, under tail-coverts more spotted. Tail may look paler than Long-billed's – browner bars, narrower than white areas between.

Adult (winter): almost identical to Long-billed – see above.

Juvenile: breast more buffy than Long-billed, indistinctly mottled and spotted. Scapulars and tertials more noticeably traced and striped (Long-billed's tertials are plainer with narrow edging).

Long-billed
winter

Long-billed
breeding

Short-billed
breeding

Long-billed
breeding

Short-billed
juv.

Long-billed
juv.

DOWITCHER

ad. winter

Long-billed

Short-billed

127

Plate 16　　　　**GODWITS**

BAR-TAILED GODWIT *Limosa lapponica*　15″　　　　p 171

Adult male (breeding): more upcurved bill, shorter legs, stockier than Black-tailed; russet under-parts, largely, unbarred Female much duller, browner than male.

Adult (winter):, more streaked above than winter Black-tailed, tail barred brown, rump white.

Juvenile: more streaked above, than juvenile Black-tailed.

Flight: no clear wing-bar, whitish rump-triangle, legs barely extend beyond barred tail – unlike Black-tailed. Flight free and rapid, flocks often seen high in lines or V's.

BLACK-TAILED GODWIT *Limosa limosa*　16″　　　　p 166

Adult male (breeding): longer, straighter bill, head and breast pinkish-chestnut, flanks variably barred. Male Icelandic race (*L.l.islandica*) has redder-chestnut clearly more extensive on breast/flanks.

Adult (winter): uniform grey-brown above (not streaked), obviously longer legs, black tail.

Juvenile: more like breeding adult – rufous tinge to neck/breast, pale pink-chestnut fringes on dark brown upper-parts, red-buff edges to wing-coverts.

Flight: bold white wing-bar, legs project noticeably beyond black-banded white tail. Flight quite fast with rapid wing-beats, flocks often seen high in lines or V's.

ad. winter

ad. breeding

juv.

♂ breeding

ad. winter

BAR-TAILED GODWIT

ad. winter

ad. breeding

Black-tailed

juv.

♂ breeding

ad. winter

BLACK-TAILED GODWIT

Plate 17   **CURLEWS**

CURLEW *Numenius arquata*   22″   p 177

Adult (breeding): largest wader, long decurved bill, no head stripes.

Flight: more leisurely than Whimbrel's, rather gull-like – often in large flocks, flies high in lines/bunches. Shows whitish triangular rump, tail barred.

SLENDER-BILLED CURLEW *Numenius tenuirostris*   25″   p 176

Adult (breeding): smaller than Curlew with shorter, thinner, decurved bill – heart shaped spots on flanks, no head stripes.

Flight: wing-beats faster than Curlew's – purer white lower back/rump, less barred whiter tail, blacker primaries contrast with white spotted inner flight feathers (more so than Curlew), under-wings/body whiter.

WHIMBREL *Numenius phaeopus*   17″   p 174

Adult (breeding): smaller than Curlew, shorter bill kinked towards tip, crown boldly striped, whiter throat, shorter legs.

Flight: wing-beats faster than Curlew's – flies high in lines or V's. Whitish rump, wings more uniform in flight. N. American race (*N. p. hudsonicus*) no white rump and browner underwing.

LITTLE WHIMBREL *Numenius minutus*   11½″   p 172

Adult (breeding): tiny curlew; very short bill, only slightly decurved, crown striped like Whimbrel's, but rest of plumage warm and sandy-buff.

Flight: wing-beats freer than larger curlews. Brown rump/tail uniform with back. Wings dark above; underwings light grey-brown, dark-barred buff coverts.

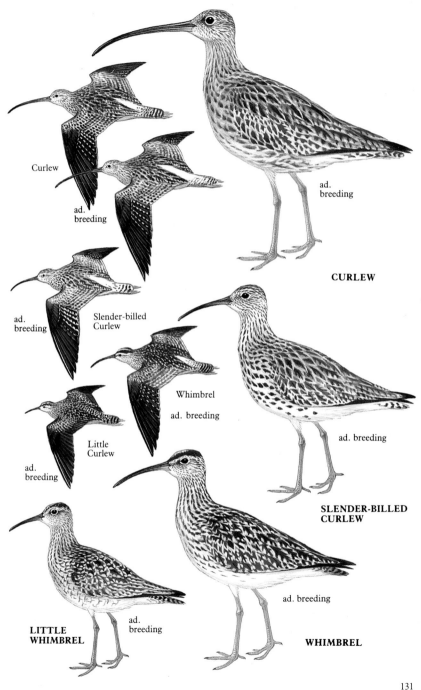

Curlew

ad.
breeding

ad.
breeding

CURLEW

ad.
breeding

Slender-billed
Curlew

Whimbrel

ad. breeding

ad.
breeding

Little
Curlew

ad.
breeding

ad. breeding

**SLENDER-BILLED
CURLEW**

ad.
breeding

ad. breeding

**LITTLE
WHIMBREL**

WHIMBREL

Plate 18   SHANKS

REDSHANK *Tringa totanus*   11″   p 182

Adult (breeding): red legs, longish straight reddish-based bill; brown above, mottled/barred dark brown below.

Adult (winter): greyer-brown above, more white round eyes, finely streaked throat/breast, less barred flanks; legs orange-red.

Flight: fast, erratic with jerky shallow wing-beats, showing conspicuous white wedge to back and white inner rear wings.

SPOTTED REDSHANK *Tringa erythropus*   12″   p 180

Adult (breeding): larger, more elegant than Redshank with longer dark brown-red legs, longer finer dull red-based bill; mainly black, spotted above with white.

Adult (winter): paler ashy-grey above and whiter below than Redshank, eye-stripe darker, longer whiter supercilium, legs orange-red.

Juvenile: upper-parts darker brown, extensively spotted and chequered with white marks and bars, legs orange-red.

Flight: stronger, often more direct than Redshank – shows conspicuous white wedge to back (lacks Redshank's white trailing edge), silhouette more attenuated – legs trailing.

GREENSHANK *Tringa nebularia*   12½″   p 185

Adult (breeding): larger, taller, greyer than Redshank; longer greenish legs, slightly upturned bill; blotched grey and black above, head/breast heavily streaked/spotted blackish.

Adult (winter): pale greyish above, whiter below, face whitish.

Flight: swift, strong – shows conspicuous white wedge up back between wings (cf. Greater/Lesser Yellowlegs).

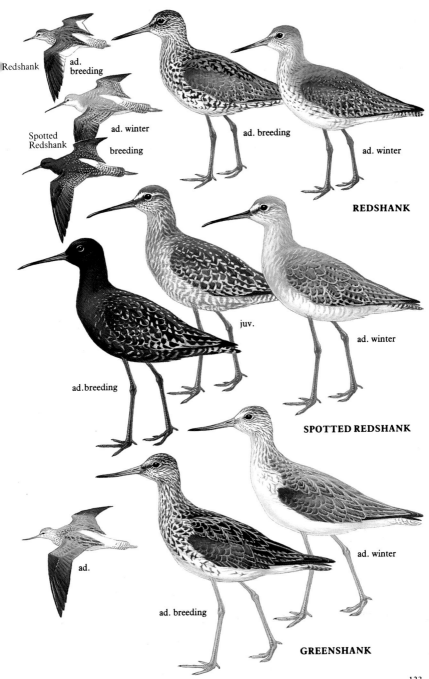

Redshank

ad.
breeding

Spotted
Redshank

ad. winter

breeding

ad. breeding

ad. winter

REDSHANK

juv.

ad. winter

ad.breeding

SPOTTED REDSHANK

ad. winter

ad.

ad. breeding

GREENSHANK

133

Plate 19   WOOD, GREEN SANDPIPER etc.

WOOD SANDPIPER *Tringa glareola*   8″   p 193

Adult (breeding): differs from Green Sandpiper in slimmer, browner and more spotted appearance above, more streaked head, clearer super-cilium, longer (usually pale) legs, shorter bill.

Adult (winter): more uniform, less spotted above, legs pale olive to ochre.

Juvenile: warmer brown above, profusely spotted rich buff.

Flight: escape flight fast, erratic, with jerky shallow wing-beats, often rising high, but less inclined to tower than Green. Also shows less cont-rasting whitish rump, more barred tail, thinner winged with lightish-grey (not black) underwing.

GREEN SANDPIPER *Tringa ochropus*   8¾″   p 191

Adult (breeding): larger, stouter than Wood Sandpiper, shorter olive-green legs, broader wings, darker above – olive-brown peppered whitish-buff.

Adult (winter): more uniform above, spotting less distinct.

Flight: has low zigzag Snipe-like escape flight, then towering with jerky wing-action, appearing more black-and-white than Wood – has blacker under-wing, purer white rump and belly.

SOLITARY SANDPIPER *Tringa solitaria*   7¾″   p 190

Adult (breeding): like a small Green Sandpiper, but slimmer outline with wings extending slightly beyond tail; obvious white eye-ring, dark rump, tail sides strongly barred white.

Adult (winter): more uniform above, less spotting, breast-sides more clouded.

Flight: lacks Green's white rump – appearing uniformly dark above, barred tail-sides whiter, heavily barred dark underwing (not quite as black as Green Sandpiper's). It is also narrower winged with wing-action more reminiscent of a Wood Sandpiper.

ad.

ad. winter

juv.

WOOD SANDPIPER

ad.

ad.
breeding

ad. winter

ad.

ad.breeding

GREEN SANDPIPER

ad. winter

ad.

ad.

ad.
breeding

SOLITARY SANDPIPER

Plate 20   TEREK, COMMON SANDPIPER etc.

TEREK SANDPIPER *Xenus cinereus*   9″   p 194

Adult (breeding): like large Common Sandpiper, but long tapering upcurved bill, short orange-yellow legs; greyer brown above with blackish bands on scapulars.

Adult (winter): greyer, more uniform above, paler head, whiter forehead, stronger supercilium, dark 'shoulders', bill orange-based.

Flight: like *Tringa* sandpipers, but often quite low over mud/water like Common Sandpiper. Shows narrower Redshank-like white patch across secondaries, rump/tail greyish-brown.

COMMON SANDPIPER *Actitis hypoleucos*   8″   p 196

Adult (breeding): smaller than Green Sandpiper, shows white wedge behind rounded brown breast-sides, rear body rather elongated – constantly wagging or 'teetering'; legs grey-green.

Juvenile: wing-coverts and tertial edges barred sepia and buff. The juvenile Spotted Sandpiper is more uniform greyish above, has tertials plainer with thin buff tips, and wing-coverts boldly barred blackish and buff.

Flight: gives flickering wing-beats, bowed in brief glides low over water shows broader white wing-bar and more white on sides of tail than Spotted.

SPOTTED SANDPIPER *Actitis macularia*   7½″   p 198

Adult (breeding): marginally smaller than Common Sandpiper with shorter tail, boldly spotted below; bill and legs flesh-pink.

Adult (winter): greyer above, indistinct blackish bars on wing-coverts, usually yellowish bill-base and legs.

Flight: wing-bar shorter, tail-sides show less white than Common Sandpiper.

MARSH SANDPIPER *Tringa stagnatilis*   9″   p 184

Adult (breeding): smaller than Redshank, needle-bill, long spindly green legs, boldly spotted blackish above.

Adult (winter): paler more uniform, whiter face and under-parts.

Flight: rapid/agile *Tringa*-like – all dark wings, white wedge up back, long trailing legs.

breeding

ad. winter

TEREK SANDPIPER

breeding

ad. Common

juv.

ad. breeding

COMMON SANDPIPER

ad. winter

SPOTTED SANDPIPER

ad. breeding

ad. winter

ad. breeding

MARSH SANDPIPER

Plate 21   **WILLET, YELLOWLEGS etc.**

WILLET *Catoptrophorus semipalmatus* 15″   p 199

Adult (breeding): a large, plump, straight-billed shorebird; greyish-brown, heavily mottled above and below.

Adult (winter): uniformly pale greyish above, whitish below, legs blue-grey.

Flight: strong, direct – shows striking black-and-white wing pattern, rump white, tail grey.

GREATER YELLOWLEGS *Tringa melanoleuca* 12″   p 187

Adult (breeding): Greenshank-size, long yellow legs, stout slightly up-turned bill; upper-parts more boldly spotted white and patched with black, under-parts more boldly marked below than Lesser Yellowlegs.

Adult (winter): greyer-brown above, sides of neck and breast narrowly streaked brown, whiter below.

Flight: strong, rapid as Greenshank – shows pale spotting on inner primaries, square white rump is cut-off sharply across lower back (Greenshank has white wedge up back).

LESSER YELLOWLEGS *Tringa flavipes* 9½″   p 188

Adult (breeding): smaller, slimmer than Redshank, straight, thin bill, long spindly yellow legs; blackish-brown above, spotted whitish (pattern similar to Wood Sandpiper).

Adult (winter): greyish-brown above with fewer spots, tertials barred, obvious white eye-ring, short white supercilium.

Flight: actions like Wood Sandpiper, but flight slower – wings uniform, white rump-patch as Greater, long yellow legs project beyond tail.

STILT SANDPIPER *Micropalama himantopus* 8″   p 146

Adult (breeding): larger than Curlew Sandpiper, longer neck, long droop-tipped bill, stilt-like greenish legs; chestnut cheeks and nape, bold supercilium, heavily barred below.

Adult (winter): greyer above whiter below, resembles Curlew Sandpiper but straighter bill, longer yellow-green legs.

Flight: shows white rump like Curlew Sandpiper, but lacks wing-bar and feet extend beyond tail.

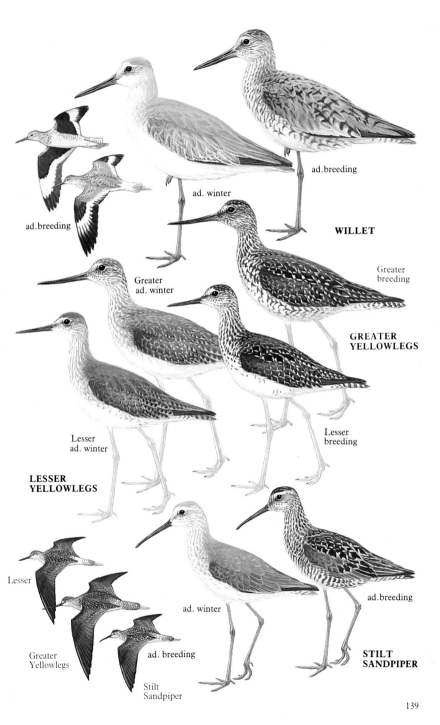

ad.breeding

ad. winter

WILLET

ad.breeding

Greater
ad. winter

Greater
breeding

**GREATER
YELLOWLEGS**

Lesser
ad. winter

Lesser
breeding

**LESSER
YELLOWLEGS**

Lesser

ad. winter

ad.breeding

Greater
Yellowlegs

ad. breeding

Stilt
Sandpiper

**STILT
SANDPIPER**

Plate 22   PHALAROPES

For comparative purposes the three species are shown standing. Phalaropes are habitually swimming waders, although Wilson's often runs and swims less than the other two.

WILSON'S PHALAROPE *Phalaropus tricolor*   9″   p 203

Adult female (breeding): the largest phalarope, longer needle-bill, longer black legs; blue-grey above, black eye-stripe extends into chestnut on back.

Adult male (breeding): smaller, duller than female; dark brown eye-stripe, dull cinnamon on neck and back.

Adult (winter): pale grey above, pure white below, legs yellowish.

Flight: wings less pointed, rounder than other phalaropes – action slower, more *Tringa*-like in flight – no wing-bar, but shows obvious white rump.

GREY PHALAROPE *Phalaropus fulicarius*   8¼″   p 207

Adult female (breeding): slightly larger, stockier than Red-necked, stouter broader bill; rich chestnut under-parts, white cheeks.

Adult male (breeding): browner cap, cheeks dingier, under-parts duller, yellow base to bill.

Adult (winter): resembles Red-necked, though paler grey, more uniform, less streaked with whitish above, stronger mark through eye.

Flight: shows white wing-bar, white sides to rump.

RED-NECKED PHALAROPE *Phalaropus lobatus*   7¼″   p 205

Adult female (breeding): smaller than Grey, slender neck, more needle-like bill; white throat, neck-patches orange-red, golden-buffy lines on back.

Adult male (breeding): duller, less extensive orange on neck.

Adult (winter):blackish-grey cap, black crescent through and behind eye, greyish upperparts narrowly fringed white.

Flight: bold white wing-bar, white sides to rump.

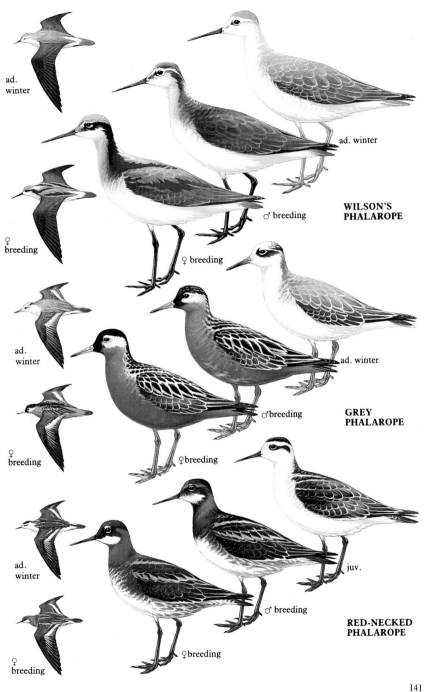

ad.
winter

ad. winter

♀
breeding

♂ breeding

♀ breeding

**WILSON'S
PHALAROPE**

ad.
winter

ad. winter

♂breeding

♀
breeding

♀breeding

**GREY
PHALAROPE**

ad.
winter

juv.

♂ breeding

♀
breeding

♀breeding

**RED-NECKED
PHALAROPE**

141

Plate 23   **CHICKS**

This plate shows a variety of ways in which patterns have evolved to break up outline and match surroundings.

Wader chicks vary markedly in general appearance, some being slim and fairly long-necked, while others are more chubby. Even in the most long-billed species, the chicks have only a moderately long bill, but legs and feet may be extremely long in some species. The colours of the down are highly cryptic, with complex patterns of mottling and lines.

For more information on the identification of downy young of waders, the reader should consult the very detailed and well-illustrated account in the *Guide to the Young of European Precocial Birds*, by Jon Fjeldså (1977), Skarv Nature Publications, Denmark.

The representative species shown here are:

1 Oystercatcher, p. 21

2 Lapwing, p. 6

3 Ringed Plover, p. 40

4 Golden Plover, p. 55

5 Snipe, p. 153

6 Woodcock, p. 164

7 Turnstone, p. 201

8 Curlew, p. 177

9 Black-tailed Godwit, p. 166

10 Redshank, p. 182

11 Dunlin, p. 95

12 Temminck's Stint, p. 81

13 Common Sandpiper, p. 196

14 Ruff, p. 149

15 Avocet, p. 26

16 Red-necked Phalarope, p. 205

17 Pratincoles, p. 35-6

18 Stone Curlew, p. 29

BROAD-BILLED SANDPIPER   *Limicola falcinellus*

Du – Breedbekstrandloper   Fr – Bécasseau falcinelle
Ge – Sumpfläufer   Sp – Correlimos falcinelo
Sw – Myrsnäppa

Pl. 10

Identification. Length 6½in. Smaller than Dunlin, with longer, broader, kink-tipped bill, steeper forehead with distinctive forked supercilium and shorter legs looking set far back. When not in breeding plumage liable to be mistaken for Dunlin or Curlew Sandpiper.

Adult summer, upper-parts blackish fringed pale chestnut to whitish, initially with broad grey-white tips, when worn becoming very black above. Thin bright stripes on edges of mantle form creamy lines, recalling Jack Snipe. The head shows a dark median stripe, bordered by thin bright lines, with a strong dark line below these, and a broad, pale buff supercilium. Under-parts white, with throat and breast heavily spotted with brown and arrow marks on flanks. Adult winter, much paler, recalling Curlew Sandpiper, with the upper-parts greyish-brown and the chest markings much reduced. The dark marks on the head are lost, but the basic pattern is still retained, including the forked supercilium, more obvious when viewed head-on (not shared by Dunlin). The characteristic bill shape is emphasised more by the paler foreface, the latter always paler than in Dunlin. Also has distinctive black 'shoulders' like Sanderling, and the black rump is even more obvious in winter.

Juvenile similar to breeding adult, with double supercilium and wing-coverts with broader buff margins. Breast more buff, faintly streaked dark brown. In early part of first winter plumage often shows blotched upper-parts. Often green tinge to dark legs and paler-based bill. In flight shows a thin, dull wing-bar, and lower back, rump and tail-centre almost black, contrasting sharply with white lateral coverts.

Voice. In flight, '*chrrreep*', or '*chr-reek*', low, trilled or buzzing. Flight song on the breeding ground is a fast, spinning '*trirr trrirrirrirr*', with a quality strongly recalling the twitter of Sand Martin. In slow-flight song gives a rhythmical buzzing trill, '*SUirr-SUirr-SUirr*' or '*dsrui-dsrui-dsrui---*'.

Habitat. Nests in wettest parts of bogs, on slough of thin peat mud lightly overgrown with sedge and cotton grass. Outside breeding season, in wet or muddy pond margins and swampy patches of lake edges, sewage farms or fresh marshes. In winter quarters further south occurs on muddy estuaries, brackish lagoons and salt pans.

Distribution. Nominate *falcinellus* breeds in Norway, Sweden and Finland, east to the Kola Peninsula in Russia, wintering in the Red Sea, Arabia, the Persian Gulf, Pakistan and western India. The range of *L.f.sibirica* is imperfectly known, but is presumably northern Siberia east of the Yenisei, wintering from China and Hainan, south to the Indo-Chinese countries, eastern India, and Australia. Accidental in Iceland and many European countries, including the British isles (99). Map **30**.

Movements. The nominate form breeding in the western Palaearctic migrates mainly south to south-east across central and eastern Europe, on a broad front, with a noticeable passage of birds through the Caspian and Black Sea areas, the eastern Mediterranean and the Middle East. A very few birds pass through western Europe in spring and a small number occur regularly on passsage in southern France in May and August. In the Persian Gulf peak numbers occur from August to November and smaller parties reach Oman at this time. Small numbers also winter in Aden, although many more birds pass through both in spring and autumn. In East Africa it has recently been found wintering in Eritrea and Djibouti, and also in Kenya. Further east it winters regularly in Pakistan and western India. Adults leave Fenno-Scandia in July, with juveniles mainly following in August, which corresponds with the main autumn passage in central Europe. In Pakistan, arrives from late July to early August (adults) and late August to early September (juveniles). August is also a peak month in Aden. In the southern Caspian, passage is mainly August to mid-September. In spring the main departures from Aden and Pakistan and the main passage through Europe is in May. Birds reach Fenno-Scandia in the second half of May, and breeding grounds are reoccupied from then until mid-June.

Feeding. Feeds by pecking, but also by probing in soft mud or in water. Also walks fairly fast, pecking at the surface, and occasionally stopping to peck repeatedly at one place, or probing by pushing bill in with skewering motion and head held slightly to one side. Invertebrates recorded from freshwater and marine habitats include insects, molluscs, crustaceans and marine worms, also seeds and vegetable matter.

Social and breeding behaviour. Breeding behaviour poorly known, and on the breeding ground the bird skulks, making it difficult to observe. Breeds in loose 'colonies' in wettest parts of marshes. The males have a territorial song flight and may either fly slowly (10–20m above ground), alternately shivering wings and gliding, giving a slower rhythmical buzzing trill, or perform faster flights accompanied by a faster song, particularly when two or more birds are involved. No details of courtship. The species has a monogamous mating system. Gregarious, but much less so on autumn passage. Associates with other waders in winter, but forms own flocks before northward migration.

Nest, eggs and young. Loosely colonial, nests on ground, frequently in the top of a tussock, and cup lined with grass. Eggs 4, pale buff, heavily speckled red-brown. Incubation period 21 days, by both sexes. Fledging period not known, and young cared for initially by both parents, but later generally by the male only.

STILT SANDPIPER   *Micropalama himantopus*

Du – Steltstrandloper   Fr – Bécasseau à échasses
Ge – Bindenstrandläufer   Sp – Correlimos zancolin
Sw – Styltsnäppa   Pl. 21

Identification. Length 7–8¼in. Larger than Curlew Sandpiper, with longer neck, long, spindly, stilt-like greenish legs and long droop-tipped bill. In flight shows white rump like Curlew Sandpiper, but lacks a wing-bar, and feet extend beyond tail.

Adult summer, reddish-chestnut ear-coverts, lores and nape, and barred under-parts are distinctive. Upper-parts blackish edged cinnamon-buff. The crown and neck are streaked and it has a prominent whitish supercilium. Rump white, obscured by barring, but contrasts with dark lower back and ashy tail. Adult winter, very different appearance, looking mainly grey above and white below. Shows prominent white supercilium and white margins to wing-coverts and tertials. Flight pattern bolder, with blackish flight feathers contrasting with greyer wing-coverts and back, and pure white rump more obvious.

Juvenile, upper-parts blackish-brown with even buff scaling. Wing-coverts grey-brown, broadly edged whitish-buff. Neck and chest buff and more obviously streaked than non-breeding adult, and under-parts white. Shows prominent white supercilium. Bill black with brown base. Legs, dull green to ochre.

Voice. Commonest call '*grrt*' or '*querp*'. In flight gives a single, whistled '*whu*' or husky '*chu*'. Flight song is a yodelling '*o-gal-ee*' repeated over and over. Also a nasal '*he-haw*', uttered rapidly, in series.

Habitat. Breeds on tundra, near marshy areas or shallow pools. Outside breeding season prefers sheltered shallow inland and sheltered coastal pools, muddy edges of water-courses in marshes and is also seen along salt-water mudflats and sandy beaches.

Distribution. Breeds in tundras of North America from north-eastern Alaska to northern Canada. Winters mainly in central South America south to Uruguay and north-eastern Argentina. Accidental, British Isles (17), Sweden and Austria.

Movements. Migratory, with adults leaving their breeding areas from mid-July and juveniles from mid-August. The main route is through the Canadian prairies and the interior of the U.S.A. (passage lasting to early October). Migrants from the interior cross the Gulf of Mexico and the Greater Antilles to South America. The Atlantic route is partly coastal, but it is thought that some transoceanic crossings take place from New England to the Lesser Antilles, or Guianas, as the species is fairly regular in Bermuda in autumn, and large numbers pass through Surinam August–September. Birds reach Paraguay and Buenos Aires in late August and are common there from mid-September. Return in spring is in March, and it is believed that most leave South America via the Caribbean coasts of Colombia and Venezuela, evidently crossing the Caribbean and the Gulf of Mexico in unbroken flight, as rare in the West Indies in spring. The main passage (from mid-March) is in April, with spring migrants almost entirely moving through the North American interior. Breeding areas are reoccupied in late May to mid-June.

Feeding. Feeds by picking rapidly from the surface of the water or below it, and by probing in soft mud, actions recalling Dowitcher, with similar 'sewing machine' motion of head and bill. Often wades up to its belly in water to feed. Foods in summer include adult and larval beetles, especially dytiscids, adult dipterans, snails and larval insects.

Social and breeding behaviour. Birds arrive on their breeding grounds singly, or in small flocks. Males establish territories quickly and begin to advertise with prolonged display flights lasting several minutes. Normally the male flies at about 20–60 metres above the ground, on shallow wing-beats, spreading the tail and sometimes gliding and singing. Before landing he sings again, then raises his wings and drops back to earth. Much of the courtship occurs in the air, with males chasing females while repeating their songs over and over and attempting to fly in front of the females, then raising their wings almost vertically and singing as they fall, while tilting from side to side. After dropping nearly back to earth they resume their chase and repeat the performance. Males also take the initiative in nest-scraping, sometimes making six or more scrapes before the final nest site is selected. There is a high degree of fidelity to previously held territories and previous mates, and the species has a monogamous mating system. Gregarious outside the breeding season.

Nest, eggs and young. Nests on the ground among grasses, usually on a slightly raised, drier site. A shallow hollow, sparsely lined with a few dead leaves and grasses. Eggs 4, pale creamy-olive, marked with reddish- or purplish-brown. Incubation period 19–21 days, by both sexes. Fledging occurs when about 18 days old, and by then both parents have abandoned them, with the female leaving first.

BUFF-BREASTED SANDPIPER   *Tryngites subruficollis*

Du – Blonde Ruiter   Fr – Bécasseau rousset
Ge – Grasläufer   Sp – Correlimos canelo
Sw – Prärielöpare

Pl. 12

Identification. Length 7–8in. An erect, short-billed, round-headed and longish-necked sandpiper, having a wholly buff face and under-parts – features obvious at all seasons. Also has a plain rump, no wing-bar, white under-wings and yellow legs (compare juvenile Ruff), while transatlantic vagrants generally prefer short-grassy habitats. Stance and movements, not unlike a slender *Pluvialis* plover. On the wing has an erratic fast flight, appearing longer-winged when head and neck drawn in.

Adult, the back has a clear-cut pattern of blackish feathers with sharply defined buff borders much like juvenile Ruff. The whole of the under-parts, including the throat and sides of the face, are buff or pinky-buff, with the lower belly and under-tail paler. Has small black spots on the crown, hind-neck and mantle, and the dark eye is emphasised by the very pale eye-ring. Sexes similar, no seasonal variation.

Juvenile is less intensely coloured than the adult, with the fringes to the upper-parts thinner, and creamy rather than buff, forming a beautiful scale-like pattern on the back and wings. Spots on side of neck, paler.

Voice. Commonest call a low, trilled '*pr-r-r-reet*'. Also a diagnostic '*tik*' and a low '*chwut*'. The species' displays are distinctive in their lack of song flights and other *Calidris* features.

Habitat. Breeds on dry, grassy, arctic tundra, and on migration and in winter prefers extensive short-grassy areas, i.e. Paraguyan chaco and Argentine pampas, but occurs occasionally on golf courses, airports and sewage farms, less frequently on beaches and shores.

Distribution. A western arctic breeding species, which is found in a restricted area of the North American arctic, from Alaska (Point Barrow) to western Canada (north Mackenzie and some islands from Banks Island to King William Island). In Russia breeds on Wrangel Island and perhaps Chukotsky peninsula (no regular movement through eastern Asia). Winters in central Argentina and Paraguay. Accidental, Iceland, Spitsbergen, several European countries, including the British Isles (443, now annual), Azores, North Africa and USSR.

Movements. Departure from breeding areas is from mid-July to mid-August, with the main passage through the U.S.A. (August–September) and the majority, including juveniles, passing through the Canadian prairies and central U.S.A. on a narrowing front, and across the Gulf of Mexico. Birds appear to fly non-stop to northern South America, as scarce in Central America or the Greater Antilles in autumn. Passage continues south through the centre of South America (east of the Andes) to wintering quarters in Paraguay and Argentina. Early birds arrive on the chaco in Paraguay in late August, and in Buenos Aires province in September (numbers increasing to mid-October). Also in autumn small numbers diverge from the main route in Canada, moving more south-east, arriving New England states (sparingly August–September), and are then believed to make a direct overseas crossing to north-eastern South America. The spring route north through central South America continues over the Gulf of Mexico, with early arrivals appearing in the southern U.S.A. from mid-March. The main passage, with halts at traditional stopping points in southern Texas (mid-April to early May), also continues through central U.S.A. with another traditional stopover near Edmonton (Alberta), before the breeding grounds are finally re-occupied in late May to mid-June.

Feeding. Feeding is by picking from the surface and from short, grassy vegetation. Takes mainly terrestrial invertebrates, especially the adults and larvae of beetles and the larvae and pupae of dipterans, also spiders, craneflies and gammarid crustaceans.

Social and breeding behaviour. On the breeding grounds males typically gather in groups of from two to ten, and exhibit true lekking behaviour, as found in the Ruff. Each male defends areas 10–50 metres in diameter, or considerably larger than the tiny lek territories of the Ruff. The display sites have no specific spatial relationship to nesting areas. Males indulge in chasing other males from their territories, concentrating their display activities in the more twilight hours. Wing-flashing or wing-waving is of prime importance, both in defence and courtship display. Birds also give flutter-jump displays, and if two birds are competing, they may rise side by side for 6–12 metres in the air, their wings fluttering and their legs dangling. In precopulatory behaviour the male tries to lead the female to a secluded site by running towards the mating site and displaying by raising one wing. Copulation is preceded by the male performing a double-wing embrace with the attracted female or females coming within the arc of his wings. The female may then spread her wings prior to copulation. The species mates promiscuously. Gregarious, feeding in small parties of five to six birds, occurring in larger numbers on migration.

Nest, eggs and young. Nest is a shallow scrape on the ground, sparsely lined with dry grasses or leaves. Eggs 4, pale creamy, tinted greenish or olive, heavily marked with medium to dark brown. Incubation by female only, period not known.

RUFF *Philomachus pugnax*

Du – Kemphaan   Fr – Chevalier combattant
Ge – Kampfläufer Sp – Combatiente
Sw – Brushane

Pl. 13

Identification. Length, males larger (10–12in) than females (8–9in), varying between Buff-breasted Sandpiper and Redshank, with small head on extended neck, short bill (slightly decurved), long body and longish orangey-yellow legs.

Adult summer, ruff and ear-tufts of breeding male are extraordinarily variable in colour and pattern, barred or unbarred, and showing white, buff, chestnut, purplish and black in different combinations. The female (reeve) lacks ruff and head-tufts, but the breast and mantle are mottled blackish-brown. Adult winter, male loses all breeding plumage and resembles female (male's greater size still obvious) and is greyish-brown above, with paler edges to the wing-coverts. Under-parts whitish, with the breast streaked grey. Legs pinkish or orange-red all year.

Juvenile is markedly warm in colour, with a rich pattern above, profusely scaled dark brown with extensive warm buff edges. Under-parts white, with breast washed golden-buff, contrasting with white rear parts. Legs usually yellowish-brown or greenish.

In flight shows white oval patches on either side of dark central area of tail (sometimes extending to form white horseshoe across base of tail), and narrow white wing-bar, with the feet extending a little beyond tail. Stance of stationary bird, upright, with head raised and drooping tail, but more horizontal posture when feeding, with characteristic hunched back.

Voice. Typically silent, even during lekking displays, other than uttering a few muted sounds. Gives a gruff '*kru*' or a short '*ga-ga*' when taking off, and a short '*gue-gue-gue*' in alarm.

Habitat. Breeds over a rather wide range of temperate to subarctic climatic zones, mainly in low-lying grassy marshes in slightly wooded, or treeless, portions of the northern birch zone, and the shrub and moss tundra habitats. Outside the breeding season it inhabits the muddy shores of lakes, pools, wide estuaries having muddy banks or exposed mudflats, wetlands behind sea-banks and salt marshes no longer exposed to tides, preferring slightly brackish or fresh waters.

Distribution. Breeds from Britain and France east through Europe and Fenno-Scandia to Russia and Siberia, to Anadyrland. Winters in small numbers from Britain and the Netherlands to the Mediterranean basin and the Middle East to Arabia, the Persian Gulf and India. The largest numbers occur in Africa (south to Cape Province), especially in Sahel and northern Savanna zones (from Senegambia to the Sudan), with numbers approaching the million mark in the Senegal delta, and even larger numbers in the Niger inundation zone (Mali); over a million birds winter in north-western Nigeria, with similar numbers around Lake Chad. Also common in East and southern Africa. Map 31.

Movements. Although the winter range extends from western Europe to India, by far the largest numbers winter in Africa, including birds that nested in north-eastern Siberia. In autumn, movement through Europe is broad-front and overland, with a general trend south to south-west, but in spring there is a more easterly shift, with birds returning more directly to their breeding areas. Long east-to-west autumn movements across Eurasia (in subarctic to temperate latitudes) are shown by eastern Siberian recoveries of birds ringed as passage migrants in Fenno-Scandia and southern North Sea areas. Ringing in East and South Africa indicates that their birds are entirely Siberian (arriving via Black and Caspian Sea areas). The main movements across Europe are from the end of July (males leave from end-June) to mid-September, continuing on a reduced scale till mid-November. The first males reach Senegal from mid-July and trans-Saharan passage noted in central Chad from third week of August (peak mid-September). In Africa and southern Europe the return movement begins in mid-February, peaking in March and early April. Breeding areas are reoccupied from mid-April around the North Sea and much later in Siberia (late May to mid-June).

Feeding. Walks with deliberate gait, sometimes wading into shallow water to probe with relatively short bill into mud; also picks prey from surface and from vegetation. In breeding season adult and larval insects, both aquatic and terrestrial, are especially important. Outside the breeding season a wide variety of invertebrates are recorded, also crustaceans, small molluscs, annelid worms, frogs, small fish and vegetable matter, including seeds.

Social and breeding behaviour. The Ruff exhibits the most remarkable social behaviour of any wader and is also probably unique in its degree of male plumage polymorphism, associated with sexual behaviour. Courtship and mating occur in common leks, which are usually raised grassy hillocks. A varying number of males assemble on the lek, which is subdivided into individual display territories. Display consists of ritualised aggression, including raising the head tufts and neck ruffs, also wing-raising, overt threats and flights. The Ruff shows considerable variation in the coloration of the head plumage, and it is only recently that the reproductive significance of such plumage polymorphism has been understood. Two groups of males occur in the lek – Independent males and Satellite males.

Independent males (mostly darkly coloured): behaviour includes much fighting and other activities associated with territory-holding. This group is split into Resident males that defend territory that they occupy, and Marginal males (do not defend territory) that stay on the edge of the lek, sometimes establishing peripheral territories and then becoming the Resident male.

Satellite males (mostly white) do not defend territories, but they do visit the territories of Resident males, avoiding aggressive behaviour towards them. Satellite males also include two types – Central and Peripheral. Central males spend more time on the lek and are less easily driven away by the Resident males.

Females visit the lek for short periods, and on their arrival the Resident males adopt a motionless squatting posture; the Satellite male also squats with the Resident male. Females that step into the Resident male's territory, particularly when he is attacking or threatening a Satellite male, usually crouch. Copulation often occurs at this time.

On the large leks Resident males that are alone on their territory are almost exclusively the successful copulating partners. On the small leks the presence of one or more Satellite males increases the chance for copulation by both Resident and Satellite males. The reproductive value of Satellite males lies in the fact that their presence increases their chance for copulation on small leks and promotes the establishment of new leks, or the maintenance of several leks in an area. The reproductive value of the two major status categories probably varies, with Independent males being favoured during periods when there are low numbers of males present, and Satellite males having the reproductive advantage when there are many males available. The species has a polygamous mating system, with no true pair-bonds. Highly gregarious outside the breeding season, with concentrations of several hundred thousand occuring on the Niger and Senegal deltas in winter.

Nest, eggs and young. Nest is on the ground, concealed in herbage, a shallow scrape lined with grasses. Eggs 4, pale olive with darker olive-brown markings. Incubation period 20–21 days, by female alone. Fledging period 25–28 days, young cared for by female only. Age of first breeding one to two years.

Displays performed on arrival of a female at the lek include the low-wing posture of independent resident males and the strut-walk display of satellite males.

SNIPES and DOWITCHERS   Subfamily Gallinagininae

Small to medium-sized robust waders with longish legs and very long bills. They have cryptic plumages, especially the snipes, which all look remarkably similar, differing mostly by the number and size of their outer-tail feathers – the latter often associated with the demands for effective acoustic advertisement in the breeding season. Some species fly up steeply and/or zig-zag when flushed. Some are highly migratory. The two species of dowitcher (breeding in the Nearctic) also show great similarity, and like some of the more difficult *Calidris* sandpipers they are separable with care.

Range. Worldwide – but only visitors to southern Asia and Australia.

Number of species. World, 20; western Palaearctic, 7.

JACK SNIPE   *Lymnocryptes minimus*

Du – Bokje   Fr – Bécassine sourde
Ge – Zwergschnepfe   Sp – Agachadiza chica
Sw – Dvärgbeckasin

Pl. 14

Identification. Length 6¾–7½in. Smallest snipe, with bill not much longer than head. When flushed normally rises silently, and flight slower, more direct than Snipe, with no real zig-zag to towering flight. Often stays hidden until almost trodden on, usually flying only a short distance, so that the dark, wedge-shaped tail, lacking any white (compare Snipe) is hard to detect.

Adult has mottled rich brown plumage and creamy lines on crown and mantle, with green and purple gloss on back, scapulars and rump. Has characteristic wedge-shaped tail of 12 pointed tail feathers, and wings show white trailing edges to secondaries and inner primaries in flight. Flanks mottled, not barred. Bill dark brown, paler at base. Legs pale greenish. Juvenile not distinguishable from adult.

Voice. Outside breeding season generally silent, but may very occasionally give a low, weak '*gach*' when flushed. Song of displaying male is remarkable, recalling sound of cantering or galloping horses – '*logitokk-logitokk*', etc; may also be given on the ground – sound carries up to one kilometre.

Habitat. Often shares same habitat as Broad-billed Sandpiper in taiga and birch or willow country, keeping to tracks of coarse sedge, with horsetail and cottongrass, in peaty ooze or soft bog. In winter found in similar habitat, where shallow or wet muddy areas with a fair cover of vegetation, avoiding more open, deep or saline waters.

Distribution. Breeds from northern Norway and Sweden east across Russia and Siberia east to the Kolyma delta. Winters mainly in western and southern Europe, North Africa, northern Afrotropics (Senegal to Ethiopia), Asia Minor, northern Middle East, Iran, Afghanistan and the Indian subcontinent to Vietnam. Map **32**.

Movements. In the autumn there is a broad-front south-west movement across Europe, and birds occurring in the British Isles include passage birds, as well as winter visitors. Those birds wintering Asia Minor and Levant eastwards are presumed to originate from Siberia, as are those reaching East Africa. The main autumn movement through Europe south to the Baltic occurs in mid-September to mid-November, with birds also appearing in Nigeria and East Africa during November. In the western Palaearctic the largest numbers are believed to winter from the British Isles to Iberia and the Maghreb, and it is unknown what percentage reach the Afrotropics (reported fairly common only in Sudan). Return passage begins in February in the southern wintering areas, but the main movement is in April, with breeding areas reoccupied from mid-April to mid-May.

Feeding. Takes food from surface and by probing. Feeding birds may move body rhythmically up and down. Feeds on insects, adults and larvae, molluscs, worms, and some seeds or vegetable matter.

Social and breeding behaviour. Although the species is quiet and unobtrusive outside the breeding season, it becomes conspicuous when the males establish territory shortly after spring arrival. In the display flight the male rises on rapid wing-beats to 50–60m, then levels out and flies on a straight line, or circles. The bird then ceases its wing-beats and dives steeply (at about 45°), sometimes performing partial or complete rolls, with wings half folded and curved downwards. It then pulls up into a steep, climbing glide, giving the unique 'cantering' calls all the while. The dive and upward glide lasts about ten seconds. At the top of the glide the male may flutter his wings briefly, then continue in level glide (wings fully spread) for ten to 30m, giving a series of thin, high-pitched, whistling calls. He then adopts a jerky, shallow, switchback flight, as if being jerked up and down on an invisible string, fluttering up and gliding down, ten or more times. The wings are held below the body and rapidly shivered, before the bird flies on in curves and sweeps, gaining height, and after a variable interval, the performance is repeated. The female may fly, calling, to join the male, giving low creaking notes, shortly after he has performed his display flight low over where she was settled on the ground. Both then fly, with the female still calling. Probably monogamous, but type of mating system not clarified. The species is markedly solitary, and even in winter quarters the birds feed quite separately from one another.

Nest, eggs and young. Nests in grassy tussock, often in very damp sites. The cup is lined with a few pieces of grass or leaves. Eggs 4, olive-buff and well marked with dark chestnut. Incubation period at least 24 days, by female only. No information on fledging period.

SNIPE   *Gallinago gallinago*

Du – Watersnip   Fr – Bécassine des marais
Ge –Bekassine   Sp – Agachadiza común
Sw – Enkelbeckasin

Pl. 14

Identification. Length 10–10½in. A rather variable species, and also very similar to Pintail and Swinhoe's Snipes, but shows clear white trailing edge to secondaries in flight. It is smaller than Great Snipe, with a longer bill, more extensive white belly and flanks fully barred; shows less white on outer-tail feathers, and lacks bold white spotting on wing-coverts. When flushed gives a very distinctive hoarse '*scaap*', with typical zig-zagging flight, often towering.

Adult (nominate form), upper-parts richly patterned in black, brown and rufous with creamy stripes down sides of mantle and scapulars. Head striped with buff down centre of crown. Neck and breast buff with lines of dark brown spots and V marks. Flanks buffish, barred dark brown, and belly white. Tail is irregularly patterned with dark bars, cinnamon and tipped pink-buff to white; comprises 12 to 18 feathers (usually 14 or 16), with broad outer-tail feathers.

Juvenile (difficult to distinguish) has buff stripes, on back usually narrower and paler, sometimes almost white. Fresh wing-coverts show completely white tips – not broken by black divide, as in adult.

Voice. Flushed birds give hoarse '*scaap*'. On breeding grounds males indulge in drumming flights (non-vocal) in display dives, with the spread outer-tail feathers producing a throbbing '*vuvuvuvu*' (1–2 seconds). The song is a regular clockwork-like '*chip-per-chip-per-chip-per …*', uttered on ground, on a post, or sometimes in flight.

Habitat. Breeds in marshy bogs and moors, grassy or marshy shores of rivers and lakes, swampy meadows, wet hayfields and marshy patches of tundra. Winters in similar sites, with more use of artefacts, such as sewage farms, reservoirs and ricefields. In frost may shift to seashore.

Distribution. *G.g.gallinago* breeds in the British Isles and Eurasia, and USSR east to Kamchatka, Bering Island and Sakhalin. Mainly winters from British Isles and Low Countries to Iberia and the Maghreb, Mediterranean basin, Middle East and southern Asia. Also winters in large numbers in Africa, south of the Sahara.

G.g.faeroeensis breeds in Iceland and the Faeroes, Orkney and Shetland.

G.g.delicata breeds in North America and winters from British Columbia and Georgia south to Central and South America. Map 33.

Movements. Icelandic birds mainly migrate (a few winter), and ringing recoveries indicate that Ireland is the main wintering area. Return migrants reach Iceland in mid-April and continue inland immediately. Departure dates uncertain, but recoveries are from October onwards in Scotland and Ireland. Faeroes birds (although some are resident) increase in March–April and September–October, reflecting emigration as well as through passage by Icelandic birds. In the British Isles partially migratory, with numbers reduced in the more northern parts in winter (wintering mainly in Ireland). Elsewhere in Britain some remain near their breeding areas or disperse south-west in the country, and a few cross to the Continent.

The Fenno-Scandian populations (where ringed as migrants) show south-west-orientated passage in the autumn (reversed in spring), with the main wintering areas in the British Isles, France and Iberia. Autumn passage begins in July, with peak numbers occurring in Denmark and the Netherlands, September–October. Spring migration starts in March and breeding areas are reoccupied April–May.

On the Continent, autumn passage (as shown by ringing recoveries) is mainly between west and south-west, including some east European birds from as far east as the Urals. Some central European birds show a tendency to move north-west in autumn. The timing of movements is about the same as for the Fenno-Scandian populations.

The Nearctic population *delicata* winters from central U.S.A. to northern South America. There is some evidence for transoceanic passage from the maritime provinces to Neotropical wintering areas. This race has twice straggled to Britain in autumn.

Feeding. Feeds mainly on wet ground or in shallow water, taking items by probing. Probes in a small area, or while walking slowly forward, sometimes up to belly in water.

In soft ground often probes to full length of bill, and food located by touch and, unless large, swallowed without bill being extracted. Essentially crepuscular, though may feed sporadically through day. In some areas earthworms are particularly important; also takes larval insects and adults, molluscs, crustacea, vegetable matter and seeds.

Social and breeding behaviour. Males arrive on breeding territory ten to 14 days before females. They are highly territorial and select areas of wetland over which they display and attempt to attract females. The male rises 80–120m, makes a circular course of his territory and then performs a 45° dive, producing a drumming or winnowing sound. When the females arrive they are promiscuous, copulating with several males, but later remaining for longer periods in one territory and forming a pair-bond with the resident male, who begins to follow the female closely. The pair-bond is only fully established when the nest site is selected and laying has begun. During incubation the male attempts to copulate with any female before finally becoming involved with the care of the young when they hatch.

On arrival in an area the female alights in an exposed place and gives rather subdued '*chipper*' calls, attracting one or several males, which fly in and alight near her in wing-arch flight, and continue to perform these flights round her while she remains crouched. When she finally flies up, one or more males follow in erratic pursuit flight, all birds giving '*chipper*' calls. The male's wing-arch flight and rolling type of flight serve as forms of enticement to the female to remain in his territory. Precopulatory behaviour involves birds circling around each other, strutting, drooping wings and cocking and fanning the tail, commonly giving the '*chipper*' calls. Females also give flutter-leaps, with tail cocked and fanned, and male may join in prior to copulation. The species has a monogamous mating system. It is not truly gregarious, though typically occurs in small groups, sometimes in large numbers where rich feeding areas.

Nest, eggs and young. Nest is a shallow scrape lined with grasses, and usually well concealed. Eggs 4, pale green to olive, with small blotches of dark or reddish-brown. Incubation period 18–20 days, by female alone. Fledging period 19–20 days, parents split brood, young fed bill to bill initially. Age of first breeding one to two years.

Territorial ownership is asserted by flights in which the bird dives at 45° with the outer tail-feathers held out to the side. The movement of air over these feathers produces the distinctive "drumming" sound.

GREAT SNIPE   *Gallinago media*

Du – Poelsnip   Fr – Bécassine double
Ge – Doppelschnepfe   Sp – Agachadiza real
Sw – Dubbelbeckasin

Pl. 14

Identification. Length 10½–11½in. Bulkier than Snipe, with larger head, stouter bill and broader wings. The upper-parts appear less striped and show a diagnostic white-edged dark central wing panel in flight. (Snipe lacks this distinctive dark, bright-edged central panel.) The wing-coverts are boldly spotted with white, and the tail shows more white around the edges than in Snipe. The flight is slower and straighter, lacking the fast zig-zagging or towering behaviour of Snipe, and is briefer, with the bill held more level, like a small Woodcock.

Adult is similar to Snipe, but differs in the more mealy appearance of its head and neck, with less pronounced loral, and cheek-stripes. It is more definitely barred above, thereby reducing the clarity of the stripes on the back, and shows bold white tips to the wing-coverts, creating regular transverse lines. The chest, flanks and lower belly are more completely barred in the form of regular chevrons and not lines. The white on the belly is more restricted, and may not be visible when on the ground. The tail shows bold white corners, almost forming a white rim to it. Under-wing, dusky and heavily barred. In winter, unlike Snipe, becomes duller and darker, losing rich buff and cinnamon fringes of summer plumage.

Juvenile resembles breeding adult but is generally duskier and less well marked. White on tail more restricted, but still shows when spread. Belly fully barred.

Voice. Generally silent away from breeding-display areas. When flushed may give a quick, gruff, gutteral croak. In the display area lekking males give all sorts of extraordinary noises (after dusk) and, unlike other *Gallinago*, have complex ground display and song, but lack only flight song. Males may give a low bubbling sound only audible at a few metres, sometimes jumping into the air. In the display proper, the male rises on tiptoes and draws himself up, with his chin resting on his chest, and produces a strange series of twittering notes (bill open), which at times are interrupted by distant 'motorboat' sounds, continuing into a clicking or drumming song, which finally develops into a strong, vibratory whizzing sound, fading off at the end. In the later stages he quickly spreads his wings once or twice, and fans his tail to display the white corners.

Habitat. Breeds mainly in boreal upper middle latitudes, on marshy and grassy ground, in generally more wooded and less swampy habitats than Snipe. It especially favours sites fringed or hemmed in by willow, alder, birch and conifers, growing as scrub. Bogs and wetlands in subalpine areas of Scandinavia are used as communal display sites, or leks. Outside the breeding season birds inhabit marshy or swampy areas that have good grassy cover; also found in drier habitats than Snipe.

Distribution. Breeds in Scandinavia, and from Finland and Russia south to the Baltic countries and east across Siberia to the Yenisei River. Winters mainly in tropical Africa (especially eastern half) south to South-West Africa and Natal. A few, probably irregularly, winter in north-western Europe. Accidental Spitsbergen, in various parts of

Europe, including the British Isles (234), the Middle East, Madeira and Canary Islands. Map **34**.

Movements. Migratory, wintering mainly in the Afrotropical region, especially in the east. The main movement of Fenno-Scandian birds is probably north to south across central Europe. Fewer birds now pass through western Europe than in the 19th century, presumably due to the decline of breeding birds in north-western Europe. In Nigeria it is most common August to November, particularly in September, and in Kenya only from mid-October to mid-November, and again on return passage in May. In Zambia it is a winter visitor in the south (staying till April) and a migrant in the north (October to January).

A broad-front overland movement across Russia and eastern Europe occurs basically in a south-western direction, and the species is not scarce on passage through eastern and central Europe (mainly August–September), but it is considerably rarer further west. Spring return is rather late, with some birds still present in Zambia in April, and the return movement through Kenya is in the second and third weeks of May. The main movement is evidently rapid, since breeding areas are reoccupied during May to early June.

Feeding. Feeding behaviour studied less than Snipe, but probably similar. Takes mainly earthworms, molluscs, insect adults and larvae, including beetles, flies, ants, caterpillars, crickets and some seeds.

Social and breeding behaviour. Towards the end of the day males gather at traditional lekking sites to display (normally about ten, sometimes 15–20 males gather together). The song display (see voice) and flutter-jumps (one or two males may leap simultaneously one to two metres) have antagonistic as well as advertising functions, and birds usually display immediately after landing. Each male advertises its presence and proclaims its territory mainly by drumming, which initially begins with a song-like twittering. The female visits the display area for copulation, so that when she is present on the territory the male moves to a display site nearer to her, and performs vigorous flutter-jumps and song displays. However, when the female is present on an adjacent territory, he similarly performs and attempts to get near to her, with the result that there is much chasing. Thus a male with a female on his territory is often thwarted in his attempts to court her. When a female eventually squats, and if the male is able to fend off other intruding males, he may mount her from the rear and successfully copulate. The species does not form pair-bonds and probably has a promiscuous mating system, with the sexes meeting for copulation at the communal display-grounds. Outside the breeding season, generally solitary, although small scattered flocks sometimes occur in winter quarters.

Nest, eggs and young. Nest is well concealed on the ground in thick vegetation, a shallow depression with a little lining of grass or moss. Eggs 4, stone to buff, covered with deep brown spots and blotches. Incubation period 22–24 days, by female only. Fledging period about 21–28 days.

At dusk, male Great Snipe gather at traditional lekking sites to display and sing. The female visits the display area and may subsequently mate with any male – the species does not form pair-bonds.

PINTAIL SNIPE   *Gallinago stenura*

Du – Stekelstaartsnip   Fr – Bécassine à queue pointue
Ge – Stiftbekassine   Sp – Agachadiza uralense
Sw – Sibirisk beckasin

Pl. 14

Identification. Length $9\frac{3}{4}$–$10\frac{1}{2}$in. Close in size to Snipe but bill slightly shorter, with narrower tip, has shorter tail and duller upper-parts. In flight wings (slightly blunter) appear more uniform, lacking a prominent white trailing edge, and the under-wing is darker. The escape flight differs from Snipe in being slower, noticeably heavier, steadier, rarely containing a zig-zag or towering escape pattern.

Adult is similar to Snipe (nominate form), but is slightly less well marked on the head and the upper-parts are browner and more vermiculated, with the pale creamy stripes more broken. The wing-coverts are duller, buff-spotted – not white-tipped. In flight the upper-wing is the dullest of any Palaearctic snipe, and the under-wing is more heavily barred. The tail is distinctive in having the outer eight pairs of feathers pin-like (1–2mm wide) in a tail of some 26.

Voice. Flushed birds give a '*scaap*', more abrupt, less explosive and rather weaker than Snipe, or a short, rasping '*squik*' or '*squok*'. In song flight (50–70m) males begin to dive, plunging more and more vertically, while uttering a short, metallic '*tcheka-tcheka-tcheka*', rising in pitch, so that the calls soon merge with the noises made by their tails. The sounds become stronger, higher and longer as each bird descends towards the ground, before pulling out and soaring back up again.

Habitat. Breeding areas cover the forested regions of Siberia, and nesting areas include grassy swamps in taiga, damp meadows along river valleys, sphagnum bogs, timberline and areas of tundra with patches of dwarf birch at 2,300m. Differs from Snipe in frequenting drier situations. In winter resorts to marshy areas of pools and wet rice stubbles, again tending to occupy somewhat drier sites than Snipe.

Distribution. Breeds just on the north-eastern border of the western Palaearctic (in the western foothills of the Urals), eastward through Siberia, western Anadyrland and the coast of the Sea of Okhotsk. Winters from south-eastern China and Taiwan south to the Indo-Chinese countries and Malaya, India and the Sundas. Occurs on passage west to Iran and recorded as a vagrant to Eilat, Oman, Socotra, Somalia and Kenya. Map 35.

Movements. Migrates from northern breeding areas, presumably on a broad front, to winter in southern Asia. Early movements occur in Siberia in late July, although the main departure is in August–September, with birds arriving in India and Malaysia from mid-August and in early September in Borneo (main influx second half September–October). Return movement from Borneo reported in February, but the main departure from southern Asia, March to mid-April. The southern parts of the breeding range are reoccupied in May, but not until early June in the far north.

Feeding. Feeds mainly by picking, but also by probing into soft mud, using long bill with its sensitive and flexible tip, which opens to seize prey. Food is largely invertebrates, mainly insects and their larvae, molluscs and earthworms, some crustaceans, seeds and vegetable matter.

Social and breeding behaviour. Shortly after arrival on their breeding grounds males perform display flights over wide areas, which are often communal. Communal flight displays (involving up to 15 birds) appear to be most characteristic of birds early in the breeding season and during migration. Later in the season, when breeding is under way, display flights occur singly, rarely three or four males together. The display flight by single birds is largely similar to that of the drumming flight of the Snipe (see Voice).

Males may also sing and land in treetops or on the ground. Territories are zealously defended by the males, and fights between them were regularly observed during the day. It is possible that promiscuous mating occurs in this species, judging from its communal aerial courtship displays. Outside the breeding season occurs singly or in small groups of two to four birds, and larger loose flocks (up to 60) where food is abundant, and before or after migration.

Nest, eggs and young. Nest is well concealed on the ground in thick vegetation. A shallow depression lined with grass. Eggs 4, olive green with dark brown spots and blotches. Incubation period about 20 days, probably by female only. No other information.

SWINHOE'S SNIPE   *Gallinago megala*

Fr – Bécassine de Swinhoe   Ge – Grosse Waldbekassine

Identification. Length 10½–11in. Plumage very similar to Snipe and Pintail Snipe, but slightly larger and upper-parts look somewhat creamier and brighter, especially on sides of face, hind neck, sides of breast and prominently barred pale buff wing-coverts. On the wing looks heavier than Snipe, paler, and shows only a narrow whitish trailing edge to secondaries (1mm wide), and under-wings are more heavily barred darker than in Snipe. In the hand it can be seen that the tail comprises 20–30 feathers (rarely 18–26), with the outermost pair 2–4mm broad, narrower than in Snipe, but broader than in Pintail Snipe. In escape flight it rises rapidly, evenly, on a straighter course than Snipe.

Voice. When flushed gives a raspy '*squik*' or '*squok*'. In display flight the male flies in wide circles giving regular '*chvi*' or '*tchiki*' notes, before performing a steep kamikaze-like dive, producing an incredible sound not unlike a falling artillery shell. Birds may also give chirpy '*tchiki*' notes in the day, whilst perched on a broken stump.

Habitat. Breeds in the taiga and forest-steppe zones of central Siberia, in well forested plains, river valleys and clearings, or margins of well wooded regions. It has also been reported in alpine meadows at the timberline. Prefers drier sites than Snipe for breeding. In winter it resorts to marshy areas and paddy-fields.

Distribution. Breeds in central Siberia from about 82°E. longitude, eastward to Lake Baikal and south-western Transbaikalia. It apparently also breeds in southern Ussuriland and perhaps on Sakhalin. It winters from the Philippines and western Micronesia to India, the Indo-Chinese countries, the Sundas, New Guinea and Australia. Has straggled to the Maldives, and the only western Palaearctic record is from the northern Caucasus in December 1898.

Movements. Movement from breeding areas is probably on a broad front overland to wintering areas in south-east Asia. Birds depart from their breeding grounds around Krasnoyarsk by mid-September, and from the Altai region by mid-August, although some stay later. Birds also leave Transbaikalia between mid-August and the third week of September, and in the maritime provinces numbers decline sharply from mid- to late September. Spring passage in southern China is from the end of April and in May, and in the maritime provinces from late April, sometimes earlier. In Transbaikalia passage occurs from the end of April till late May, and from April in the Altai region. Birds appear in the Yenisei River region in mid-May and around Irkutsk during the first half of May.

Feeding. Feeding actions probably similar to other *Gallinago*, often foraging amongst hummocks in grass and on mudflats around seepage areas. Its food consists of earthworms, adult and larval insects and terrestrial molluscs.

Social and breeding behaviour. In spring birds arrive on their breeding areas, but spend some time in small groups in the river valleys before finally settling down in the more open areas of the taiga. Males indulge in high display flights over large territories, which persist well past the appearance of young birds, having a more prolonged courtship-display period than most other snipe. In the display flight the males fly around their territory and then plunge dramatically towards the ground, producing a loud rushing noise and calling, before pulling out and soaring upwards again. While the male flies around and over the female perched in the grass, she calls to him from time to time. These flights continue day and night at the height of the breeding season. The species has a monogamous mating system. In winter occurs singly, or in small loose parties.

Nest, eggs and young. Nest is a shallow hollow well hidden in short vegetation or shrubbery, lined with grasses. Eggs 4, creamy with irregular-shaped blackish-brown markings, mainly on the larger end. Fledging period 18–20 days. No other information.

SHORT-BILLED DOWITCHER   *Limnodromus griseus*

Du – Kleine Grijze Snip   Fr – Bécasseau à bec court
Ge – Kleiner Schlammläufer   Sp – Agujeta gris
Sw – Mindre beckasinsnäppa

Pl. 15

Identification. Length 9½–10½in. Distinguished with difficulty from Long-billed Dowitcher, with some overlap in bill length (varies from 1½ to 1¾ times head length). Has diagnostic call, a soft, rattled '*tu-tu-tu*' (compare thin '*keek*' of Long-billed), given with a somewhat Turnstone-like quality. Has distinctive summer and juvenile plumage, which with care are separable from Long-billed. Also differs from the latter in having the tail-bars browner, usually narrower than the white areas between. Has more spotted sides to the neck and chest and less barring on flanks, which are reduced to small spots and Vs on the under tail-coverts. Long-billed is darker and more heavily barred on the sides of the flanks and usually more distinctly barred on the under tail-coverts (rather than spotted).

Adult summer, the upper-parts are blackish-brown, marked rufous and buff. The under-parts are salmon (paler than Long-billed), with fine dark spotting on the neck and sides of the breast, with a few broken brown bars on the sides of the flanks and a whitish belly. Adult winter, upper-parts including wing-coverts, uniform greyish-brown, with darker crown contrasting with long white supercilium. Under-parts white, neck and upper breast suffused pale grey-brown, often with indistinct fine streaking.

Juvenile separable from Long-billed, with dark brown upper-parts broadly edged and vermiculated bright buff-brown. The breast is also more buffy, with indistinct mottling or spotting (Long-billed has the head, neck and upper breast much greyer). The scapulars and tertials are more noticeably traced and striped than the mantle (tertials 'tiger-striped'). In the Long-billed the tertials are plain with narrow edging.

In flight it appears stout, carrying its long bill pointed slightly downward. Shows white trailing edge to secondaries and inner primaries, with the lower back white, and rump/tail white, barred dark brown. On ground, chunky appearance, long bill and feeding behaviour recall *Gallinago* Snipes.

Voice. Still incompletely known and some calls apparently shared with Long-billed. However, flight call diagnostic, a quiet, rattling, musical '*tu-tu-tu*'.

Habitat. Breeds largely in the interior coniferous forest and muskeg zone, boggy and marshy areas with low vegetation often close to a small tree, extending to swampy coastal tundra, where it nests on dry ground in wet areas. After breeding moves to prairie lakes and sloughs, but in winter, in contrast to the Long-billed, it shows a strong preference for coastal mudflats, estuaries or shallow pools on salt marshes.

Distribution. Breeds in three separate areas in sub-arctic North America, in northern Quebec, central and north-western Canada and southern Alaska. Winters in southern U.S.A., Central America, West Indies, and South America to Peru and Brazil. Accidental Britain (2), also Norway, Sweden and Spain.

Movements. Migratory, with three distinct populations, *L.g.griseus* (breeding Labrador Peninsula (Ungava) to James Bay) and *L.g.hendersoni* (breeding Canadian interior west of Hudson Bay) have different migration patterns, but overlap in their winter quarters (southern and south-eastern U.S.A., Caribbean area south to Brazil). The Alaska population, *L.g.caurinus*, migrates south along the Pacific coast (some inland) to winter from California to Peru. Nominate *griseus* follows the Atlantic route in spring and autumn, while *hendersoni* follows the Great Plains and Mississippi valley route through the interior (some migrants move south-east to reach the Atlantic coast in autumn from Long Island southwards, where they are outnumbered by *griseus*). In New Jersey three main peaks occur in the autumn (both races), from early to mid-July (females), late July to early August (males) and mid-August to early September (juveniles). Birds show low weights on arrival, which suggests that they made non-stop flights from Ungava (*griseus*) and the Canadian interior (*hendersoni*) to New Jersey, and from there to Florida or the Caribbean. Many nominate *griseus* passing through the Gulf of St. Lawrence and the Canadian maritime provinces are thought to make non-stop flights to the Lesser Antilles or north-eastern South America. (Large numbers arrive there from mid-August to early October.) Spring passage is thought to be mainly from the Guianas over the outer Caribbean to the U.S.A. Breeding areas are reached in late May-early June.

Feeding. Feeds by jabbing, in which the bill is thrust into the mud and immediately withdrawn, or by probing with a fast up-and-down vertical motion of the head and bill, recalling sewing machine. Both Dowitchers forage by probing while standing in rather shallow water and probably take very similar foods on their breeding grounds, with larvae and pupae of dipterans forming a significant part of their diet. However, the Short-billed consumes a larger proportion of marine polychaete worms and molluscs in winter, while the Long-billed eats more insects, a difference that is to be expected in view of their winter habitat preferences.

Social and breeding behaviour. Breeding behaviour has been little studied, but it is known that the male performs a hovering flight with a warbling or gurgling song, becoming more mechanical towards the end. Copulatory behaviour has not been described, but it is known that strong pair-bonds are formed and nesting pairs often remain close together. Pairs invariably defend their nesting territory against intruders in concert. Gregarious outside the breeding season, in flocks, with even larger flocks on migration.

Nest, eggs and young. Nest is well concealed in vegetation and is a shallow hollow lined with dry grasses. Eggs 4, pale greenish or buff, marked with dark brown and pale grey. Incubation period 21 days, by both sexes. Fledging period not known, female taking little part in the care of the young, which are left to the male to tend.

LONG-BILLED DOWITCHER *Limnodromus scolopaceus*

Du – Grote Grijze Snip Fr – Bécasseau à long bec
Ge – Grosser Schlammläufer Sp – Agujeta escolopacea
Sw – Större beckasinsnäppa

Pl. 15

Identification. Length 10–11in. Easily confused with Short-billed Dowitcher, but is slightly larger and longer-billed (bill length variable, but many obviously long, and over $1\frac{3}{4}$ times head length). Has diagnostic flight call, a shrill '*keek*' (compare Short-billed's '*tu-tu-tu*') and distinctive juvenile plumage. Tail feathers evenly marked, with dark brown bars wider than the white ones. Flight pattern similar to Short-billed Dowitcher.

Adult summer, differs in looking much darker below, with whole under-parts, including belly and vent, dull red-chestnut, looking darker and richer-toned than Short-billed. Barring more obvious from the side of the chest to the rear flanks, with complete bars of distinct Vs on under tail-coverts. Adult winter, as moult progresses becomes noticeably greyer-headed, but in full winter almost identical to Short-billed, and only the tail feather pattern and stronger marks on the vent and under tail-coverts, plus distinct call, may help to separate it. The breast averages slightly darker and is more extensively grey and less speckled.

Juvenile differs from Short-billed in having the head, neck and upper breast much greyer. The back, scapulars and tertials are mainly dark brown, narrowly fringed or scalloped chestnut-brown, and darker than the buff-brown of the Short-billed. Tertials are rather plainer, with narrow edging. The difference in feather pattern between the two dowitchers is most obvious on the scapulars and tertials, and clearly visible at close range. The under-parts are similar to the non-breeding adults, with the breast indistinctly marked and not as buff or speckled as the Short-billed.

Voice. Commonest call, a shrill, penetrating '*keek*', which may be given up to three times. In the display flight the male has a prolonged song, '*peet-peet*'; '*pee-ter-wee-too*'; '*wee-too*'; '*pee-ter-wee-too*'; '*pee-ter-wee-too*'; '*wee-too*'; '*wee-too*'.

Habitat. In Siberia breeds in low, moss-sedge tundra having an abundance of lakes or pools during spring. In North America breeds in grassy and sedgy areas with or without scattered low, woody vegetation and usually near shallow fresh water. In winter prefers fresh-water habitats, while the Short-billed is more common on salt-water or brackish-water habitats.

Distribution. Breeds in north-eastern Siberia and in North America on St. Lawrence Island and the coasts of northern and western Alaska, and in northern Mackenzie. Winters from California and Florida southward through Mexico to Guatemala (which is mainly north of the Short-billed Dowitcher's wintering range). Accidental in several European countries, including the British Isles (105 identified of 230 dowitchers); a high proportion of indeterminate records of *griseus/scolopaceus* in western Palaearctic. Surprisingly enough, the Alaskan Long-billed Dowitcher occurs more often in Europe than the central and east Canadian Short-billed, which is presumably a consequence of overshooting after a long south-east autumn movement towards the Atlantic coast. British and Irish autumn arrivals are normally associated with Atlantic depressions.

Movements. In north-eastern Siberia females flock from late June and move away, while males tending chicks depart in late July to early August. Siberian birds cross the Bering Sea to North America and migrate with the latter population. In North America the main southward movement (July–September) is through the western provinces to winter from central California southwards to Guatemala. Other birds pass further east of the Rockies and some go south between the Rockies and the Mississippi valley as far as the Gulf of Mexico. Others continue south-east over the Great Lakes to reach the Atlantic states, from about Massachusetts southwards (wintering southern New Mexico to Florida). In New Jersey (where scarce) it does not occur regularly until mid-August (adults) or September to early October (juveniles), so that Atlantic passage begins five to six weeks later than the Short-billed (Long-billed has already flown about 6,500Km from far western breeding grounds). Return passage through western U.S.A. is in April, with breeding areas in Alaska reoccupied from third week of May, and in early June in north-eastern Siberia.

Feeding. Feeding actions similar to Short-billed Dowitcher. In spring eats a variety of insect larvae, seeds and vegetable matter, later taking abundant cranefly larvae during the summer, also small gastropod molluscs.

Social and breeding behaviour. Shortly after arriving on their breeding grounds in spring males perform song-flights over their territories, until the time that the first broods appear. The song flight is performed about 15 metres above the tundra, the male hovering on quivering wings, singing all the while. Often only parts of the song are given, especially if the male is chasing a female. No information on any ground displays or copulatory behaviour. Outside the breeding season the species is gregarious, feeding in flocks on shallow, muddy, fresh-water pools with some marginal vegetation. Sometimes mingles with Short-billed Dowitcher on the shore on migration.

Nest, eggs and young. Nest is in a hollow, sparsely lined with grasses and small leaves, amongst grasses or sedges. Eggs 4, pale greenish, or olive and marked with dark brown and purplish-grey. Incubation period 20 days, by both sexes at first, later by male alone. Fledging period, not known.

WOODCOCKS   Subfamily Scolopacinae

Robust, long-billed, highly cryptic scolopacid waders adapted to nesting on the ground in forests. Plumages are soft and thick, the wings are short and rounded, and flight owl-like. Eyes set even further back on the head than Snipe – allowing vision through 360°. Crepuscular and nocturnal.

Range. Holarctic, southern Asia, Indonesia and New Guinea.

Number of species. World, 6; western Palaearctic, 1.

WOODCOCK   *Scolopax rusticola*

Du – Houtsnip   Fr – Bécasse des bois
Ge – Waldschnepfe   Sp – Chocha perdiz
Sw – Morkulla

Pl. 14

Identification. Length 13½in. Larger than Snipe and rounder winged, with russet coloration and long bill; rises from cover in open woodland and flies off with twisting flight through the trees. On the ground appears rather large and bulky, while upper-parts are beautifully marked with rufous-brown and buff below, with intricate marbling and barring, obvious at close range; head crossed with thick bars – not striped like Snipe. Sexes similar. Juvenile closely resembles adult, but not always distinguishable with certainty.

Voice. A harsh '*schaap*' sometimes given when flushed after dark. At dusk the male performs a display flight, known as roding, and repeatedly traverses a regular circuit just above treetop height, giving a '*quorr-quorr-quorr tsiwick*'. Alarm calls, '*pier*' and a quiet '*uk-uk-uk*' – rarely uttered. The female calls down the roding male with a softer version of the male's sneeze-note.

Habitat. Chiefly frequents extensive moist woodland, either broad-leaved, mixed or coniferous, with open glades and rides and a good cover of bracken, brambles and bushes, especially evergreens. Also woods with swampy hollows and overgrown ditches, although the bird requires dry ground to rest in by day. At dusk flies to feed on marshes, boggy ground and spongy places about ditches and streams.

Distribution. Breeds in the Azores, Madeira, the Canaries, the British Isles and on the mainland of Eurasia from Scandinavia south to Spain and eastward across Russia and Siberia to Sakhalin and Japan. Also breeds in China, probably northern Burma, in northern India, Russian Turkestan and the Caucasus. Winters south to the Mediterranean, Iraq, Iran, Afghanistan, India and Indo-Chinese countries. Map **36**.

Movements. Mainly migratory, although many birds are resident in Ireland, Britain and probably France. These areas also receive large influxes of winter visitors from Scandinavia etc. A few also winter in Denmark, The Netherlands and West Germany, but the main wintering areas are in western and southern Europe, North Africa and from Asia Minor east to Japan.

Ringing recoveries of Fenno-Scandian birds show autumn movement S–WSW. Autumn migration begins in the first half of October in Finland and from mid- to late October in Scandinavia, with departures closely related to the onset of frosts. By the end of November the majority of birds have occupied their winter quarters. Later in cold weather, birds may move further west or south to milder areas. Return movement begins in the first half of March, with the breeding areas reoccupied during April in Scandinavia. In Finland passage lasts until mid-May. Continental populations have similar west to south autumn orientation as shown by Fenno-Scandian birds. Some Russian birds undoubtedly occur west to the British Isles, although it is assumed that the west Siberian birds normally winter in the south-west of southern Asia.

Feeding. Takes food from ground surface and from under leaf litter, or by probing in puddles and damp ground. When probing, at each step the bill is inserted for about a third of its length. Once prey is detected by the sensitive bill tip, the bill is inserted to its full length. It probably takes small prey by suction, but when a worm or other large item is encountered, the distal third of the upper mandible is bent upwards and the prey is seized and slowly extracted. Food is largely earthworms, but it also takes insects and their larvae, particularly beetles; also takes plant food.

Social and breeding behaviour. The male has a self-advertising display flight and roding occurs primarily at dusk and dawn, throughout the breeding season. The primary function is evidently to attract or discover females ready to mate. Flying males may also be called to earth by females, which utter shrill notes that cause the male to drop like a stone. A ground display by the male follows, which has been described as strutting with dropped wings, the tail raised and spread. In one observation the male followed the female with a low crouching gait and swaying motions, until the female crouched and copulation followed. The male remains with a single female only until her clutch is complete and then resumes roding, indicating a mating system approaching polygyny. The species is typically solitary.

Nest, eggs and young. Nest on ground in woods, concealed by low vegetation, or in heathland with medium-height cover: shallow depression, lined with dead leaves, dry grass and a few feathers. Eggs 4, pale buff with brown or chestnut markings. Incubation period 22 days, by female only. Fledging period 15–20 days, young cared for by female only. Age of first breeding, one year for females, two years for most males.

GODWITS, CURLEWS and other SANDPIPERS   Subfamily Tringinae

Most species breed at high latitudes in the northern hemisphere and include many of the largest waders. Many are long-distance migrants, and are remarkably strong fliers. Godwits have very long, straight, or slightly upcurved bills and most have distinct breeding and winter plumages. The Curlews are the largest members and are characterised by moderate to very long decurved bills and brown mottled plumage, which shows little change from summer to winter. The *Tringa* sandpipers range from two of the largest, the Greenshank and the Greater Yellowlegs to two of the smaller, more compact and short-legged members, the Green and Solitary Sandpipers, both of which lay their eggs in the arboreal old nests of other birds. The Common and Spotted Sandpipers also breed in more temperate latitudes than most. Females are usually larger than males, especially in the larger species.

Range. Holarctic (more northern areas) and wintering further south in more temperate zones, often south of the Equator.

Number of species. World, 29; western Palaearctic, 22.

BLACK-TAILED GODWIT   *Limosa limosa*

Du – Grutto   Fr – Barge à queue noire
Ge – Uferschnepfe   Sp – Aguja colinegra
Sw – Rödspov

Pl. 16

Identification. Length 15½–17in. Large, rather graceful wader similar in body size and wing length to Bar-tailed Godwit, but is taller with longer legs and straighter, longer bill. In flight easily distinguished from the latter by bold, broad, white wing-bar extending right across blackish flight feathers, and long legs projecting conspicuously beyond the black-banded white tail; from the Hudsonian Godwit by bolder white wing-bar, broader area of white across the lower rump and upper tail-coverts, and white, not black, under-wings and axillaries.

In summer, head, neck and breast pale pinkish-chestnut, with flanks and belly white, variably barred blackish. Bill, with basal two-thirds yellowish-pink, remainder blackish-brown. Winter plumage more like a dark Bar-tailed, but wing and tail pattern unchanged. Upper-parts more uniformly pale greyish-brown, lacking darker shaft streaks of Bar-tailed. Under-parts white with breast washed greyish.

The juvenile has a rufous tinge to the neck and breast, with pale pinkish-chestnut fringes to the dark brown upper-parts, and red-buff edges to the wing-coverts. Bill colour in non-breeding and juvenile plumages, fleshy-pink basal half, with distal part dark brown to black on tip. Legs lead-grey to black.

Voice. Flight call, head chiefly from flocks on the wing, a loud clear '*weeka-weeka-weeka*'. A short '*däät*', uttered singly or in short series, is characteristic of the summer flock period. Noisy when nesting, and on the breeding ground the main call is a disyllabic '*kwee-yit*', recalling Lapwing's note. '*Krru-wit-tew*' song in display flight.

Habitat. Breeds in water meadows, rough pastures, rushy bogs and marshes. In eastern England has successfully recolonised grazing-fields or washes, a type of water meadow rich in rough grasses. In the non-breeding season sheltered coastal inlets and salt marshes are favoured more than the open shore, and it is much more of an inland bird than the Bar-tailed Godwit, visiting fresh-water marshes, lakes and sewage farms on passage.

Distribution. The Islandic race (*L.l.islandica*) breeds in Iceland, Scotland and northern Norway, wintering in large numbers in Ireland. Britain and Western France. The nominate form breeds in England, western and central Europe, and USSR east to the Yenisey river. Winters in part in southern Europe and south-western Asia, but mainly in Africa. The oriental form (*L.l.melanuroides*) probably breeds from Mongolia and perhaps the upper Yenisey east to the sea of Okhotsk and Sakhalin, and from Anadyrland south to Kamchatka, wintering in south-east Asia from the Bay of Bengal to Taiwan and the Philippines and south to Australia. Map 37.

Movements. Birds are present on Icelandic breeding grounds from late April to August, with the first returning migrants reaching Ireland in late June. Numbers build up slowly until mid-August, then there is a sudden influx which is completed in about the first ten days of September. In French Vendée some birds arrive in July, but the main influx is in the second half of August and September, with adults averaging earlier than juveniles. Small numbers of birds also reach south-west Norway both in spring and autumn, and a few *islandica* probably occur sparingly on passage in West Germany and the Low Countries.

Departures from European breeding grounds begin in late June with the major exodus in July, continuing till September. The European population winters mainly in Africa, north of the Equator, but most in West Africa from Morocco to Sierra Leone. Many adults pause in northern Morocco in July to moult. The small numbers that occur in southern Morocco and on the Banc d'Arguin, Mauritania, indicate a mainly non-stop crossing of the Sahara by those wintering further south. Enormous numbers occur on the flood plains of Lake Chad from September to December; also numbers in excess of 10,000 in the Senegal delta and over 100,000 estimated in the Niger inundation zone, Mali, have been recorded in January. Small numbers also winter in north-western Europe, with increasing numbers in Iberia. Estonian birds are known to move south to south-east in autumn in the direction of the Black Sea and some may winter in the eastern Mediterranean. Large numbers of Russian birds are also presumed to winter in the Afrotropics. Return movement begins in February, with the largest numbers occurring from late February to mid-March at an important staging area in Maine et Loire (France). In north-western Europe, breeding sites are reoccupied from mid-March to mid-April, and April to early May in the USSR.

Feeding. Locates food by touch and sight. Feeds more leisurely then Bar-tailed Godwit, with a preference for deeper water, often probing with head completely immersed. Typically, walks forward slowly, holding head down with almost vertical bill, making several exploratory probes, then suddenly probes deeper, pulling out prey, usually swallowing it immediately. Also pecks food from the surface and vegetation. Takes a wide range of invertebrates, including insects, annelid worms and molluscs. Also plant material and some seeds.

Social and breeding behaviour. Pair formation occurs generally on the breeding grounds, although a few may already be paired on arrival. Birds arrive in groups of five to 30 individuals, soon dispersing, and song-flights by males become frequent. The male begins with a steep ascent on rapidly beating wings, uttering a loud, quick repeated, trisyllabic note. Around 50–60m the call changes to a more disyllabic song-note, the wing-beats are slower and more clipped, with the wings markedly bent downwards. The flight becomes more undulating as the bird pitches from side to side with spread tail. Finally the rolling flight and call stop simultaneously and the bird glides on rigid wings, before suddenly nose-diving with wings and tail almost closed. About 15m above the ground the wings are opened and the bird sideslips downward, finally spreading the tail and raising the wings in an extended wings-high display just before landing. A second type of display flight is performed by both sexes, in which the female typically takes the lead, with both sexes calling. This flight may take the form of a pursuit, especially when other males join in. Additionally, pursuit flights are directed at other Godwits that fly over the male's territory. There are several threat-display postures that are performed towards rivals on the ground, which include tail-spreading, ruffling of the back feathers and bill-crossing. The male may include several of these elements, including wing-raising, in his display towards females. In the nest-scrape ceremony the male runs to a depression in the grass, crouches in it, tilts his tail high in the air and rubs his breast against the ground. Sometimes the pair nest-scrape alternately. Copulation is preceded by the female standing fairly still while the male approaches from behind. He spreads his tail, calls, and begins vibrating his wings, eventually fluttering above his partner with legs dangling and wings still vibrating. He settles on to her back and copulation follows. The birds have a monogamous mating system.

The species is highly gregarious, often forming flocks of several thousand in late summer, or early spring.

Nest, eggs and young. Somewhat colonial, with nests frequently found only three to ten metres apart. Nests are usually in rather luxuriant grass cover, although in sandy areas the nest may be sheltered by more scrubby vegetation. Eggs 3–4, olive green to dark brown, marked and blotched darker brown. Incubation period 22–24 days, by both sexes. Fledging period 25–30 days, young cared for by both parents. Age of first breeding, two years or older.

During the early stages of the breeding cycle, the male frequently performs the quiver-flight as an invitation for the female to follow.

HUDSONIAN GODWIT   *Limosa haemastica*

Fr – Barge hudsonienne

Identification. Length 14–16½in. Similar to Black-tailed Godwit, but shorter-legged, with a slightly more upturned bill, and showing a narrower white wing-bar (not showing beyond the coverts on the secondaries), narrower white band across the upper tail-coverts, with the axillaries and most of the under-wing black. Breeding plumage darker, richer and more rusty coloured, this colour also extending on to the belly and under tail-coverts. Also has a distinctly streaked neck and throat, unlike the Black-tailed Godwit. Under-parts narrowly barred black, heaviest along side of body and under tail-coverts. Upper-parts blackish, flecked with buff. Throat and sides of head whitish, freckled dark grey or blackish, and showing a whitish eye-stripe.

Adults in winter are uniformly greyish-brown on the upper-parts, with the inner wing-coverts fringed whitish. Juveniles are brownish-black above, with buffy to whitish fringes, and the wing-coverts are brown fringed buff. Juveniles and winter-plumaged adults tend to be washed with tawny on the under-parts and edges of the tertials, while similarly plumaged Black-tailed Godwits look cleaner and whiter below, with the tawny or greyish-brown wash restricted to the breast, and tend to have whitish edges to the tertials. The Hudsonian Godwit is also darker capped than the Black-tailed in winter plumage. The bill is blacker at the tip and pinkish towards the base. Females have a purplish-flesh bill colour in spring, compared with a clear bright orange in males. Legs and feet bluish-grey.

Voice. In flight '*ta-it ta-it*', a subdued version of the noisy '*toe-whit toe-whit*' calls constantly heard on the nesting grounds.

Habitat. A typical nesting habitat is at tree-line, a few miles back from the coast, or the banks of rivers, where the last few stunted trees run out into the tundra, with willow thickets and sedge meadow lying between. Outside the breeding season, mudflats, sandy beaches and shallows of fresh, brackish and salt water.

Distribution. Breeds in three apparently disconnected regions: the south and west shores of Hudson Bay from Cape Henrietta Maria to Eskimo Point (largest numbers); the north-western corner of arctic Canada, including the lower reaches and deltas of the Anderson and Mackenzie rivers (small but substantial numbers); and western Alaska (probably no more than a few hundred breeding pairs). Winters in northern Argentina, northern Chile, Paraguay and southern Brazil, Uruguay, to Tierra del Fuego and the Falkland Islands. In autumn occurs south along the Atlantic seaboard to New Jersey and Virginia. It has wandered to Australia, New Zealand and the British Isles (September 1981–January 1982, April 1983).

Movements. In mid-July non-breeding sub-adults and failed breeders begin to gather on the tidal flats of Hudson Bay and move south-east. Later the successful breeders which have left their chicks behind them, join them. During the first week of August the first fully fledged juveniles appear on the Hudson Bay flats and soon gather into flocks of their own. Unlike the adults they do not begin at once to move south-east. It is probable that the Anderson-Mackenzie and Alaskan populations also gather here, as there is little evidence of their being found elsewhere. For a period of a week or more in mid-August, virtually the whole species, old and young, are concentrated in a narrow coastal strip, stretching some 1,600km from Eskimo Point to the foot of James Bay. At favoured gathering spots they form flocks of many hundreds, or even thousands. The major southward departure of adults takes place during the last ten days of August. Their spectacular long-distance flight takes them on a great circular course, projected roughly south-east from James Bay, out over the south coast of New England, passing west of Bermuda, down the outer curve of the Lesser Antilles, and after some 4,800km they reach the northern coast of South America. It seems certain that the birds fly non-stop, as there are virtually no records or sightings anywhere along this route.

Although there are records of small parties arriving on the Guianan coasts, the numbers do not match the James Bay departures, and only in northern Argentina are large numbers reported. The necessity for birds to replenish their fat reserves before undertaking a flight across the Amazon Basin suggests a restaging area somewhere on the Guianan seaboard, and a further indication is that birds are known to arrive in Paraguay and Argentina in late September to early October, but so far such an area remains undiscovered. On spring migration the returning flocks are traceable as far as northern Argentina, where they virtually disappear, until in late April they reach the coasts of Texas and western Louisiana. Spring passage up the western side of the Mississippi drainage is more dispersed than the autumn migration down James Bay. The Alaskan population reaches Prince William Sound in early May, but there are few clues as to their route. By early June all nesting grounds are reoccupied.

Feeding. Feeds by touch and sight, rapidly probing in mud with long bill, which is sometimes immersed to eye level. Often wades and feeds in water so deep that the head is completely under water while feeding. Feeds on marine worms, molluscs, particularly *macoma* species and crustaceans; on the nesting grounds, insects, including flies and mosquitoes.

Social and breeding behaviour. Breeding behaviour is rather similar to that of the Black-tailed Godwit, with males performing song flights and pursuit flights over their territories. The male climbs steeply for the first 30m, giving low calls, after which he remains silent, while he continues to climb in a series of spirals up to some 250m. Then, after levelling off, he begins a series of '*toe-whit*' calls, gradually increasing in intensity. After some distance he turns back, gliding with the wings held in a V, circles about calling loudly and starts to lose altitude. Suddenly he stops calling and plummets downward on closed wings until about 12m above the ground. Then spreading his wings, he glides, and alights gracefully on a tussock, folding his wings quite deliberately. It is not known how other aspects of breeding behaviour differ from those of the Black-tailed Godwit. The species is markedly gregarious (see *Movements*).

Nest, eggs and young. A depression near or under a dwarf birch or small willow, often with little lining except a few dead leaves. Eggs 4, dark olive green, sparingly spotted brown. Incubation period 23 days, by both sexes. Fledging period 30 days, young cared for by both parents.

BAR-TAILED GODWIT   *Limosa lapponica*

Du – Rosse Grutto   Fr – Barge rousse
Ge – Pfuhlschnepfe   Sp – Aguja colipinta
Sw – Myrspov

Pl. 16

Identification. Length 14½–15½in. Similar in body size to Black-tailed Godwit, but shorter legged and more stocky, with rather shorter bill which is noticeably more up-curved (has pinkish or orange base). No clear wing-bar or marked tail pattern, the latter brown and obscurely barred. Main feature in flight is the white rump; feet barely projecting beyond the tail. Russet breeding plumage (largely unbarred) extends over the entire under-parts, including the under tail-coverts. Upper-parts blackish-brown, feathers with reddish notches; wing-coverts greyish-brown with paler edges. Female much browner and duller than the male.

Adults in winter plumage are obviously more streaked above than winter Black-tailed Godwit. The upper-parts are greyish-brown with darker shaft streaks, recalling Curlew. Under-parts whitish, with the breast faintly streaked brown. Under-wing and axillaries white, barred brown. The juvenile is more brown and buff, and more streaked than the juvenile Black-tailed.

Voice. Rather quiet, but flying flocks give low barking '*kirruc*' or '*yak*' notes. Often highly vocal on breeding grounds. Male in song-flight gives a series of sweet, soft, rapid notes – '*a-wika-wika-wik*', '*ku-wew ku-wew*'. Prior to display, a very rapid '*tivvy-tivvy-tivvy*', ending with '*wee-it*' has been noted.

Habitat. Breeds in marshy places in moss and shrub-tundra, swampy heathlands in the willow and birch zones near the tree-line. Outside the breeding season it is found on both muddy and sandy shores of sea coasts and estuaries. Occurs inland less frequently than Black-tailed Godwit.

Distribution. Nominate '*lapponica*' breeds in Lapland from northern Norway and Sweden east to the Taimyr Peninsula. Winters in the North Sea and Atlantic coasts of Europe and Africa, and to a lesser extent in the Mediterranean, Red Sea, Persian Gulf, and coasts and islands of the western Indian Ocean. The eastern race, *L.l.baueri*, breeds in northern Siberia, east from the Khatanga river, also in western Alaska. Winters from south-east Asia to Australia and western Polynesia. Map **38**.

Movements. The major passages of nominate *lapponica* in spring and autumn are through the Baltic and North Seas, and involve birds as far east as the western Taimyr. These birds winter on coasts from the British Isles and the Waddenzee, south to South Africa. The largest numbers winter on the Banc d'Arguin, Mauritania (i.e. 543,000, February 1980). Migrants occur in Scandinavia and West Germany from July–October, peak numbers late July–early August. Some birds pass through the Waddenzee rapidly without moulting, many of these presumably moving on to Morocco and Mauritania.

The main arrivals occur in August in the Wash and at Morecambe Bay (England). Many birds stay to moult, with some adults leaving afterwards. During late March and April birds leave their wintering areas in north-east England and Morecambe Bay (still in winter plumage) and presumably return to their moulting areas. At the same time large numbers of birds build up on the Waddenzee for pre-breeding moult and fat deposition, prior to departure.

Small numbers of birds also presumably cross western Siberia, since the species in winter is not scarce in Pakistan and north-western India.

Feeding. Feeds mainly by probing, though some prey is captured at surface. Usually moves briskly over mud, making frequent test probes, sometimes in rapid series. When prey is detected, probes rapidly and deeply, often continuing forward movement around bill as it is driven in. On mudflats takes mainly bivalves and marine worms; on breeding grounds, beetles, flies and worms are major items, with some plant material (seeds and berries).

Social and breeding behaviour. Territorial and display behaviour have only poorly been described, but the male's song-flight is apparently much like that of other Godwits, circling on stiff, decurved wings, twisting and turning, with wing-beats slow or erratic and interspersed with short glides. Additionally, communal aerial display also occurs on the wintering grounds and during spring migration. Individual birds sometimes dive out of flocks and plummet several hundred feet, while calling loudly. There are probably several types of aerial displays, including song-flights and pursuit flights, but these remain to be clarified. Similarly there appears to be no description available regarding copulatory behaviour. The species has a monogamous mating system. Gregarious, flocks may reach several thousand birds in winter.

Nest, eggs and young. A shallow scrape is made in short vegetation, on a dry ridge or mound within swampy terrain, and lined with plant material, building being probably by both sexes. Eggs 3–4, green to olive, spotted or blotched dark brown and grey. Incubation period 20–21 days, by both sexes. The fledging period has not been determined. The young are cared for by both parents. Age of first breeding, two years.

LITTLE WHIMBREL   *Numenius minutus*

Du – Kleine Regenwulp	Fr – Courlis nain
Ge – Zwergbrachvogel	Sp – Zarapito chico
Sw – Dvärgspov	

Pl. 17

Identification. Length 11–11¾in. A tiny Curlew, only slightly larger than Redshank, with long legs, upright stance and delicate carriage. The noticeably slender, short bill (about half the length of a Whimbrel's) is only slightly decurved for the last third of its length. As in Whimbrel, the crown is dark brown showing a narrow buff median stripe, but unlike the Western Palaearctic race of that species, the rump and tail are brown, uniform with the back. Its close relative the nearly extinct* Eskimo Curlew (*N. borealis*) of North America is only slightly larger than *minutus*, but shows more cinnamon and less buff in its plumage. It is also more boldly and coarsely marked, with heavier streaking to the sides of the face and neck, and shows distinctive dark brown chevrons on the breast and flanks. The Little Whimbrel is buffier on the face, neck and breast and more finely streaked, the chevrons being few in number and confined to the flanks, and the belly is whiter. In both species the under-wing coverts and axillaries are barred with dark brown, but in *borealis* these feathers are rich cinnamon, whereas in *minutus* they are a much paler buff, or sandy colour. At rest, the tail of the Little Whimbrel extends noticeably beyond the folded wings, whilst in *borealis* the wing tips cover the tail. The pinkish base to the lower mandible is more extensive in *minutus*, reaching to or beyond the middle of the bill. In *borealis*, the bill, which is slightly longer, heavier and fractionally more decurved, is darker, with the pale area occupying less than half the bill length.

Voice. Feeding flocks give a soft '*te-te-te*'. In alarm gives a rather harsh, '*tchew-tchew-tchew*', similar to the note of the Greenshank, but lower – or when flushed, a hoarse but musical '*klee-klee-klee*'. In song-flight gives a short, melodious, fluting trill, which is sometimes immediately followed by a bubbling Curlew-like trill.

Habitat. Breeding habitat is mainly clearings in subarctic forest, often in areas which have been affected by fire, but where the vegetation has rejuvenated. Also along valleys and steppe-like foothills in upland areas. Said to associate with breeding Golden Eagles, presumably gaining some protection thereby. In winter prefers extensive grasslands, especially wet ones, but is also found on dry open grassland, including airfields.

Distribution and Movements. Breeds in central Siberia in the upper reaches of the Moyero and Kochechum rivers, and in north-eastern Siberia in the middle reaches of the Yana River and mountains to the Indigirka River. Flocks begin to form in the second half of July. Apparently migrates overland to eastern China, and from there to winter quarters, mainly in northern Australia, but also in Borneo, Sulawesi, the Moluccas and the Philippines. Birds are on their wintering grounds in Australia from September–October to March–April, and reoccupy their breeding grounds again during the last few days of May. The species has strayed to Britain twice (Aug–Sept 1982 and 1985), Norway (July 1969) and the Seychelles (October 1972–April 1973).

Feeding. Obtains prey on the surface or by shallow probes, often making swift runs to seize it. Insects predominate in the recorded diet. In the summer the birds also take a number of berries, such as blueberries and their related species.

Social and breeding behaviour. Forms small isolated breeding colonies, each pair taking up a territory some 200–300m from its neighbour. In the display flight the male climbs for some 200–300m before levelling out and then performs an alternate wing-shivering and slow-sailing flight, flying in irregular circles of some 100–200m in diameter. From time to time he gives a short, melodious, fluting trill. Immediately after the trill he may close his wings and plunge downwards at an angle of 30–40° for some considerable distance, at the same time producing a whistling sound with his flight and tail feathers.

---

*The Eskimo Curlew (*N.borealis*) formerly bred in western Canada and probably Alaska; wintered in South America from Paraguay and southern Brazil to Patagonia. Excessive shooting was undoubtedly the main cause of its decline and by the early 20th century it was feared extinct. However, the species continues to be reported in ones and twos at irregular intervals. Accidental, British Isles (7, last 1887).

Subsequently he climbs back up again to his original level. Often the display flight, sometimes involving two males, will last for 40 minutes or more. It often ends with the bird's diving down and alighting on top of an old larch tree, before flying down to the ground. Other details of breeding activity and pre-copulatory behaviour are not known. The species is gregarious in winter, with flocks sometimes numbering thousands.

Nest, eggs and young. Nests in open grassland with scattered willow bushes and dwarf birch. A depression lined with dry bents and grasses. Eggs 4, pale greenish with dark reddish-brown spots and blotches. Incubation period 22–23 days, presumably by both sexes. Fledging period, not determined.

WHIMBREL   *Numenius phaeopus*

Du – Regenwulp
Fr – Courlis corlieu
Ge – Regenbrachvogel
Sp – Zarapito trinador
Sw – Småspov

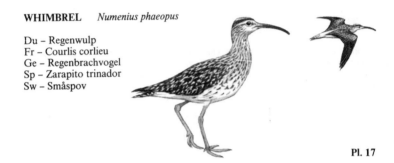

Pl. 17

Identification. Length 15¾–16½in. Smaller than Curlew, to which it bears a general resemblance, with proportionally shorter legs and bill, the latter abruptly bent. It also has a strongly marked head pattern, with two dark bands on the crown separated by a pale central stripe, a feature shared only by the much smaller Little Whimbrel and Eskimo Curlew, both of which have dark brown rumps. The Whimbrel generally looks darker brown than the Curlew, with denser markings on the back, chest and flanks. In flight the under-wing appears darker than the Curlew's and the flight action is more buoyant, with faster wing-beats. The rump is white, although the Nearctic race *hudsonicus* is separable at long range by having the lower back and rump uniform with the rest of the upper-parts and a browner under-wing. Call note distinctive (see below). The juvenile differs from the adult by having contrasting pale spots on the crown, scapulars and tertials.

Voice. Usual call is a rapid, far-carrying, rippling titter lasting one to one-and-a-half seconds. On the breeding grounds display calls include a bubbling trill very like the Curlew's, and a distinctive, long-drawn, whining '*teeeeee-ooo*'.

Habitat. Breeds on northern and subarctic heaths and moorlands, ranging from dry lava desert (Iceland) to dwarf birch and willow scrub or open heaths in forested regions. On passage, mainly confined to coasts, occurring in similar places to Curlew, but more often on rocky shores. In tropical wintering areas may be found on coral reefs or mangroves, as well as open shores.

Distribution. The nominate race breeds in Iceland, the Faeroes, Scotland and continental Eurasia from Sweden to central Siberia. *N.p.alboaxillaris* breeds in the southern USSR.

N.p.variegatus, breeding in north-eastern Siberia, winters from the Bay of Bengal to Melanesia, Micronesia and Australia. The race breeding in North America, *N.p.hudsonicus*, winters from the southern U.S.A. to Chile on the Pacific coast and Brazil on the Atlantic side. This race has been identifed in the British Isles (4) and West Africa. Map **39**.

Movements. Breeding birds from Iceland, Scandinavia and north-western Russia occur on autumn passage through western Europe and winter mainly in West Africa, some as far south as South Africa. Some also winter on the islands and coasts of East Africa and the western Indian Ocean (in latter region overlapping with *alboaxillaris*). Migration to and from these areas evidently takes place by long flights, often overland, between a few major staging points. The autumn exodus from breeding areas begins in July, with peak numbers occurring in western Europe in August, in September in Iberia, with rapid movement continuing down the Moroccan coast to Mauritania (where a good many overwinter). It is thought that some Icelandic breeders may reach West Africa direct by a long oversea flight. Many summer in African wintering areas and probably all one-year-olds do so. Spring passage in the Afrotropics begins in March, including a long diagonal Saharan crossing from Ghana. Early birds reach Europe in late March, though the main passage is in the last half of April to mid-May. The interior of The Netherlands and Hungary both provide important staging areas, although autumn routes are less well known. The large numbers of birds which migrate to and from East and south-eastern Africa via the Middle East are presumably of Siberian origin. Breeding grounds are reoccupied in May, or in June in the northern USSR.

Feeding. In all habitats relies more on visual clues than Curlew, with consequent preponderance of surface-living prey. Crabs, shrimps, sandhoppers and marine snails (periwinkles, dog whelks) are important items on the shore. Inland, snails, slugs and insects are major prey items, as well as earthworms and insect larvae. Some individuals wintering in Mauritania hold territories of 1,000–3,000 sq.m, evenly spaced along the shore and related to the presence of a crab which forms a major food source. In breeding areas berries are a frequent food, in addition to insects and other animal prey.

Social and breeding behaviour. On arrival at the breeding grounds, strong territorial fidelity appears to facilitate the re-pairing of returning birds. The display flight is similar to the Curlew's; as he rises from the ground at 45° to about 150–300m, the male begins flying in a circle of some 200–400m in diameter, often describing the same course repeatedly. During the circuit he alternately climbs at 45°, flapping rapidly, and then breaks off, making a shallow downward glide with wings held stiffly out from the body and arched, head erect and retracted close to the body, for several seconds. The female sometimes flies up to join the male while singing, and high-flying displays have been reported to last up to one hour. On landing after displaying, the male may give a whining call several times, leaning forward with lowered breast and tail raised. Ground-threat and advertisement postures are similar to the Curlew's, and tail-fanning and the exposure of the white rump are a feature of courtship. The pair may sing and call together in ground courtship. A copulatory attempt involved the male following closely behind the female whilst performing head-jerking and wing-lifting movements. The species has a monogamous mating system. On the breeding grounds nests solitarily, or scattered about in loose groups. Highly gregarious in winter, often forming large flocks.

Nest, eggs and young. The nest is a shallow depression on bare ground or in short vegetation, lined with fragments of vegetation. Eggs 4, olive-green to buff, with dark brown spots and blotches. Incubation period 27–28 days, by both sexes. Fledging period 35–40 days, both parents caring for the young. Age of first breeding two years.

SLENDER-BILLED CURLEW   *Numenius tenuirostris*

Du – Dunbekwulp
Fr – Courlis à bec grêle
Ge – Dünnschnabelbrachvogel
Sp – Zarapito fino
Sw – Smalnäbbad spov

Pl. 17

Identification. Length 14–16in. About the size of a Whimbrel, but with slimmer build, plain crown and general colour pattern of Curlew, though paler than most individuals of the latter (see below). Bill more delicate than that of either Curlew or Whimbrel, tapering to a fine point and with very even curvature – appearing black and lacking the Curlew's pinkish colour on the basal half of the lower mandible. At close range distinctive heart-shaped spots on the flanks can be seen, better marked in breeding plumage and lacking in juvenile. In flight differs from adult Curlew in almost-black outer primaries, contrasting with white spotted inner flight feathers and greater coverts. It also has a pure white lower back and rump, dark brown and white bars on the tail and an almost pure white under-wing, so that overhead the bird appears nearly white. Flight action similar to Whimbrel's. At times the identification of *tenuirostris* can be far from easy, particularly with the variability shown by some *arquata* in size and plumage, and especially the eastern race *N.a.orientalis*. Some small pale Curlews closely resemble *tenuirostris* and differ only in the usually smaller white chin, abrupt change between the clouded streaks on the chest and the spots of the flanks and forebelly, usually paler inner primaries and secondaries, and diffuse brown bars on the tail. Legs dark grey, darker than blue-grey legs of Curlew.

Voice. Similar to Curlew, but calls higher pitched and shorter, a '*cour-lee*' lacking Curlew's gutteral quality. Also '*kew-ee*' in flight, presumably given in alarm and much less drawn out than Curlew's, quite distinctive. Gives Curlew-like bubbling notes and a strikingly unusual '*truiiii*', or '*truiii-ti-ti-ti-ti*'.

Habitat. Breeding areas are in extensive peat bogs with cover of sedges, marsh horsetail, dwarf birch and osier. Wintering habitat generally similar to Curlew's. It has been recorded on saline tracks on *Artemisia* steppe, *Salicornia* and crops; also shows a fondness for damp meadows with dense herbage and areas of standing water.

Distribution and Movements. A rare and declining species, currently known to breed only in the USSR, east of the Urals, on the steppes of western Siberia and northern Kazakhstan from the region of Uralsk, north-east to the drainage of the upper Ob, and east to the steppes of Lake Balkash. Migrates across the Aral-Caspian steppes, Turkmeniya, Ukraine and south-eastern Europe. A few still migrate across Turkey, the Balkans and southern Hungary August–November and March–May. Winters in Mediterranean areas, probably mainly Tunisia and Morocco. Accidental in a number of European countries (not Britain), the eastern Mediterranean and the Middle East including the Northern Yemen (Jan 1984), also in the Azores and the Canary Islands. Map **40**.

Feeding. Insects, molluscs, crustaceans and worms form the recorded diet, but the delicacy of the bill suggests a bias towards smaller prey and perhaps softer feeding substrates than is the case with the Curlew and Whimbrel.

Social and breeding behaviour. No information, although displays and sexual behaviour are presumably much like those of the other large Curlews. Gregarious in winter, occasionally being found in small flocks.

Nest, eggs and young. The nest is a depression in the ground, lined with dry vegetation. Eggs 4, greyish-olive, ochre or brown, with darker spots and blotches. No further information.

CURLEW   *Numenius arquata*

Du – Wulp   Fr – Courlis cendré
Ge – Grosser Brachvogel   Sp – Zarapito real
Sw – Storspov

Pl. 17

Identification. Length 20–24in. Largest wader, with extremely long curved bill, streaky brown plumage, and prominent white rump and lower back are evident in flight. Apart from the Eastern Curlew (*N.madagascariensis*), not yet recorded in the western Palaearctic (see below), it can only be confused with the Slender-billed Curlew (see that species), or the Whimbrel. Compared with the latter it is larger and more coarsely marked, with a longer bill, and lacks the distinctive boldly striped crown. The head, neck, breast and upper-parts are pale buff-brown, with dark streaks and markings. The dark streaked cheeks contrast with the pale chin and upper throat, while the streaks on the lower chest are heavy, with the under-parts becoming increasingly white, though well streaked and marked with Vs on the flanks. Under-wing mainly white, whereas the Eastern Curlew shows heavily barred dark brown under-wings, a brown rump and an even longer bill.

The adult in winter is duller and drabber than in summer, losing its buff tones and much of the intricate notching on the feather margins. The juvenile resembles the breeding adult, but the buff tones are paler, under-parts are whiter and the bill is obviously shorter.

Voice. Familiar notes on the breeding or winter quarters are a rich loud ringing '*COURli-COURli-COURli*'. The song is not necessarily limited to the breeding areas. It starts with slow, low-pitched '*courli*' notes, gaining speed and rising in pitch, to merge into a bubbling trill. The vocabulary is extensive, and many other calls are described, some rather like the Whimbrel's, though not frequent enough to cause confusion.

Habitat. Breeding habitat is typical grassy moorland, interspersed with patches of boggy ground, but also, increasingly in Britain, lowland heaths, grasslands or cereal fields. Outside the breeding season feeds mainly on estuarine mud-flats and salting edges, or adjacent fresh marsh.

Distribution. The nominate race breeds from the British Isles and France across western Europe north to about the Arctic Circle and south to the Caspian Sea, and east to about the Urals, where it intergrades with *orientalis*. The Siberian Curlew, *N.a.orientalis*, breeds in south-eastern USSR east of the lower Volga and Ural steppes, eastward to Transbaikalia and central Manchuria. Map **41**.

Movements. Mainly migratory, although some birds in Ireland and perhaps parts of Britain are virtually resident. There is a general tendency for most northern European populations to disperse south-west, to the coasts, from Britain south to Iberia, Morocco and Mauritania. Autumn passage of Scandinavian and west European birds begins in late June (main arrival July–August), with adults arriving on the North Sea estuaries, i.e. the Wash, the Waddenzee, and the East Frisian Wattenmeer (West Germany), where they begin their moult. Juveniles from the continent arrive later in the Wash, from mid- to late September. Most birds are thought to winter on their moulting grounds. Birds from central and south-eastern Europe appear to winter largely on the Mediterranean coasts. Return migration by adults to western and southern breeding areas is from February to March, and at the end of April in the northern USSR. Many first-year birds remain in their winter quarters.

Typical Siberian *orientalis* and some intergrades are believed partly to winter in the eastern Mediterranean and on the Red Sea coasts. Others winter across southern Asia from the Persian Gulf to the Philippines and Japan, also in the Afrotropical and Malagasy regions.

Feeding. Feeds by both touch and sight, the proportion of each varying with habitat and season. On the breeding grounds takes worms and insect larvae by probing in grass roots and soil, other insects (e.g. craneflies) by direct capture on the surface. Passage and wintering birds feed both on coastal fresh marsh and estuarine mud. During autumn the prey is likely to include small shore crabs on the mud and craneflies on the fresh marsh. Later in the winter earthworms, marine worms and small bivalve molluscs become important. Feeding by touch is carried out by making a regular series of shallow trial probes while moving forward; when the prey is detected, a deeper probe to capture it follows. Capture of some deep-lying prey, especially worms, involves vigorous movements of the head and neck to make use of the bill curvature. Worms are often removed piecemeal. Crabs may be shaken, dropped and picked up again, thus breaking off limbs, but surprisingly large ones can be swallowed whole. Short runs may be made to take surface prey. Piratical attacks by one bird attempting to steal food from another are common when large prey requiring prolonged handling is discovered.

Social and breeding behaviour. A prominent feature of behaviour in breeding areas is the display flight, which may function to mark territory or as an advertisement for a mate. The male flies over a regular, roughly circular route, starting low over the ground, then rising steeply, hovering for a moment, then gliding down with the wings held in a shallow V, before repeating the same. The bubbling song may occur at any time in this flight, or as the bird glides down to land. On the ground, approaches intruders in a 'hunched threat' posture, with head stretched forward, bill down, slightly drooped wings and raised and fanned tail. Mock fights and sometimes real ones occur; in mock fights pieces of grass are often pulled up and dropped.

Courtship may begin with rather similar postures to the 'hunched threat', proceeding to more elaborate displays and eventual copulation. Displays are more marked in birds pairing for the first time than in established pairs re-uniting on territory. Aerial displays by pairs may include high-soaring flights and aerial chases. Later the male may make several scrapes, of which the female chooses and lines one. The species has a monogamous mating system, pair-bond probably re-established in successive years.

Commonly solitary, but often forms large flocks outside the breeding areas. Some individuals maintain small, well defined feeding territories in successive seasons, while other birds are non-territorial. Feeding territories are usually on areas of medium food abundance rather than really rich ones, which may attract too many birds for defence to be practical.

Nest, eggs and young. Nest a depression amongst grass or crops, occasionally more exposed, lined with dry grasses and a few feathers. Eggs 4, green to olive, with small spots and blotches in darker brownish and grey. Incubation period about 28 days, shared equally by both sexes. Fledging period 32–38 days, young cared for and brooded by both parents while young. Age of first breeding probably two years.

UPLAND SANDPIPER   *Bartramia longicauda*

Du – Bartrams Ruiter   Fr – Bartramie à longue queue
Ge – Prärieläufer   Sp – Correlimos de Bartram
Sw – Piparsnäppa

Pl. 12

Identification. Length 10¼–11in. A slim, graceful sandpiper, having a small, dove-like head and long neck and wings, with plover-like actions and plumage recalling a tiny curlew. It has a straight, short, fine bill (tip of the upper mandible decurved) which is bright yellow with a blackish culmen. On the ground it appears mainly pale yellow-buff, with a dark brown crown showing a buffish central stripe. The mantle and coverts are brown and barred darker brown, tipped buffish. It shows a dark eye prominent on a buffish face, which is virtually unmarked, as is the creamy throat. At close range shows fine, intricate brown streaking on the sides of the hind-neck, lines of droplets on the fore-neck, with a diffuse chest-bib and small, dark brown chevrons on the fore and middle flanks. The belly and vent are creamy buff, paler than the chest and neck.

Distinctive in flight, showing long wings, long tail, with head kept well tucked in, and contrasting dark crown and mantle, very dark outer wings and an almost black panel down the back, rump and centre of the tail. The longish, well rounded tail has all the feathers barred dark brown, bordered with white, and covers the longish yellow legs in flight; primaries blackish-brown and unbarred. Flight swift, with strong wing-beats. Perches regularly on posts, tree-stumps etc, often holding wings extended upward for a second or so after alighting, showing black-barred wing linings.

Voice. Common call in a variety of circumstances is a rapid '*quip-ip-ip-ip*', also a loud, mellow '*qua-a-ily*' and a liquid, bubbling '*whee-di-li*'. A loud '*whip-whee-ee-you*' in song-flight.

Habitat. Breeding habitat is either rough grassy areas in prairies or meadows, or clearings in spruce muskeg in the northern parts of its range. In winter frequents savannas and open fields, with migrants also using airfields and golf courses.

Distribution. Breeds from north-western Alaska, the Yukon and British Columbia south to Oregon and south-east through the Great Plains and Lake States to West Virginia and Maryland. Winters from southern Brazil to southern Argentina and Chile. Accidental, Iceland, and in several European countries, including the British Isles (38), also in the Azores.

Movements. Breeding grounds are vacated by late August to early September. Migration occurs mainly through the North American interior east of the Rockies, with staging over the prairies and plains before moving down through eastern Central America, or crossing the Gulf of Mexico to South American winter quarters. More eastern birds migrate through the interiors of the eastern states and over the Greater Antilles. Birds reach their chiefly pampas winter quarters from late September onwards. Return passage begins in mid-February in Argentina, with migrants reaching the southern U.S.A. from early March and the main passage occurring from late March to late April. Breeding grounds in North Dakota and Minnesota are reoccupied during the first ten days of May, while the most northerly breeding areas may not be reached until June.

Feeding. Diet consists largely of insects, particularly grasshoppers, crickets and weevils, also wireworms, beetle larvae, moths, spiders, snails and earthworms. Prey items are mostly obtained from the surface, often after sudden runs and passes.

Social and breeding behaviour. Birds returning to their mating areas are mostly paired on arrival. Nesting territories may be generally grouped, and some aggressive behaviour apparently associated with territories is typical early in the season. The song-flight of breeding birds is often performed at such a height that the bird is barely visible as it slowly circles about calling. Sometimes after circling for some time, the bird will suddenly plunge to earth with folded wings. Another type of display flight is performed low over the ground, with wings fluttering in rapid shallow strokes. In pre-copulatory behaviour the male is reported to court by raising his tail feathers and running towards his mate, giving a short guttural whistle. If the female allows the male to approach copulation follows, otherwise she runs away. Outside the breeding season occurs singly, or in small parties.

Nest, eggs and young. The nest is a depression with a lining of dry plant material. Eggs 4, creamy or pinkish-buff with darker reddish-brown spots. Incubation period 24 days, by both sexes. Fledging period 32–34 days, young probably tended mainly by the male.

SPOTTED REDSHANK   *Tringa erythropus*

Du – Zwarte Ruiter   Fr – Chevalier arlequin
Ge – Dunkler Wasserläufer   Sp – Archibebe oscuro
Sw – Svartsnäppa

Pl. 18

Identification. Length 11½–12¼in. Slightly larger and more elegant than Redshank, with longer, finer bill and legs. Has a conspicuous white wedge up the back and, unlike Redshank, lacks a broad white trailing edge to the wing, while flight silhouette is more attenuated, with feet obviously trailing behind tail. In summer the adult is mainly dusky black, spotted above with white, and white under-wings contrast strongly with black body. The female shows paler fringes to the crown and under-parts, and more white under the tail. Base of blackish-brown bill dull red, and legs dark reddish-brown. In winter adults are mainly ashy-grey above (not brown as Redshank) and show a prominent greyish-white supercilium, a dark eye-stripe, with a paler lower face and throat. The wing-coverts show white fringes and the edges of the tertials are notched white. The chest is pale grey and mostly unmarked, unlike Redshank, which is streaked brown. Remainder of under-parts white, with a few faint bars on the flanks and more noticeable ones on the lateral tail-coverts. Bill colour at the base is more orange-red and legs paler orange, or orange-red.

The juvenile has the upper-parts darker brown, extensively spotted and chequered with white marks and bars. Under-parts whitish, heavily washed and barred brownish-grey.

Voice. Most familiar call a loud clear '*chuit*'. In song-flight, or occasionally uttered on the ground, '*tjuitt-tjuee-tjuee-tjuee*', also various '*chip*' calls and harsher notes resembling Arctic Tern's '*krri-krri-krri*'.

Habitat. Breeding areas consist mainly of marshy and swampy places and heathlands in lightly wooded regions near arctic timberline, ranging from open pine and birch forests northward well into shrub tundra. Outside the breeding season less marine than many congeners occurring on estuarine mudflats, salt marshes, lagoons, pools, reservoirs, salt pans, irrigated rice fields and sewage farms.

Distribution. Breeds from northern Scandinavia west across the Kola Peninsula and brushy tundras of northern USSR and northern Siberia to the Anadyr Basin, and south to the northern limits of dense forest. Winters from western Europe (north to The Netherlands and Britain) and West Africa to the Persian Gulf, India, the Indo-Chinese countries and south-eastern China. Map **42**.

Movements. Adult females form flocks and leave the breeding grounds while the males are still incubating (about 10 June in Finland), reaching Denmark and the Waddenzee by mid-June. Males and juveniles follow in the second half of July and August. Important staging areas occur in the German–Dutch Waddenzee and Dutch delta region, in southern Hungary, on the Evros delta in south-eastern Greece, and also in central Turkey. Smaller concentrations occur elsewhere in various parts of Europe, and others in the southern USSR (Black and Caspian Seas). In European staging areas numbers increase until early September, dwindling thereafter till mid-October. Early arrivals reach Ghana (an important wintering area) in West Africa in August–September, but the main arrival is in October. In the spring there is an influx of returning migrants to Ghana in March, and few are left by the end of April. Return movement through Europe takes place in April and May. The first arrivals reach Finland in very early May (females present in breeding range for only four to five weeks). A few non-breeding birds summer in West Africa, but others return to Europe and remain in flocks south of their breeding range.

Feeding. Feeds by picking or jabbing forward, often after a short dash. Occasionally probes quite vigorously. Forages in deeper water than any other *Tringa* species; swims confidently, often immersing head and neck completely, or up-ending like a surface-feeding duck. Also uses side-to-side scything movements like Avocet. Prey located visually, and in water also by touch. Prey items are chiefly adult and larval insects; also crustaceans, molluscs, frogs, tadpoles and small fish.

Social and breeding behaviour. Breeding behaviour in this species is virtually unknown, while pair formation probably occurs upon arrival on the breeding grounds. Aggressive displays include strong wing-lifting, exposing the white under-wing, sharply contrasting with the black body, which presumably serves in an advertisement role. The song-flight is similar to the Redshank's, consisting of an undulating display flight, given while calling. Adults with young frequently perch on dead trees and limbs, giving '*chip*' calls when disturbed. Although monogamy is probably the more normal system of breeding, there have been a few observations of apparent polyandrous matings. On the breeding grounds nests of this species are generally well dispersed. Does not form large congregations on passage. In winter sometimes gregarious, forming small flocks, but occasionally large flocks are recorded.

Nest, eggs and young. The nest is a shallow depression on the ground in the open in short vegetation, lined with a few leaves, stems and feathers. Eggs 4, olive to pale green, with dark brown blotches and spots. Incubation period not recorded; most reports – by male only; female may leave breeding site up to a week before hatching. Fledging period not recorded; in some cases young believed to be cared for by both parents at first, but female leaves brood well before fledging. Age of first breeding not known.

REDSHANK   *Tringa totanus*

Du – Tureluur   Fr – Chevalier gambette
Ge – Rotschenkel   Sp – Archibebe común
Sw – Rödbena

Pl. 18

Identification. Length 10½–11½in. Slightly smaller, more compact and with slightly shorter legs and bill than Spotted Redshank. Brown or greyish-brown above, showing a triangular white rump and white secondaries in flight. A nervous, noisy and restless bird, with distinctive notes (see below) and strident alarm calls.

The adult in summer is brown above and marked with dark brown or black spots, streaks and notches. The dark brown streaked head shows a short buff supercilium and a white eye-ring. The under-parts are white, with variable amounts of dark brown barring and spotting. Under-wings white, and tail barred brown and white. The adult in winter is greyer brown above, lacking the intense spotting and streaking of breeding dress. Under-parts white, with the breast washed grey and finely streaked brown. Bill black with an orange-red base to the lower mandible. Legs orange-red, but deeper red when breeding.

The juvenile is warmer above than the adult, with many buff fringes. The chest is also suffused with buff-brown. Legs orange-yellow, so that their colour may invite confusion with several other *Tringa* sandpipers.

Voice. A noisy bird at all times of the year. Commonest call a single '*tuuu*' and a ringing triple '*teu-huhu*'. Has a wide variety of calls, including whistles, squeals, yelps and yodelling song. The display-flight song is given rapidly and is a regular loud yodelling '*tu-udle*', often sustained for several minutes. In alarm an incessant high, sharp '*tyuk-tyuk-tyuk*', or scolding '*chip-chip-chip*' notes.

Habitat. Breeds in grassy marshes, natural and cultivated wet meadows, coastal salt marshes and swampy heathlands, or moors. Outside the breeding season it frequents muddy flats, tidal estuaries, marshes, borders of lakes, reservoirs or sewage farms.

Distribution. The form *T.t.robusta*, which breeds in Iceland and the Faeroes, winters mainly in the British Isles and along the North Sea coasts. Nominate *totanus*, breeds from the British Isles to northern Finland and the Kola Peninsula, also in Iberia, France, northern Italy, Turkey and from Belgium and Greece east to western Siberia. *T.t.ussuriensis*, breeds in USSR east of the Urals to south-eastern Siberia, Manchuria, Mongolia and northern Tibet. *T.t.eurhinus*, breeds in northern India and the Himalayas. This and other Asian races winter in south-eastern China, the Philippines, southern Asia south to India and the Indo-Chinese countries, and south to the Sunda Islands. Map **43**.

Movements. Icelandic birds are present on their breeding grounds from April to August, and migrants reach Britain and the continental coasts from early July to August, returning mainly in March–April. British breeding birds are only partially migratory and after June inland breeders move to coasts. There is a general southward movement within Britain, with some birds from Scotland and northern England wintering in Ireland. Some also continue south to continental coasts, from the Netherlands to western France and Portugal. Fenno-Scandian and Baltic populations (including Denmark) are nearly all migratory, and ringing recoveries indicate that Danish birds winter mainly in the west Mediterranean basin. Many Fenno-Scandian birds probably regularly winter on West African coasts, and some presumably cross the western Sahara to and from

West Africa. The main passage of Fenno-Scandian birds through Europe occurs in July to September, with peak numbers occurring on the Banc d'Arguin, Mauritania, in October. Return movements may begin in February, but the main passage through western Europe is in April and early May, with northern breeding grounds re-occupied a month later than in Britain and Denmark. Birds from central Europe appear to winter mainly in the Mediterranean, and birds from the USSR presumably winter in the eastern Mediterranean, Red Sea, Persian Gulf, southern Arabia and western India, also eastward to the Philippines.

Feeding. Locates prey by sight and touch, moving forward at a brisk walk, with occasional runs. Feeds by pecking, jabbing and probing, and also moves forward holding the bill nearly vertical and its tip in contact with the mud, while the head is usually moved from side to side detecting the food by touch. Pecking is probably the most common of these movements, so that most prey is probably obtained at or near the surface visually. *Hydrobia* gastropods are one of the items thus obtained in large quantities, while the amphipod *Corophium* is primarily obtained by probing. Much of the species' foods are very small invertebrates, and during the winter months birds often feed well into the night to fulfil their energy requirements. Breeding birds also feed mostly on invertebrates, including insects and earthworms, although there are considerable seasonal differences in the specific items that Redshanks eat.

Social and breeding behaviour. Although some display between birds may occur before arrival, it is probable that pair formation takes place on the breeding grounds. The male has two ways of securing a mate: ground-chasing or indulging in display flights. In ground-chasing, males tend to behave indiscriminately and promiscuously, chasing and unsuccessfully attempting to copulate with any female. In the display flight the male rises to some 40m, and at the end of the climb changes to a switchback flight, repeatedly gliding down on depressed wings and rising again, by vibrating the wings rapidly below the horizontal, and calling. A successful display flight attracts the female into the air, usually flying behind the male, who may then alight on the intended nesting area, or at some distant feeding point, with the female following. On landing the male performs a wing-lifting display, and may continue singing for up to three minutes. In pre-copulatory behaviour the male performs a high-stepping run or dance, which includes wing-lifting, exposing the silvery-white under-side to the female, whilst calling. Then the male begins fluttering his wings, vibrating them more rapidly and performing high-stepping movements, before finally fluttering off the ground and landing on the female's back, with copulation following. The species has a monogamous mating sytem. Outside the breeding season it is not highly gregarious, often solitary, especially when feeding, though it occasionally forms small parties or loose flocks, particularly at high-tide roosts.

Nest, eggs and young. Nest amongst vegetation, or in a hollow in a tussock, often with overhanging leaves and stems intertwined to form a partial or complete canopy, lined with grass stems and leaves. Eggs 4, cream to buff, with brown and red-brown spots and blotches. Incubation period 24 days, by both sexes. Fledging period variable, 25–35 days, young cared for by both parents to start with, but often male only in later part. Age of first breeding is one, sometimes two years.

Ceremonies preceding mating include the male's wing-lift display.

MARSH SANDPIPER   *Tringa stagnatilis*

Du – Poelruiter   Fr –Chevalier stagnatile
Ge – Teichwasserläufer   Sp – Archibebe fino
Sw – Dammsnäppa

Pl. 20

Identification. Length $8\frac{1}{2}$–$9\frac{1}{2}$in. A noticeably slim, long-legged sandpiper with a long, fine bill and body bulk close to Wood Sandpiper, but standing as high as a medium-sized *Tringa*. In breeding plumage upper-parts are buff – or pinkish-grey, with bold dark chequering, while the under-parts are white with dense blackish spotting on the breast and chevrons on the flanks. Shows pale face, with only faintly streaked white forehead, supercilium and cheeks. Winter and juvenile plumages have pure white under-parts, white face and greyish upper-parts, recalling miniature Greenshank. Juvenile, distinguishable by browner upper-parts with buff spotting. Wades freely, often in quite deep water. In flight, dark flight feathers and greyish coverts contrast with conspicuous white wedge extending from rump to centre of back, and olive-green legs project well beyond tail.

Voice. Song consists of a melodious, repeated '*tu-ee-u*' or '*tyurlyu*'. Other calls include a metallic, sharp '*tew*' (given on passage) and a sharp '*chik*', used in alarm.

Habitat. Breeds on wet open lowlands, near rivers, lakes or pools, occasionally near a few small trees such as alder. On passage and in winter quarters, frequents swampy margins of pools or lakes, paddy fields and, to a lesser extent, brackish lagoons and salt pans, avoiding direct exposure to breaking waves.

Distribution. Breeds in south-eastern Europe from Bulgaria and Romania east to the Ukraine, Crimea and eastern USSR; also in western Siberia and Transbaikalia and possibly east to Lake Khanka in Ussuriland. It has bred in Finland, Hungary, Austria and elsewhere in Europe. Winters in warmer latitudes from Africa and across southern Asia to Vietnam, Indonesia and Australia. Accidental in many parts of Europe, including the British Isles (59) and Cape Verde islands. Map **44**.

Movements. Migratory; moves by long overland flights on broad fronts to winter over most of Africa south of the Sahara and the Indian sub-continent. Russian breeding birds are believed to migrate mainly east of the Black Sea (main passage August to mid-September). In south-westerly autumn movements from the USSR birds are regularly recorded in eastern Czechoslovakia, Hungary, the Balkans, Italy and thence the eastern Mediterranean. These western-orientated birds mostly cross the Sahara to and from their Afrotropical winter quarters. Many more birds use the more eastern route through the Caspian area and across the Middle East, to winter in eastern and southern Africa. The East African Rift Valley is an especially important staging area for migrants (main influx late September–October). Birds return during mid–March and April, with passage through the southern USSR from early April to early May. Some non-breeding birds summer in East Africa.

Feeding. Feeds mainly while wading, picking food from water, mud surface or off plants; occasionally probes. Agile and active while foraging, with frequent quick darts to seize prey. Sometimes associates with larger birds, e.g. ducks and egrets, to find prey disturbed by their activities. Prey found by these means are mostly small to medium aquatic insects, such as water beetles, water boatmen and fly larvae. Also small crustaceans and molluscs.

Social and breeding behaviour. Song is delivered by the male during the descending phases of a circling 'switchback' flight like that of other *Tringa* sandpipers. It may also be given during a ground display in which the male runs to and from the female performing a wing-lift display. Display flights start three to four days after arrival on the breeding grounds, and pairing occurs after five to seven days; during this early phase, the male spends a large proportion of daylight hours in such flights. Other aspects of the birds' breeding behaviour have not been described. The species has a monogamous mating system.

Sociable outside the breeding season, generally feeding scattered, but sometimes in quite dense flocks, which may number several hundred or thousand. However, also quite commonly seen solitarily. Associates freely with other waders, especially Greenshank.

Nest, eggs and young. Breeds solitarily or in loose colonies of (formerly) up to several hundred pairs. The nest is a shallow depression amongst short vegetation, lined with a few scraps of grass. Eggs 4, creamy or buff, with reddish-brown or blackish blotches and spots. Both sexes incubate, but the incubation period is not recorded. The young are tended by both parents. Breeds in first year, or older.

GREENSHANK   *Tringa nebularia*

Du – Groenpootruiter   Fr – Chevalier aboyeur
Ge – Grünschenkel   Sp – Archibebe claro
Sw – Gluttsnäppa

Pl. 18

Identification. Length 11¾–13in. Larger, taller and greyer than Redshank, with longer, greenish legs, slightly upturned bill and lacking white in the wing. The breeding adult is dull grey above, streaked and blotched blackish-brown. Head, neck and upper chest are also strongly streaked and spotted blackish-brown. The throat, remainder of the underparts, centre of the back and rump are white, the latter forming a prominent white wedge up the back, between the wings. Tail white, barred greyish-brown and black. In winter, paler and greyer above, losing black chequering on mantle, face and supercilium whiter, and cheeks paler. Juveniles tinged browner, with buff feather edgings. Flies swiftly and strongly, sometimes erratically; uses characteristic flight call freely.

Voice. Commonest note in flight, especially when flushed, is a loud, ringing '*tew-tew-tew*'. The song is a rich '*ru-tu-ru-tu-ru-tu*', uttered in display flight. A repeated '*chip-chip-chip ...*' is frequently heard on the breeding grounds, especially from bird returning to the nest.

Habitat. Generally selects open ground for breeding, with or without scattered trees, and within reach of lakes, pools or streams for feeding. In Scotland breeding habitat is commonly treeless moorland, often fairly low, but in Scandinavia pairs appear to prefer areas with a few trees, posts or rocks as lookout posts, and also nest at higher altitudes. In the USSR generally nests not far from stands of mature forest.

Outside the breeding season frequents a wide variety of water margins, both coastal and freshwater, requiring only open surroundings and shallow edges. Thus tidal pools, salt marsh, flooded meadows, sewage farms and mangrove swamps are all suitable.

Distribution. Breeds in Scotland, and from Norway east across Scandinavia, Estonia, the USSR and Siberia to the northern limits of the taiga and the Bering coast, south through Kamchatka and southern Siberia to the mouth of the Amur. Winters in small numbers in western Europe and the Mediterranean, but most cross the Sahara to winter in Africa, south to Cape Province. Birds from the eastern Palaearctic winter on Asian coasts, the Philippines, Melanesia and Australia. Map **45**.

Movements. Migratory. In Scotland adults begin leaving breeding areas in early July, with adults tending young following three to six weeks later. Passage through Britain and Ireland occurs from the second week of July to late October, and includes continental birds. Probably the main Scottish breeding population winters in Ireland and western Britain, as Scottish breeding areas are reoccupied a month earlier than the main influx of Fenno-Scandian birds returning through the North Sea countries. The latter depart from their breeding areas at about the same time as the Scottish birds. Autumn movement across Europe is mainly SSW–SW. Large numbers build up in July to September in the Danish/German/Dutch Waddenzee and in the Dutch delta region, where adults start wing moult. Moulting adults are also present from July to September in Morocco, with trans-Saharan passage through central Chad beginning in mid August (maximum passing in mid-September). Return movement in Africa begins in March, with arrivals reaching Europe in April, though the main movement through the North Sea countries and into Fenno-Scandia is in early May. The large numbers of birds wintering in central, eastern and southern Africa are presumably birds from the USSR, which use the Great Circle route vie East Africa on passage.

Feeding. A highly active feeder, frequently employing runs or agile changes of direction. Although probing is sometimes used, as well as touch-foraging techniques such as 'mowing', the main emphasis is on hunting by sight, and simple feeding actions, most of the prey being seized from water or the surface of mud or plants. The active feeding behaviour is related to the speed and activity of much of its prey, among which small fish, shrimps and crabs figure prominently on passage or in winter quarters. Sometimes 'dances' through shallow water with a high-stepping action, presumably to make prey move and reveal itself. Cooperative feeding with other individuals or other species of waders is also recorded. Insects are important prey on breeding grounds, including waterside leaf beetles, water beetles, dragonfly nymphs, pondskaters and water boatmen. Small vertebrates and fragments of bone picked up loose may contribute usefully to the calcium needed for eggshell formation.

Social and breeding behaviour. Members of a pair commonly re-unite in successive breeding seasons and reoccupy the same territories. Nests are widely dispersed, generally between 1.2 and 2.4km apart, occasionally much closer, exceptionally 200m. Birds maintain four distinct (but often overlapping) territories for mating, nesting, feeding and chick-rearing. There is often more than one feeding area, which may be several Km from the nest. Usually a substantial surplus of non-breeding birds, some of which may establish territories.

Intruders in a territory are challenged by the resident male. If they fail to depart, ground displays occur involving loosened wings, tail fanning and showing white rump, and may develop into fights. Fleeing intruders may be pursued in flight with clipped wing-beats, twisting and diving, and bursts of faster flying. Display flight and song function chiefly for self-advertisement to attract a mate and maintain pair-bond; performed by both sexes, though more frequent and intense by the male. Display flight consists of a typical *Tringa* 'switchback' type, with alternating rises (to at least 60m, often much higher) on beating wings, followed by downward glides during which song is uttered.

When the female enters territory, the male challenges; another male would fight or flee, but the female will fly off in a straight line if unreceptive, or stay if she is interested. If she stays, swerving courtship chases are likely to follow. Continuation of courtship involves ground pursuits, with wing-lifting, strutting and '*chip*' calls by the male, leading to copulation. The mating system is usually of a monogamous type, rarely bigamous. Outside the breeding season occurs singly, or in small flocks.

Nest, eggs and young. Nest a shallow scrape on open ground, usually near some marker such as log, rock or stump. Lined with scraps of plant material and a few feathers. Eggs 4, off-white to buff, with heavy blotches and streaks of red to chocolate. Incubation period 24 days, by both parents. Fledging period 25–31 days, young cared for by both parents. Age of first breeding, two years.

GREATER YELLOWLEGS   *Tringa melanoleuca*

Du – Grote Geelpootruiter
Fr – Grand chevalier à pattes jaunes
Ge – Grosser Gelbschenkel
Sp – Archibebe patigualdo grande
Sw – Större gulbena

Pl. 21

Identification. Length 11½–12¼in. Nearly a third larger than Lesser Yellowlegs, close in size to Greenshank, but with yellow legs and square white rump, cut off sharply across the lower back. (Greenshank has white V extending up back.) Lacks a wing-bar, but coverts, secondaries and inner primaries show more distinct white spotting than Greenshank. Has a stout, slightly upturned bill and similar calls to Greenshank. The breeding adult is similar to Greenshank, but the upper-parts are boldly spotted with white and patched with black, and the white under-parts are marked with black arrowheads and chevrons. Adult in winter is more uniform greyish-brown above, losing strong black-and-white markings of breeding dress. The foreneck and breast are narrowly streaked brown, and the sides of the flanks are irregularly marked greyish. The juvenile is browner on the upper-parts, with extensive buff spotting, and the legs are pale orange to bright yellow.

Voice. Commonest call a sharp, penetrating '*tew-tew-tew*'. In song-flight gives a yodelling '*too-whee, too-whee*' or '*whee-oodle, whee-oodle*'.

Habitat. Breeds on the edge of subarctic coniferous forest, in swampy muskeg or bog, and also on hills or ridges near swamps that are mostly burned over and grass-covered, or which are still covered with forest. In winter frequents various wetlands, especially ponds, shallows along margins of standing water, or sluggish streams. Also prefers muddy creeks and estuaries, and areas on tidal flats with vegetation nearby, rather than the open shore beaches.

Distribution. Breeds in southern Alaska, British Columbia, the northern prairie provinces of Canada to northern Ontario, central Quebec, Labrador, Newfoundland and Nova Scotia. Winters mainly in the southern U.S.A., the West Indies, central America and South America to Tierra del Fuego. Accidental in Iceland, British Isles (28) and Sweden.

Movements. Adults leave the breeding grounds from mid-July, juveniles following a month or more later. Autumn passage is prolonged, lasting till mid-November. Many migrate overland through the North American interior on both passages, although they are less numerous in the autumn, when they are also common on and near the Atlantic and Pacific coasts. While a few may make a long direct flight over the western Atlantic from the Canadian Maritimes to the Lesser Antilles and north-eastern South America, the majority make a more leisurely passage along the Atlantic seaboard, and from Florida across the Greater Antilles to South America. Birds reach Paraguay and northern Argentina from late August, and they are common there in September, departing in March. In spring it is one of the earliest returning waders to the U.S.A., and passes through the Gulf States from mid-March. Most of the breeding areas are re-occupied within the final third of April.

Feeding. Does not probe with bill, but pecks at water and picks up food. While walking through water swings bill from side to side, skimming it. May also run about rapidly chasing and catching small fish in its bill. Sometimes forages on the shore, running through grass to snatch insects such as small grasshoppers. Eats aquatic and other insects and their larvae, snails, crabs, worms, tadpoles and berries.

Social and breeding behaviour. Birds probably pair shortly after arrival on the breeding grounds. They become highly dispersive, with breeding pairs nesting some distance apart. This species has a typical *Tringa* switchback type of display flight, which lasts for some ten to 15 minutes. Wing-lifting has been noted in ground courtship, but other aspects of breeding behaviour are lacking, and little has been written on the species' biology. It is only moderately social on migration and on the wintering grounds. It occurs in flocks of up to about ten, but more commonly individuals forage alone, with many birds defending feeding territories.

Nest, eggs and young. Nest a shallow hollow in moss or dry peat, unlined, or scantily lined with some grasses and dead leaves. Eggs 4, pale creamy-buff, speckled, spotted and blotched with dark brown and grey. Incubation period, 23 days. Young tended by both parents.

LESSER YELLOWLEGS   *Tringa flavipes*

Du – Kleine Geelpootruiter
Fr – Petit chevalier à pattes jaunes
Ge – Gelbschenkel
Sp – Archibebe patigualdo chico
Sw –Mindre gulbena

Pl. 21

Identification. Length 9–9¾in. Smaller, markedly more slender and less stocky than Redshank, with shorter, straight, fine black bill and long, slender bright yellow legs, which project well beyond the tail in flight. On the ground lively and graceful, moving in an active walk or run with legs strongly flexed. In flight wings uniform, but white rump-patch is cut off more or less square above the tail-coverts and not prolonged as a wedge up the back between the wings as in Greenshank.

The breeding adult is dark blackish-brown above, mottled and spotted grey or white, producing a pattern similar to Wood Sandpiper. The head, sides of the neck and upper breast are streaked and spotted dark brown, and the flanks barred, with the remainder of the under-parts white. The winter adult is paler, more uniform greyish-brown above and less spotted, tertials barred. The sides of the head and foreneck are white, narrowly streaked grey. The bird shows a short white supercilium running from the base of the bill to above the eye, and has an obvious white eye-ring. The chin and throat are white, with the chest, sides of the breast and flanks closely freckled with paler grey; the remainder of the under-parts – pure white. The juvenile has the back and tertials brown with extensive buff spotting, and the streaking on the chest is more diffuse.

Voice. Typical calls are single or double notes '*cu*', '*tu*', '*whew*', recalling Redshank or Greenshank, but quieter. In song-flight gives a nearly continuous yodelling '*pill-e-wee, pill-e-wee, pill-e-wee*'. Also clipped '*tuk-tuk-tuk*' notes in alarm.

Habitat. To the edge of the tundra in more open muskeg-spruce forest, preferring grassy marshes and bogs between patches of black spruce. Nests in drier places than Greater Yellowlegs, in natural clearings or burned-over areas of forest with fallen dead trees. Outside the breeding season frequents grassy marshes, margins of ponds, lakes or reservoirs and coastal mudflats; sometimes also dry meadows.

Distribution. Breeds in north-central Alaska and much of Canada, east to James Bay. Winters in small numbers in the Gulf States, eastern Mexico, central America, but most from the West Indies and south America, south to Chile and Argentina. Accidental in Iceland, the Azores and many European countries, including the British Isles (187).

Movements. Adults leave their breeding grounds early, arriving in the U.S.A. from the first week of July (peak from mid-July to mid-September), with juveniles following later. Many birds move south through the interior of North America. However, large numbers also occur on the Atlantic coast, with migrants common in the Maritime Provinces. This substantial south-east movement from breeding areas in the autumn across Canada probably accounts for the greater frequency of records of this species in Europe than those of its cousin, the Greater Yellowlegs. Migrants are presumably more liable to overshoot the Canadian coast and continue out to sea into the paths of Atlantic depressions. Some birds fly direct from the Canadian Maritimes to the Lesser Antilles and north-eastern South America. Others travel south down the Atlantic coast to complete their moult, before onward movement to their winter quarters. While some take the transoceanic route to the Antilles, others move in more leisurely stages, south along the Atlantic seaboard. Birds arrive in Paraguay and Argentina from late August (peak in mid-September), returning in March. The main spring passage through the U.S.A. is through the interior, with fewer following the Atlantic coast. Southern breeding areas are reoccupied in early May, with more northerly ones reached by the end of the month.

Feeding. Similar to Greater Yellowlegs, but does not swing bill from side to side in water when feeding. Feeds mainly by picking and snatching food with bill. Eats mainly insects, especially aquatics such as water boatmen, diving beetles, dragonfly nymphs – also land beetles, grasshoppers, ants, small crustaceans, worms and small fish.

Social and breeding behaviour. In spring, birds arrive on their breeding grounds in groups, ranging from two to three to as many as 20, and quickly disperse over the available habitat. They indulge in typical *Tringa* 'switch-back' song-flights, gliding up, then levelling, and then down, fluttering the wings rapidly on the descent before rising up again to repeat, whilst continuously calling. Both sexes may indulge in the song-flight, and pairs have been seen flying close together during the display. At the end of it the bird frequently alights on a dead tree and continues calling. Copulation often occurs on a dead tree stump. In winter the species is more gregarious than the Greater Yellowlegs.

Nest, eggs and young. Nest is a shallow depression lined with a few dry leaves and grasses, often placed beside a branch, log or stump. Eggs 4, creamy-buff or tinted olive, and speckled or blotched with purplish-brown. Incubation period probably 22–23 days, by both sexes. Fledging period, not recorded.

SOLITARY SANDPIPER   *Tringa solitaria*

Du – Amerikaanse Bosruiter
Fr – Chevalier solitaire
Ge – Einsamer Wasserläufer
Sp – Andarríos solitario
Sw – Amerikansk skogssnäppa

Pl. 19

Identification. Length 7–8¼in. Slightly smaller than Green Sandpiper, with uniformly dark upper-parts and lacking white rump, sides of latter and tail strongly barred white. Has a distinctive white eye-ring and short dull white supercilium. In flight the lack of white rump or wing-bar makes the bird look uniformly dark. Under-wing heavily barred blackish-brown, but not quite so black as Green Sandpiper. On the ground has long tapering silhouette, with wings extending beyond the tail. The short legs are olive-green and the bill is blackish. The breeding adult is olive-brown above, mottled with small, pale buff spots. Neck and upper chest are streaked dark brown and sides of the chest more clouded. Throat and remainder of under-parts, white. The winter adult is more uniform above, with reduced pale spotting and the chest marks are less distinct. Juveniles resemble the breeding adult, but have buffier chest marks and the small marks on the upper-parts are brighter.

Voice. Commonest call a piping '*peet*' or '*pleet-weet-weet*'; passage birds give soft '*twick*' or '*pit*' calls. Gives a highly pitched, repetitive song on the ground, or in display flight.

Habitat. Breeds in wet muskeg country, in typically wet open areas amongst scattered mature trees, often bordering an open bog, or beside a lake. Frequently nests in the same areas as the Rusty Blackbird, sometimes utilising their nests. In winter frequents wooded streams, small pools, bogs, lake and river edges, creeks and irrigation ditches.

Distribution. *T.s.solitaria* breeds from Labrador and Quebec west across Ontario to the southern parts of the Prairie Provinces and eastern British Columbia. Winters from the southern U.S.A. south through Central and South America to Argentina; also in the West Indies. *T.s.cinnamomea* breeds from central Alaska and Mackenzie south to northern British Columbia, southern Yukon and north-eastern Manitoba. Winters from northern South America to Argentina. Accidental, Iceland, British Isles (24), France and Spain.

Movements. It is a freshwater species which migrates overland on wide fronts. The eastern race passes through the U.S.A. mainly from the Atlantic states west to Montana and Utah, whilst western *cinnamomea* migrate mainly through the regions between the mountains of the western U.S.A. Both populations mix in their South American winter quarters.

   Birds depart from their breeding grounds singly or in pairs, some reaching the U.S.A. in the second week of July and others arriving in the West Indies from the third week of July. The main passage through the U.S.A. is from early August to the first week of September, with few birds remaining at the end of the month. Some migrants reach their winter quarters in Paraguay from the end of August. Birds depart from their wintering areas in March to early April, with peak numbers occurring in the U.S.A. late April to early May. Most breeding areas are reoccupied by the second and third weeks of May.

Feeding. Feeds along the edge, or wades in shallow stagnant pools, snatching various aquatic insects with its bill. Probes for food in water and mud; also shakes or trembles the forward foot to stir up aquatics from the bottom. Takes dragonfly nymphs, water beetles, water boatmen, grasshoppers and caterpillars; also spiders, worms, small crustaceans and small frogs.

Social and breeding behaviour. Birds indulge in song-flight displays shortly after arrival on their breeding territories. Both sexes sing, and the song may be given on the ground, perched on a limb, in direct flight, or during the song-flight display. The male flies some distance before rising on shallower and more rapid wing-beats, then dipping for some one to two metres and repeating. Males perform wing-raising displays prior to copulation. The species, as its name implies, is non-gregarious and is rarely seen in groups of more than two or three birds.

Nest, eggs and young. Utilises the old nest of a Rusty Blackbird or American Robin, or similar-sized bird, in a tree (normally coniferous) up to 13 metres or more above the ground. Eggs 4, creamy, tinted pale greenish or buff, and speckled purplish or reddish-brown. Incubation and fledging periods not known.

GREEN SANDPIPER *Tringa ochropus*

Du – Witgatje
Fr – Chevalier cul-blanc
Ge – Waldwasserläufer
Sp – Andarríos grande
Sw – Skogssnäppa

Pl. 19

Identificaiton. Length 8½–9½in. Larger and stouter than Wood Sandpiper, with shorter legs and broader wings. In flight the upper-parts appear black, in sharp contrast with the pure white rump, tail and belly, and the blackish under-wings readily separate it from the latter. The breeding adult is dark olive-brown above, freely spotted and peppered with whitish-buff. The fore-neck, chest and upper flanks are streaked and spotted greyish-brown, and the throat and remainder of the under-parts are white. The white tail shows four blackish-brown bars across the central tail feathers. The winter adult has the upper-parts more uniform, without profuse spotting, and the under-parts are less marked and whiter. The juvenile has the olive-brown upper-parts marked with distinct deep buff spots. At all ages bill dark brown with an olive-green base, legs olive-green.

Voice. When flushed utters a clear '*tweet-weet-weet*' or, if very startled, a hysterical-sounding clamour of similar notes. Towering bird gives a series of '*klu-wit*' or '*too-wit*' notes. Song delivered in flight is a combination of short tittering and fluty notes, '*tittitti-looidee-looidee-titlooidee …*' etc. A rather different and shorter version is given on the ground or from a perch.

Habitat. Breeds on marshy areas or water margins within forested areas. Outside the breeding season frequents borders of lakes, pools and watercourses, including quite small streams and ditches. Less often on coast, where it is confined to creeks of salt marsh; hardly ever on open shore.

Distribution. Breeds from Scandinavia including Denmark east through eastern Europe, the USSR and Siberia to the Sea of Okhotsk. Sporadic or local breeding has also occurred to the west and south of these limits. Breeding proved twice in Scotland (1917 and 1959). Winters sparingly in western and west-central Europe. The main winter range lies in the Mediterranean basin and Africa, and across southern Asia, from Turkey and Iran to eastern China, the Philippines and Borneo. Map **46**.

Movements. Migrates on a broad front overland, rather than following any coastline (essentially a freshwater species). Adults leave their breeding areas earlier than most waders, with the females preceding the males. The first migrants arrive in north-western and central Europe from the second half of June, with the main passage occurring in July–August. The first arrivals reaching Africa (south of the Sahara) are recorded from early August, although they are not common there until the following month. Further south they are not recorded until early October in Zambia. Spring passage begins in March to early April, and is virtually completed by mid-May.

Feeding. Feeds principally by picking prey out of shallow water or mud surface. Majority of prey items are very small indeed, including many water beetles and tiny crustaceans and mosquito larvae.

Social and breeding behaviour. Birds return to their breeding grounds fairly early, and they sing from the time of arrival until about the time the young are fledged. Has a typical *Tringa* 'switchback' flight, very similar to that of Wood Sandpiper, though apparently used less often. The main song is delivered during this flight and the shorter version used while on the ground, sometimes by both members of the pair. Unpaired birds of either sex may be attracted to the display flight, but are driven off by the established individual of the same sex. Copulatory behaviour is still only very poorly described – the courting bird's head is lowered, the tail is partly spread and raised, and the wings are drooped. The species has a monogamous mating system. Relatively solitary, but small flocks may occur at migration halts and in winter.

Nest, eggs and young. Usually lays in an old nest of another bird, often a Thrush or Woodpigeon, and sometimes in a squirrel's drey. Less often nests on ground, preferring a mound, or a situation among tree roots. A few scraps of plant material, if within reach, may be pulled into the nest site. Eggs 4, pale cream to olive, marked with small blotches and streaks of red-brown or purplish. Incubation period appears to be 20–23 days, by both parents, though mainly by the female. Fledging period about 28 days; young cared for by both parents at first, the female tending to leave earlier. Age of first breeding not known.

WOOD SANDPIPER   *Tringa glareola*

Du – Bosruiter
Fr – Chevalier sylvain
Ge – Bruchwasserläufer
Sp – Andarríos bastardo
Sw – Grönbena

Pl. 19

Identification. Length 7½–8¼in. Can be confused with Green Sandpiper, but it is a rather smaller and distinctly slimmer bird, with longer legs that project noticeably beyond the tail in flight. Bold buff-and-white chequering on the upper-parts is distinctive in breeding plumage, but may look much more uniform in winter, though never as dark as Green Sandpiper, lacking its pied appearance. In flight distinguished by light greyish, not blackish, under-wing and less conspicuous white rump. Less inclined to 'tower' when flushed than Green Sandpiper. The breeding adult is dark brownish-black above, barred and spotted brown and white. The head is well marked, with dark streaked crown separated by white supercilium, the latter becoming streaked behind the eye, dark ashy eye-stripe, grey streaked cheeks and white throat. The upper breast is streaked and spotted dark brown. The rest of the under-parts are white, but with a few faint streaks on the under tail. The winter adult is more uniform, less obviously spotted above, and the chest markings are less heavy. The juvenile is warmer brown above, profusely spotted rich buff, and the chest is heavily suffused greyish-brown. Bill blackish, tinged green at the base in the adult. Legs, pale olive to ochre, or even ochre-yellow.

Voice. Usual call when flushed or in flight is a high '*chiff-chiff-chiff*', much less liquid than Green Sandpiper's calls. A more liquid double note used as an anxiety call is chiefly heard on the breeding grounds. Song consists of a repeated '*wHIrrru-wHIrrru-wHIrrru ...*' etc, sometimes ending with notes recalling Woodlark. Also a low '*tyuli-tyuli-tyuli*' by male in ground courtship.

Habitat. During breeding season, wet ground in northern forests, either around lakes, pools or rivers. At other times frequents pools, lakes, etc. with muddy edges, including sewage farms. Often close to coast, but not usually on shore.

Distribution. Breeds throughout the northern Palaearctic, excluding the High Arctic. Extreme southern and western breeding places include the Scottish Highlands, where small numbers have bred since about 1960, and scattered locations in Denmark. Western Palaearctic birds winter mainly in tropical Africa, a few remaining on Mediterranean coasts, and the coast of Morocco. More eastern birds winter from the Persian Gulf and east across southern Asia to southern China and Taiwan, south to the Philippines, New Guinea and Australia. Map **47**.

Movements. Migrates mainly overland on a broad front across Europe and the Middle East. Relatively few pass along the western seaboard of Europe, so that passage numbers in Britain are small. Much larger numbers pass through France, however, and daily aggregations exceed 1,000 birds in the Camargue during autumn. Small numbers of adults begin leaving their European breeding areas from the end of June, with juveniles following in August. In the Camargue, adults arrive in July (a month ahead of juveniles) and may spend up to a month feeding and accumulating fat, prior to departure for the

Mediterranean-Saharan crossing (usually overflown in continuous flight). Adults arrive in tropical Africa in August and juveniles from September, numbers increasing in October. Spring departure from winter quarters begins in late March to early April. Birds pass through Europe and the Middle East fairly quickly in April–May and breeding grounds are reoccupied from late April to early May, or early June in the northern USSR.

Feeding. Feeds both by deep probing and by picking from surface or sweeping from side to side in shallow water. Sometimes feeds while immersed up to belly. Prey taken includes insects, especially water beetles and fly larvae, small crustaceans, molluscs, worms and occasionally small fish.

Social and breeding behaviour. Both sexes arrive on the breeding grounds about the same time, some already paired beforehand. In the 'switchback' display flight, the bird commences each ascent with a bout of wing-fluttering, then ascends further on set arched wings before gliding downwards again while delivering song. Both sexes may perform this flight, though more often the male, and it is not confined to the breeding territory. The song may also be given from a perch or on the ground. Ground displays include pursuits with wings raised or half raised; and just prior to copulation the male flutters up with hanging legs, calling, before landing on the female's back. The species has a monogamous mating system.

Outside the breeding season, moderately sociable, though flocks tend to scatter when flushed.

Nest, eggs and young. Nest, a hollow on ground in dense vegetation, lined with scraps of plant material. Occasionally lays in old nests of other birds, such as Fieldfare. Eggs 4, greenish, buff or olive with bold dark spots and blotches. Incubation period 22–23 days, by both sexes. Fledging period about 30 days; both parents care for the young at first, but the male takes the greater share, the female ceasing the task sooner. Age of first breeding not known.

TEREK SANDPIPER   *Xenus cinereus*

Du – Terek Ruiter
Fr – Bargette de Terek
Ge – Terekwasserläufer
Sp – Andarríos de Terek
Sw – Tereksnäppa

Pl. 20

Identification. Length 8½–9½in. Like a large Common Sandpiper, grey above and white below, but having a long and distinctly upturned bill and rather short deep-yellow to orange legs. In flight shows a white patch on the trailing edge of the secondaries suggesting miniature Redshank, but has greyish-brown rump and tail. Flight generally like *Tringa* sandpipers, but quite often low over mud or water like Common Sandpiper. Has a bobbing action and a dashing gait. The breeding adult is grey-brown above with blackish streaks on the scapulars and dark shoulder patches. It has an indistinct pale grey supercilium separating the streaked crown from the dark line through the eye. The sides of the chest are dusky and faintly streaked, and the remainder of the under-parts, including the under-wings, are white. The winter adult is greyer, more uniform above, with paler head, almost white forehead and more obvious supercilium. Chest patches only indistinctly streaked, appearing uniform grey. The juvenile resembles the breeding adult, with scapulars streaked blackish, coverts fringed buff and chest faintly washed buff.

Bill black, tinged dull red at base, in breeding adult, more yellowish-brown base in non-breeding birds. Legs vary from ochre-yellow to yellow-orange.

Voice. Usual contact and flight call is a fluty, rippling trill. Apart from this has a wide range of other vocalisations, but most involve some trilling component. Song is a repeated, three-syllabled '*per-rrrrr-EEEEE*'. An excitement warble, quiet and resembling subsong of many passerines, is used between members of a pair during nesting activities.

Habitat. Preferred breeding habitat is wet grassland with plentiful willow shrubs or aspens, flooded meadows, lakesides or boggy areas; shows liking for boggy ground stained reddish by iron. Generally avoids mountainous or heavily forested areas, but has recently colonised new, more open, habitats in some localities. Exploits human disturbance in some places, as around reservoir sites or fields. Sometimes associates with Tern colonies.

During winter, mainly coastal, usually on mudflats, which may be in proximity to coral reefs or mangroves. Rarely seen on freshwater habitats, other than largest rivers.

Distribution. Breeding range has extended westwards in Russia and Finland. Has bred in northern Norway (1967) and now breeds regularly in small numbers in Finland (c.30 pairs in 1980). However, breeds mainly in the USSR and Siberia in the higher and middle latitudes extending eastwards to about the mouth of the Amur. Winters from the southern Red Sea to southern Africa, the Persian Gulf, India, the Indo-Chinese countries, the Sundas and Australia. Accidental in many European countries, including the British Isles (24), also Middle East and North Africa. Map **48**.

Movements. With the main breeding areas centred in Siberia, the largest numbers winter in India and Malaysia eastwards. However, a significant minority cross the western Palaearctic to winter in Africa. Moves overland through Eurasia, with an important route passing between the Volga and Ural rivers, also through Transcaucasia and the Ukraine. Adults begin to leave breeding areas in the first half of July, with juveniles departing mainly in August; exodus from USSR continues into September. Some adults may reach Arabia by mid-July, though the main passage in Arabia is August to September, with numbers increasing further south in coastal East Africa up to November. Return movements begin in Africa in late March and continue through April. Breeding areas are reoccupied in Finland around mid-May, and during the first week of June in the USSR.

Feeding. Feeds both by picking from surface and probing, sometimes deeply. Highly active while feeding, moving in a brisk walk, with occasional runs and frequent abrupt turns, indicating a high reliance on visual clues, even for subterranean prey. Runs often end in lunge at mud surface with bill nearly horizontal. Diet includes various small crustaceans, molluscs and fly larvae; on breeding grounds midge larvae are important, but seeds are also taken.

Social and breeding behaviour. Song is delivered both from the ground and in the air, but it is not certain if a 'switchback' flight, as in other *Tringa* sandpipers occurs. The only display flight recorded is very simple; after uttering repeated cries from the ground, the bird rises steeply, hovers for a short time, then glides down. At nest relief, the 'excitement warble' is often given, but other details about courtship or pairing behaviour are lacking.

The species has a monogamous mating system. Outside the breeding season it is moderately gregarious, but often solitary.

Nest, eggs and young. The nest is a hollow in bare ground or short vegetation, lined with scraps of vegetation. Eggs 4, buff with blackish-brown spots or blotches. Incubation period 23 days, but the roles of the sexes are not clear; however, it seems that both participate in care of the young. During incubation and with young chicks, notable for highly developed injury-feigning behaviour. May also scold intruders from a distance (often a tree perch) or fly near them, then settle into grass. A distinctive piece of distraction behaviour is 'chick imitation', in which the sitting bird flies a short distance, then lands, giving piping calls like a chick, fluffs out feathers and stretches neck forward.

COMMON SANDPIPER   *Actitis hypoleucos*

Du – Oeverloper
Fr – Chevalier guignette
Ge – Flussuferläufer
Sp – Andarríos chico
Sw – Drillsnäppa

Pl. 20

Identification. Length 7½–8¼in. Smaller than Green Sandpiper, with white wedge behind rounded brown breast sides, more elongated rear body and constantly wagging or 'teetering' movements. In flight shows a brown rump with barred white sides to the tail, broad white wing-bar, and rear edge to the secondaries. Has flickering wing-beats, bowed in brief glides low over the water, accompanied by shrill echoing calls. Its rarer American counterpart the Spotted Sandpiper (see that species for comparison) requires to be separated in non-breeding and juvenile plumages from *hypoleucos*.

The breeding adult is olive-brown above, intricately marked with dark brown streaks, arrowheads and irregular bars. On either side of the chest there are clouded olive-brown oval patches, and the remaining under-parts are white. The winter adult is more uniformly olive-brown above, with the wing-coverts obscurely barred and the sides of the chest thinly streaked. The juvenile is brown above, barred darker and tipped buffish, with the wing-coverts and tertial edges barred sepia and buff and the sides of the chest mottled. At all ages has a dark brown bill with an ochre base and the legs are grey-green, rarely yellow-green.

Voice. Flight note is a shrill '*swee-wee-wee*' or '*seep-seep-seep*'. The song, uttered in flight or on the ground, is a rapid pulsating '*kitti-WEEwit, kitti-WEEwit*' etc.

Habitat. On the breeding grounds frequents the edges of clear, gravelly or rocky streams and the pebbly shores of rivers, lakes or ponds. Outside the breeding season will visit almost any kind of fresh water, both standing and flowing. On the coast frequents mangroves, coastal lagoons, tidal creeks, rocky shores and docks.

Distribution. Breeds in the British Isles and on the mainland of Europe from Spain and Scandinavia eastwards across the USSR and Siberia to Kamchatka, as well as on

Sakhalin, Japan, and adjoining islands. Winters in western Europe and the Mediterranean basin, with the majority wintering in Africa south to Cape Province. More eastern birds winter in Arabia and across southern Asia to Melanesia and Australia. Map **49**.

Movements. Essentially a freshwater species migrating overland on a broad front, singly or in very small parties. Larger numbers may occur at favoured staging areas, such as reservoirs or sewage farms, exceptionally reaching 200 in autumn. Autumn migration is SSW–SW for European birds (reversed in spring) beginning from early July. In West Germany adult passage occurs during July and August, with a peak in late July, and juveniles following from late July to late September, peaking in August. The major arrivals of birds in West and East Africa occur during August–September. Spring return begins in March, with trans-Saharan passage occurring from late March or early April. The first arrivals reach Europe during the first half of April, with the main passage from mid-April to mid-May. More southerly breeding areas are reoccupied from mid-April, but not until mid-May, or even early June, by northern Scandinavian and Russian birds. Many immature birds summer in Africa.

Feeding. Locates prey visually, feeding primarily by picking from ground or from low vegetation, rarely probing, confining its activities to wet edges, rather than wading, as is typical of many *Tringa* species. Often washes prey before eating. Feeds mainly on insects, including water beetles, dipteran flies, stoneflies, mayflies, mosquito larvae; also takes water spiders, small crustaceans, molluscs, annelid worms, small frogs and tadpoles, small fish and occasionally some plant material and seeds.

Social and breeding behaviour. Males generally return to breeding territories slightly ahead of females. Pairs hold linear territories on suitable stretches of river or shore, with display flights usually performed over the water's surface. The displaying bird flies some distance, then circles back, often indulging in tight loops and figures of eight. Display flights involve slow flying close to the surface of the water, with sudden rapid bursts of very shallow wing-beats, interspersed with stretches of gliding on decurved wings, the performance lasting usually two to four minutes. Often two birds are involved, presumably the singing male chasing the female. The male may also circle round the settled female in his display flight. In ground displays, holds wings up in a brief double wing-salute, interspersed with ground chases. In the wing-salute, one or both birds of the pair may lift one or both wings, while facing or at right angles to each other, one or both birds singing. Copulation follows ground chases, with extended wing-saluting and song by the male. The female stands still while the male runs round her giving wing-salute, fluttering wings and singing, finally springing on to her back, still with wing-salute. The species has a monogamous mating system. Largely solitary, except on migration and at nocturnal roosts.

Nest, eggs and young. Nests on or near banks of streams or lakes, often close to water. A slight hollow sheltered by vegetation and lined with a few grasses and pieces of debris. Eggs 4 (3–5), pale buff to cream, with red-brown spots, speckles and streaks. Incubation period 21–22 days, by both sexes. Fledging period 26–28 days, cared for by both parents. Age of first breeding, probably two years.

Wing-saluting, with one (*right*) or both wings in an important component of many displays between members of a pair.

SPOTTED SANDPIPER   *Actitis macularia*

Du – Amerikaanse Oeverloper
Fr – Chevalier grivelé
Ge – Drosseluferläufer
Sp – Andarríos maculado
Sw – Amerikansk drillsnäppa

Pl. 20

Identification. Length 7–8in. Shaped like Common Sandpiper, but marginally smaller, with shorter tail. Although boldly spotted on the under-parts in summer, winter adults and juveniles closely resemble the latter, but with care they are separable at close range. The Spotted Sandpiper is rather more greyish above and has more boldly patterned wing-coverts. In flight it also shows a narrower and shorter white wing-bar and less obvious tail pattern, showing less white to the sides. Gives distinctive sharp '*peet-weet*' notes (Common Sandpiper gives a ringing '*swee-wee-wee*').

The breeding adult is brownish-grey above and more boldly barred than *hypoleucos*, with distinct white supercilium. The white under-parts are heavily spotted blackish-brown. Bill and legs, flesh pink. The winter adult closely resembles *hypoleucos*, but the upper-parts are slightly greyer, more uniform, and show indistinct blackish-brown bars on the wing-coverts. Also shows a more distinct eye-ring and supercilium and has paler yellow-ochre to greyish-olive legs. The juvenile is more uniform greyish above, with the wing-coverts boldly barred blackish-brown and buff (bold patterning rarely matched by *hypoleucos*), and the tertial edges lack the white notches present in *hypoleucos*. The head is well marked, showing a prominent almost white supercilium, bright white eye-ring, uniform cheeks and unstreaked throat, remainder of under-parts white. Bill dark with greyish-pink base, and legs pale yellow to ochre-yellow.

Voice. Commonest call '*peet-weet*'. When flushed a more extended '*tweet-weet-tweet-weet-weet-weet-weet...*'. Other calls include a quiet '*pit*', considered diagnostic. The song consists of a long series of '*weet*' notes.

Habitat. At all seasons virtually identical with Common Sandpiper.

Distribution. Breeds widely in North America from Alaska across Canada to Newfoundland, and south to southern California, central Texas, western North Carolina and Maryland. Winters in small numbers in southern U.S.A., but mainly from Central America and the West Indies to northern Chile, Bolivia and northern Argentina. Accidental in Spitsbergen, Iceland, the Azores, Madeira and several European countries, including the British Isles (78). Nested in Scotland in 1975, laying four eggs, but subsequently deserted.

Movements. A freshwater species which migrates on broad fronts across North America, adults departing in July and juveniles following in August. There is some evidence for some south-east movement in autumn, suggesting some use of a direct transoceanic passage from New England to the eastern Neotropics, probably accounting for some transatlantic vagrancy. There is a more westerly emphasis in spring return from South America, suggesting a greater use of the interior route through the U.S.A. There is also a lack of any transoceanic movement at this time. Spring passage through the U.S.A. is from early April, with peak movement recorded in Maryland from late April to the third week of May and the most northerly breeding areas being reoccupied by early June.

Feeding. Forages in much the same manner as Common Sandpiper, working the water margins rather than wading. Eats a vast variety of aquatic and terrestrial insects, occasionally also small molluscs, crabs and fish.

Social and breeding behaviour. Breeding behaviour markedly different from Common Sandpiper. On the breeding grounds the female is the more dominant, displaying to the male, who may display in return. Two or more females may compete for a newly arrived male. The female may either approach the male on the ground, or glide down on quivering wings, calling, to land beside him. The female may make short runs near the male, with head held high, wings drooping and tail fanned and lifted or depressed. During pair formation both sexes sing repeatedly. While one of the pair may perform wing-fluttering actions, there is an apparent absence of wing-saluting as exhibited by the Common Sandpiper. The male may allow himself to be pecked repeatedly and the pair may then subsequently retire to inspect potential nest sites. The female solicits in a tail-up posture, and the male flutters his wings in order to keep his balance during copulation. The species is monogamous, or has a successively polyandrous mating system. (The male incubates and rears young while the female re-mates). The female may mate with up to three males per season. Mainly solitary, with small flocks gathering prior to migration.

Nest, eggs and young. Nest on ground in thick vegetation, a shallow cup lined with available vegetation. Eggs 4 (3–5), light buff, heavily spotted and blotched red-brown. Incubation period 21–22 days, by both sexes, but mainly by the male. Fledging period 18–21 days; young cared for by male and assisted by female in monogamous matings. Age of first breeding, one to two years.

WILLET *Catoptrophorus semipalmatus*

Fr – Chevalier semipalmé   Ge – Schlammtreter

Pl. 21

Identification. Length 14–16in. A large, greyish-brown, straight-billed shorebird, close in size to godwits *Limosa* but more thickset. In flight shows a striking black-and-white wing pattern (broad white panel across upper-wing, broad white panel across black under-wing), has black axillaries, white rump and grey tail. Flight strong and direct. The breeding adult is grey-brown above, streaked and mottled dark brown. Under-parts white, with breast spotted and flanks barred brown. Bill black, legs blue-grey. The winter adult is more uniform greyish above, with paler fringes to the feathers. The under-parts are white and the breast greyish. The juvenile is grey-brown above, showing broad buff fringes and subterminal dark bars to the feathers. Under-parts white with a greyish breast.

Voice. In breeding season a distinctive '*pill-will-willet*'. Other notes include a loud '*kay-ee*' and a rapidly repeated '*kip-kip-kip*'. In flight a '*whee-wee-wee*'.

Habitat. The two races of Willets (see *Distribution*) have rather different breeding habitats. The eastern form is a coastal breeder, nesting in salt marshes, while the western form is associated with prairie marshes and semi-permanent ponds and lakes, with the highest numbers being found on brackish to subsaline semi-permanent ponds and lakes. In winter occurs in coastal habitats, such as open mudflats, estuaries and coastal marshes.

Distribution. Eastern nominate *semipalmatus* breeds locally on the Atlantic and Caribbean coasts from Nova Scotia to Florida, Texas, Tamaulipas (Mexico) and the West Indies. Winters locally in the Atlantic coastal states, the Gulf of Mexico, the West Indies and along the Atlantic coast of Mexico and Central America to northern South America. Western *inornatus* breeds inland in the Canadian prairies and adjacent regions of the U.S.A. Some winter in the south-eastern U.S.A. and on the Caribbean islands, but most on the Pacific coasts from California to Peru and on the Galapagos Islands. Accidental France (one, undated), one Azores (1979) and Finland (Sept 1983).

Movements. Adults migrate early, leaving their breeding areas in June–July, while the young are still flightless, juveniles following later. In spring returning birds arrive in the southern U.S.A. from mid-March, and by late April most of the breeding grounds are reoccupied.

Feeding. Feeds by probing, or pecking from the surface; also by 'mowing', during which the bird walks over the mud, rapidly opening and shutting its bill and moving the head up and down very quickly. Birds also sometimes do this while wading in water. They frequently stalk fiddler crabs or small fish and also take small molluscs, marine worms, aquatic insects, some vegetable matter and seeds.

Social and breeding behaviour. Aggressive and noisy birds during the breeding season and the distinctive '*pill-will-willet*' call of the male is a conspicuous part of territorial behaviour. It is often given during the display flight, which consists of flying in circles with the wings arched downward and moving with short and rapid beats. Courtship is usually initiated by the male as he approaches the female on the ground, giving distinctive '*dik-dik*' notes, with closed tail depressed and wings raised and waved above the back in a narrow arc as the calling intensifies. If the female is receptive she crouches slightly and the male flutters up and copulates. The species is a semi-colonial nester, is moderately gregarious and has a monogamous mating system.

Nest, eggs and young. Nests on the ground, in the open on bare ground or in short grass, or well concealed in grass-tufts or low bushes. A shallow scrape, lined to a varying degree with grasses or other debris. Eggs 4, pale greenish to buff, finely spotted and blotched medium to dark brown, or purplish-brown. Incubation period variable, 22–29 days, by female, possibly by male at night. Fledging period not recorded; young tended by both parents, but deserted at a fairly early stage.

TURNSTONES Subfamily Arenariinae

Moderately small, robust, short-legged and short-billed shorebirds with pied plumages, bustling gait and stone-turning habits. Highly migratory.

Range. Breeding, virtually circumpolar; in winter the Turnstone reaches the southern extremities of the continents and New Zealand.

Number of species. World, 2; western Palaearctic, 1.

TURNSTONE *Arenaria interpres*

Du – Steenloper   Fr – Tournepierre à collier
Ge – Steinwälzer   Sp – Vuelvepiedras
Sw – Roskarl

Pl. 5

Identification. Length 8½–9½in. A robust shorebird with 'tortoiseshell'-like plumage, short orange legs and a stout, pointed, black bill. Summer male has the upper-parts rich chestnut and black, and white head is streaked on the crown; patterned with black on the face and breast. Rest of under-parts white. The female is duller, with streaked head, buffish on nape and mantle, and breast pattern is duller.

In winter the sexes become similar, losing clear-cut pattern and rich chestnut colours of breeding plumage. Head, upper-parts and breast mottled grey-brown and blackish. Juvenile resembles winter adult but is even browner above, with upper-parts scaled buff. Legs duller yellow-brown.

In flight unmistakable, showing two white patches in the wing, with bold white lower back and base to tail.

Voice. A staccato '*tukatuk*', a metallic '*teuk*' or '*keu*'. The bird has a chattering alarm call, used mainly in the breeding season, a strong, metallic '*TiTwooo-TiTwooRiT-ititittititit* …*', which may function as a form of song. A twittering '*kitititit*' may also occur as an extended purring rattle.

Habitat. Virtually circumpolar on the arctic coasts and tundras, usually breeding near the sea on gently sloping or terraced ground with sparse vegetation and occasional boulders. Also on tundra sites that are dry and stony with or without sparse vegetation. Almost anywhere outside the breeding season, on stony shores and reefs, and even sandy beaches or mudflats provided they have some pebbles, stones or shells.

Distribution. The nominate form breeds from Ellesmere Island, Greenland, and in Eurasia from Scandinavia and Estonia east across Russia and Siberia to Anadyrland, also in north-western Alaska. Winters from California to Mexico and southern South America, and from the British Isles, the Mediterranean coast, India, China, Japan and Hawaii, south to southern Africa, Malaysia and Australia. *A.i.morinella* breeds from north-eastern Alaska east to Baffin Island, wintering from South Carolina and the Gulf of Mexico to southern South America; straggler to England. Map **50**.

Movements. The north-western populations breeding in north-east Canada and Greenland winter in western Europe, and are present on their breeding grounds from late May to early June, till early August (adults) or early September (juveniles). Some birds make a temporary stopover in Iceland, and the eastern fringe of autumn migrants touches south-western Norway. European wintering areas are reached from late July, with a few reaching Morocco, where a slight overlap occurs with Fenno-Scandian birds. Return passage is in April–May and there is evidence of northward movement through Britain, prior to departure of birds to Iceland or Greenland.

Fenno-Scandian and west Russian birds migrate mainly through the Baltic (some following the Norwegian coast) and western Europe to winter in Morocco and West Africa. Birds are present on their breeding grounds from May or June, till August. The main movement in autumn follows the continental coasts (even more pronounced in spring), and large numbers pass along the British east and west coasts in July–August (adults) and in mid-September (juveniles). A few winter around the North Sea and western Mediterranean, but the bulk of the birds winter in West Africa, from Morocco south to the Gulf of Guinea.

The tundra populations breeding from the White Sea eastwards to central Siberia are assumed to comprise those birds which migrate through the Kazakhstan lakes and Caspian and Black Seas, to winter in the eastern Mediterranean, Red Sea, Persian Gulf and coasts of the Indian Ocean, south to Cape Province.

Feeding. An active feeder using diverse methods which vary with habitat, season and availability of food. Overturns stones, molluscs and weed to peck up prey sheltering beneath. Rolls up mats of seaweed by moving briskly forward and pushing with bill and forehead under weed. Commonly searches diligently in cracks between rocks, and along shore and tideline, rapidly pecking up prey. Probes into soft sand, raising bill to push ground upwards or sideways. Molluscs (limpets and mussels) lifted up and opened by vigorous thrusts of the bill at the edge of the shell, levering from side to side. Opens barnacles with one or two rapid blows of closed bill into upper plates. Also feeds on dead organisms washed up along the tideline. During most of the summer, dipterans (especially adults and larvae of midges) are the prime food source for both adults and young birds. They also take crustaceans, marine invertebrates and plant material, especially crowberries.

Social and breeding behaviour. Birds arrive on their breeding grounds in mixed-sex flocks within a short period each year. Pair formation occurs either before or after arrival on the male's territories or on coastal beaches. Pairing is completed by early June and males exhibit well developed territorial behaviour until the time of hatching. Associated behaviour includes ground displays, calls, aerial displays and territorial boundary patrolling. Males frequently perch on rocky outcrops for territorial advertisement, crouching, vibrating their tails and giving metallic clicking notes. Noisy sexual chases have also been recorded. The male performs a song-flight ten to 50 metres above the ground, with slow, deep wing-beats, giving a series of '*tjy-tjy-tjy*' calls, finally settling on a prominent rock, where he may remain calling for up to three minutes. Most displays and territorial encounters occur before incubation, with territorial boundaries recognised by neighbouring birds thereafter. Copulation is preceded by the male lifting both wings vertically one to three times, and holding them in this position for one to five seconds. He then flies over the female's back and settles before mating. The species has a monogamous mating system. Outside the breeding season gregarious, forming close independent groups, but still consorting with other *Charadrii* throughout the year.

Nest, eggs and young. Nest on ground, usually on a slight ridge or hummock, or in a fissure, often with surrounding plants. Shallow depression lined with small leaves. Eggs 4, olive-buff heavily marked with dark brown spots. Incubation period 22–24 days, by both sexes, but much less by male. Fledging period 19–21 days. Age of first breeding two years.

PHALAROPES   Subfamily Phalaropodinae

Phalaropes are small swimming sandpipers, and they are the only small shorebirds that habitually do swim. Their toes are equipped with lobes and there are small webs at their bases, and the tarsi are laterally flattened. Females are larger and brighter than males and take the initiative in courtship, males incubating the eggs and caring for the young. Two species winter pelagically in nutrient-rich waters of tropical seas.

Range. Virtually circumpolar, also breeding in the interior of western Canada. Winter off the western coasts of South America and West Africa, in the Arabian Sea and among the East Indies, also in the interior of South America.

Number of Species. World, 3; western Palaearctic, 3.

WILSON'S PHALAROPE   *Phalaropus tricolor*

Du – Grote Franjepoot
Fr – Phalarope de Wilson
Ge – Wilson-Wassertreter
Sp – Falaropo de Wilson
Sw – Wilsonsimsnäppa

Pl. 22

Identification. Length 9½in. Larger than other phalaropes, with longer, needle-like bill, longer blackish (summer) or yellowish legs, no wing-bar, but white rump. Unmistakable in breeding plumage or when swimming, but in winter very pale above and liable to confusion with several other waders, e.g. Marsh Sandpiper or Lesser Yellowlegs. Often runs, swimming less than other phalaropes, with neck noticeably extended, looking more erect and longer-bodied. In flight wings are less pointed, more round and broader than other phalaropes, and the flight action is looser and slower, recalling a small *Tringa*.

Adult male in summer (smaller and duller than female), grey-brown cap contrasts with white forehead and whitish-buff supercilium. Eye-patch dark brown with a small area of chestnut on the side of the neck. Back, grey-brown with chestnut tones, and under-parts white.

Adult female in summer has cap and upper back blue-grey, with black eye-patch turning down the side of the neck, narrowing beside a bold chestnut patch. Lower face and throat white, isolated by a black blaze and rich orange-and-buff suffusion on the sides of the neck. Back, grey and chestnut.

Adult winter, uniform pale grey and almost pure white below, legs becoming yellow. Juvenile, similar to winter adult, but upper-parts more brownish, with extensive buff fringes. Under-parts white, with sides of the breast washed buff.

Voice. When alarmed usually silent as a migrant, has a soft nasal grunt or subdued 'aangh'.

Habitat. Breeds in the interior of North America, centred on the prairie region, but also within taiga where broken up by moist grassy muskegs with many small pools and lakes. Outside breeding season avoids pelagic zones and maritime coasts, except for tidal pools and lagoons, being found chiefly in inland wetlands, lakes or marshes.

Distribution. Breeds in the interior of western Canada from central British Columbia, Alberta and Manitoba south to California, northern Utah, central Kansas and northern Indiana, also locally in southern Ontario. Winters in South America from Peru and

Bolivia to Chile and Argentina. Accidental, Iceland and many parts of Europe, including the British Isles (188 – annual in recent years); also Morocco.

Movements. Transequatorial migrant differing from congeners in its preference for inland aquatic habitats, which is reflected in its migration pattern and choice of winter quarters. Birds leave their breeding areas late June to early July (adult females), with the males and juveniles following later. In August there is a heavy passage in the U.S.A., dwindling in September. Passage is overland across the western U.S.A., and in small numbers east of Oklahoma. Some reach Mexico through the Gulf of California, while there is also regular passage over the western Gulf of Mexico and across the isthmus of Tehuantepec. The main movement is over the eastern Pacific from the Gulf of Tehuantepec direct to south-western Colombia and Ecuador (August–October), with passage continuing through coastal Peru and the high Andean lakes (to 4,500m) in Peru, western Bolivia and Chile, then presumably fanning out eastwards to reach Paraguay (from early September) and Argentina (mid-September). Not recorded in north-eastern South America in the Guianas, thereby indicating the absence of Caribbean crossings (occurs as a vagrant in the West Indies). In spring flocks of migrants occur in coastal Peru in March, passing Ecuador in late April and arriving in the southern U.S.A. mid-April to mid-May. Prairie breeding areas are reoccupied mainly in the second half of May. It is a rare visitor (mainly autumn) to the Canadian maritime provinces and the Atlantic states of the U.S.A., so that European records (142 to 1979) are perhaps an extreme case of eastward vagrancy that involved birds overshooting the western Atlantic coast.

Feeding. Most terrestrial phalarope, foraging to a considerable extent on muddy margins of pools. It also wades and submerges its head and neck to feed below the surface, or on the bottom. Spins on the water like other phalaropes, picking food from surface or just below with rapid actions, scarcely slowing when striking at prey, and moving either clockwise or anti-clockwise. While wading in shallow water, or walking along muddy shorelines, it constantly performs side-sweeping movements with the bill. Feeds mainly on insects, adults and larvae of beetles, flies, midge larvae being particularly prevalent in the breeding season; also small crustaceans, spiders and seeds of aquatic plants.

Social and breeding behaviour. Females tend to arrive earlier than the males on the breeding grounds, unlike most shorebirds, though mixed-sex flocks and courtship displays are common among spring flocks. A female will select a male and defend his position against other females. Several short basic calls are used for communication, but the female exclusively uses one '*chug*' call which is directed towards the male, whilst at the same time expanding the neck feathers and extending the bill forward. This call seems to be associated with pair formation and also occurs before copulation. Aerial chases are frequent and are often initiated by the male taking flight, followed closely by the female. As she overtakes the male in flight in a rather hunch-backed posture, she gives a series of loud '*wa*' calls. Copulation mainly occurs among well established pairs, typically while standing in shallow water. The most frequent precopulatory display given by the male is the adoption of an upright posture, which he holds for several seconds. The female may also assume this posture and give the '*chug*' call. The male quickly hovers up and lands on the female's back and copulates while holding the wings lifted up. The pair-bond breaks immediately after the clutch is completed, and whether sequential polyandry then occurs in this species is still somewhat speculative. Outside the breeding season solitary to moderately gregarious.

Nest, eggs and young. Nests on the ground, concealed by overarching grasses, usually a number of pairs nesting in close proximity. Sex roles reversed, as in other phalaropes. Nests in a hollow lined with dry grasses. Eggs 4, creamy-buff profusely marked with blackish-brown or purplish-brown. Incubation period 21 days, by male alone. Fledging period not known; young tended by male alone.

RED-NECKED PHALAROPE *Phalaropus lobatus*

Du – Grauwe Franjepoot   Fr – Phalarope à bec étroit
Ge – Odinshühnchen   Sp – Falaropo picofino
Sw – Smalnäbbad simsnäppa

Pl. 22

Identification. Length 7–7½in. Smallest and daintiest of phalaropes, distinctly smaller than Grey Phalarope, with needle-like bill. A small-headed, slender-necked, habitually swimming wader. Breeding plumage of adult female, brighter and more clearly patterned than in the male, with slate-grey head above white throat, wide orange-red horseshoe collar on foreneck, and clouded grey chest. Slate-grey back shows golden-buff lines.

Summer breeding male resembles female, but has crown, neck and back brown or brownish-grey, with little red on neck and indistinctly whitish face. Back shows prominent pinky-buff and whitish lines, forming V on mantle. Sides of chest and flanks duller and more streaked. Legs dark slate-grey.

Non-breeding adult, both sexes become much paler grey above, although not as uniformly marked as Grey Phalarope. Has black mark through eye, white face and under-parts. Narrow crown and centre of hind-neck ashy, with the rest of the upper-parts pale grey, with white margins and tips.

Juvenile, resembles winter adult, but has the crown and upper-parts dark brown-black, with prominent golden-buff lines on the back. Under-parts white, with a pinkish-buff wash on the throat. Legs yellowish-flesh to blue-grey.

On the water it is remarkably buoyant, normally holding the neck up straight, with the body line slanting from a high shoulder downwards toward the tail. Flight action over long distance recalls that of a small *Calidris*, but over short distances more flitting and often erratic, with bird suddenly jumping off the water, fluttering over the surface and then suddenly settling again. In flight shows white wing-bar and white sides to the tail-coverts, with golden-buff V on the mantle in summer.

Voice. Commonest call '*twick*' or chirping '*prek*', and a repeated '*chek-chek-chek*' when alert. Also a more rapid '*pri-ri-rip-pri-ri-rip*' from a party of feeding birds, and female has similar call in 'pairing flight'.

Habitat. In Europe typical habitat may either be a marshy depression with small shallow pools and watercourses, or rich lowland vegetation. In Scotland, usually breeds by shallow pools created by peat cutting, and on small pools and shallow bays of lakes, with emergent vegetation. Winters mainly at sea, in warm low latitudes, often far from land.

Distribution. Breeds Greenland, Iceland, Spitsbergen, Scotland, Scandinavia, northern Russia and northern Siberia to the Chukotski Peninsula. In North America from the Aleutians and Alaska east through northern Canada to southern Labrador. Winters off the west coast of South America, in the Arabian Sea and among the East Indies, southern Philippines and Moluccas east to the Bismarck archipelago. Map **51**.

Movements. Migrates extensively overland, wintering pelagically. The European and west Siberian populations make up the bulk of the very large numbers which migrate overland via the Caspian Sea and Kazakhstan lakes, to winter in the Arabian Sea. Fenno-Scandian birds migrate south-east through the Gulfs of Bothnia and Finland, across eastern Europe to the Black and Caspian Seas. Numbers crossing the Black Sea and Turkey are relatively small in comparison with the thousands which pass through the Caspian Sea. Reports of 600,000 (May 1959) on Lake Tengiz, Kazakhstan, suggest that very substantial numbers of west Siberian birds were involved. Major passage continues across Afghanistan, Iran and Iraq to the Persian Gulf, entering the Arabian Sea, via the Gulf of Oman. By late October birds have spread west to the Gulf of Aden, with 100,000 birds recorded in one transect off southern Arabia in January 1954. By early April the main concentrations are again present in the Gulf of Oman and its approaches. Winter quarters of North Atlantic populations (Iceland, the Faeroes and Scotland) are still unknown and there is no evidence of regular movements in the eastern Atlantic.

Birds leave their northern breeding areas from the end of June (females), with males following a month later and juveniles following in August (some till early September). The main departure in spring from the Arabian Sea is in April, though substantial numbers may still be present in early May. Passage is northward through Iraq, Iran, the Caspian Sea and Kazakhstan, continuing till early June. Breeding grounds are reoccupied from mid-May, to late May and early June in Lapland and Russia. East Siberian birds migrate partly overland and partly offshore to winter among the East Indies, migrating through the Philippine seas to winter in thousands off northern New Guinea.

Nearctic birds winter mainly in the Humboldt current off South America, and are present in vast numbers off Peru (October–March).

Feeding. Forages whilst swimming or wading, taking prey from surface or just below. Occasionally up-ends briefly, or may seize flying insects in a short flutter-leap. Also spins on the water like other phalaropes. In summer feeds chiefly on insects, especially dipteran flies and their larvae, also springtails, beetles, caddisflies, molluscs, crustaceans, spiders and annelid worms.

Social and breeding behaviour. Pair formation is initiated by the female, and a frequent display is the 'imposing posture', with the neck enlarged, breast puffed out and tail depressed. A female seeking a mate has an advertising flight in which she suddenly flies up with a wing-whirr, flies a short distance close to the water, then re-alights in an 'alert posture'. She approaches the male calling, swims round him and attempts to induce him to follow her, swimming away in the 'alert posture'. The male is usually not interested, so that the female has to repeat persistently. At times she performs advertising flights and wing-whirring. When the male eventually shows interest he joins her, and their close association thereafter marks the establishment of the pair-bond. Copulation occurs on water and can be initiated by either sex, but frequently the female initiates by giving a wing-whirring display, in which she rises in the water, beating her wings rapidly for a short time. This is followed by her lying motionless on the water, with tail facing the male. He may respond with wing-whirring, then he rises in the air and copulates, with the female being almost entirely submerged. She may perform nest-scraping displays at potential nest sites, with the male usually following her, or he may make nest scrapes of his own. The female finally deposits her eggs in one of the scrapes, and thereafter the male becomes progressively attached to the nest, and less to his mate. Nest-tending may begin as early as the laying of the first egg, so that the female becomes free to begin a second clutch. Evidently successive polyandry is a regular feature in this species, provided excess males are present. Outside the breeding season, gregarious, often forming large concentrations of several thousands of birds, particularly on the sea, where upwellings produce a high biomass of accessible food organisms.

Nest, eggs and young. Nests colonially. Nest is a hollow, built into a grass tussock, with grass lining and grass pulled together over the nest. Eggs 4, olive-buff, irregularly spotted and blotched black-brown. Incubation period 17–21 days, by male only. Fledging period 20 days, young cared for by male only. Age of first breeding, one year.

GREY PHALAROPE   *Phalaropus fulicarius*

Du – Rosse Franjepoot   Fr – Phalarope à bec large
Ge – Thorshühnchen   Sp – Falaropo picogrueso
Sw – Brednäbbad simsnäppa

Pl. 22

Identification. Length 8–8½in. Slightly larger and stockier than Red-necked Phalarope, with stouter, broad bill (often yellow base), with heavier head and thicker neck. In winter plumage, mantle always plainer and identified by size and bill, swims with back more level and tail held higher than Red-necked.

Male summer, resembles breeding female, but crown and mantle streaked sandy and has smaller, less cleanly marked white cheeks. Under-parts duller, often showing some white. Bill black with yellow base, and feet pale blue with yellow lobes.

Female summer, has a blackish-brown cap and fore-face, contrasting with white cheeks. Upper-parts blackish-brown with broad margins of cinnamon and pink-buff, forming conspicuous pale streaks. Under-parts rich chestnut.

Adult winter, becomes pale uniform blue-grey above and white below. Shows more contrasting dark mark around and behind eye than Red-necked.

Juvenile, is blackish-brown above, streaked with buff (but looks less distinctly striped than juvenile Red-necked). Plumage quickly acquires pale grey feathers on mantle from early October. Under-parts white, with pink-buff on face and chest. Bill blackish, with dusky yellow base. In flight shows white wing-bar, and rump and tail pattern like Red-necked.

Voice. A shrill '*twit*' or '*wit*' and in alarm '*cruit-cruit*' or '*tchirr-lik*'. In self-advertisement circle flight female gives a Dunlin-like '*zhee*', a '*preep*' or a buzzing, vibrating '*zeeet*'. Paired birds make twittering or chirping calls.

Habitat. The most arctic-adapted of the three phalaropes, breeding near coasts on flat, low tundra with numerous pools. In Iceland nests on dry, sandy ground with stunted vegetation, on saltings, or by pools and brackish lagoons. outside the breeding season almost entirely pelagic.

Distribution. Breeds in North America from St. Lawrence Island and north-west Alaska east across northern Canada to Hudson Bay and the Canadian arctic islands, Greenland, Iceland, Spitsbergen, Novaya Zemlya and arctic Siberia from the Taimyr Peninsula to the Chukotski Peninsula. Winters at sea off the west coast of Africa, between the tropic of Cancer and Sierra Leone latitudes, especially off Mauritania; also in the Benguela current off Namibia and South Africa. In South America, along the coast of Chile. Map 52.

Movements. The most oceanic of all phalaropes, migrating almost exclusively by sea-routes, although occasionally forced inland by severe gales. Birds depart from their breeding areas from the first half of July (females), with males and juveniles following out to sea from late July to August. A few arrive in wintering areas south of the Equator in late August. 'Wrecks' on the European coasts occur mainly in September–October, and involve a good many juveniles. Probably most birds are in their winter quarters by the end of November. Birds leave their southern wintering areas in March–April and reoccupy their breeding areas from late May to mid-June, following movements along arctic coasts.

North Atlantic passage is normally well offshore, and a few birds probably enter the North Sea. Vigorous Atlantic depressions in the autumn occasionally sweep large numbers further east into the Western Approaches. (Several thousand reached the coasts of south-west England and southern Ireland in October 1960.) Many pelagic records spanning the North Atlantic suggest major south-east movements by the Nearctic population, to winter off West Africa. There is no evidence to suggest that eastern Siberian birds reach the Atlantic, though Novaya Zemlyan birds may do so. Observations in the central Pacific suggest that Siberian birds migrate south-east to winter in the Humboldt current, which would explain their rarity in south-east Asia.

Feeding. Feeding actions similar to Red-necked Phalarope, including stalking insects on land, or by standing on floating masses of seaweed, probing or pecking for invertebrates. In the breeding season takes insects and their larvae, molluscs, crustaceans, annelid worms and some plant material and seeds. In winter quarters gathers where ample food concentrations well up to the surface of the sea.

Social and breeding behaviour. Females return to breeding areas before males and, as in other phalaropes, the usual sex roles are reversed, with the female performing courtship and most of the aggression, and the male incubating and caring for the young. Has a wide variety of displays and calls in the breeding season, and behaviour pattern is largely similar to the Red-necked Phalarope. Females perform self-advertisement flights by flying round in wide circles with rather slow wing-beats, sometimes tilting the body from side to side, calling constantly and usually ending by landing beside male, leading to various ground displays. If the male flies off, the female chases him, attempting to get below and slightly ahead of him, exhibiting her white upper-wing markings. In courting on the water the female swims whilst lowering her head, pressing it down between her shoulders, with bill pointing forward, and calling. A variant of this is to withdraw the head into the shoulders and point the bill downwards in a 'pushing display'. The latter often occurs in a precopulatory situation. Copulation occurs on land, unlike the Red-necked Phalarope, with the female stretching her head and neck forward and raising the hind-parts. The male then hovers over her before settling. The mating system is basically monogamous, although flexible, so that where the pair-bond lasts only until the start of incubation (exclusively by male), the female is free for a second mate if the opportunity arises (i.e. where an excess of males is temporarily available). Gregarious throughout the year.

Nest, eggs and young. Usually a number of pairs nest in a colony. Nest, a shallow hollow, material varying from sparse fragments of vegetation in an open site to a substantial structure of grass and leaves in a grassy site. In the latter the grasses are pulled down to hide the nest. Eggs 4, light olive or green with irregular blotches and spots of blackish-brown. Incubation period 18–20 days, by male only. Fledging period 16–18 days, young cared for by male. Age of first breeding, one year.

Distribution Maps

The following 52 maps cover those species which breed or winter regularly in Europe, the Middle East and North Africa. However a regular autumn passage migrant like the Curlew Sandpiper is not mapped here, because it breeds in N. Siberia outside the book's area and winters even farther south in Africa etc. There are also no maps for vagrant Siberian, American or a few fringe southern species.

The coloured areas indicate *breeding* range. The *winter* range is the area below the dotted lines, or enclosed by them. The captions include brief notes on habitat and references to text descriptions and colour plates.

Remember that within their ranges the birds occur only in areas providing their proper habitat; that both breeding and winter densities can vary enormously from one location to another; and that areas between the breeding and winter quarters may be visited on passage.

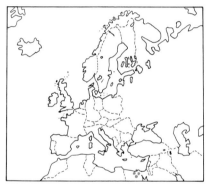

1. **Painted Snipe.** Resident around Nile Delta. Margins of pools, swampy areas with thick shrubby vegetation or reedbeds. p 19, **Pl 1**

2. **Oystercatcher.** Partial migrant, wintering south of dotted line. Breeds coastally, also inland. Winters from estuarine mudflats to rocky coasts. p 21, **Pl 1**

3. **Black-winged Stilt.** Mainly summer visitor. Opportunistic breeder in shallow, still waters. Winters mainly in Africa north of the Equator, fewer in Middle East. p 24, Pl 2

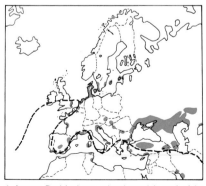

4. **Avocet.** Partial migrant, wintering mainly south of the dotted line. Breeds colonially among scrub and tussocks near shallow water. Winters on exposed mudflats, estuaries and sandbanks. p 26, **Pl 2**

210

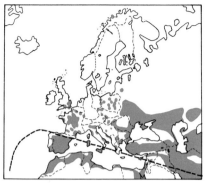

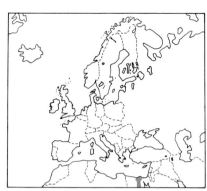

5. **Stone Curlew**. Partial migrant, breeding on stony, sandy and chalky open ground, bare downs, heaths etc. Also increasingly in cultivation. Formerly bred in Holland and Germany, has wintered in England. p 29, **Pl 2**

6. **Senegal Thick-knee**. Resident in Egypt. Unlike Stone Curlew avoids deserts, preferring vicinity of water especially sandy river beds and riverside mud-banks. p 31, **Pl 2**

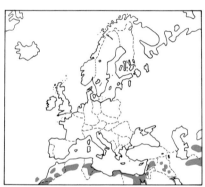

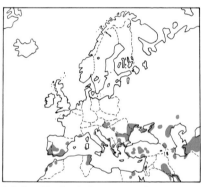

7. **Cream-coloured Courser**. A desert-haunting species. After breeding, flocks form and wander extensively, some reaching the Mediterranean coast. p 33, **Pl 3**

8. **Collared Pratincole**. Summer visitor. Frequents open, bare areas, stretches of sun-baked mud in marshy places and river flats. Winters in Africa south of the Sahara. p 35, **Pl 3**

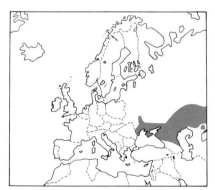

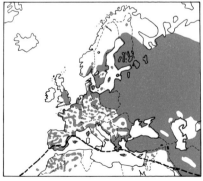

9. **Black-winged Pratincole**. Summer visitor to steppe zone. Often in denser herbage than Collared. Winters in Africa south of the Sahara, occurring further south than Collared. p 36, **Pl 3**

10. **Little Ringed Plover**. Summer visitor. Frequents sand and gravel river banks, stony river beds, gravel pits. Unlike Ringed Plover, rarely coastal, preferring fresh water with shallow muddy edges. p 38, **Pl 4**

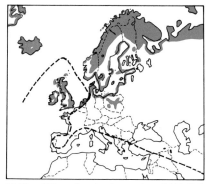

11. **Ringed Plover**. Largely migratory (some British birds are resident). Most northerly populations winter furthest south. Essentially a coastal species but in some areas breeds inland on sandy heaths and along rivers. p 40, **Pl 4**

12. **Kittlitz's Plover**. Resident in breeding areas in Egypt. Margins of lakes, saltpans, sandy river beds, also mudflats – less attracted to coasts than Ringed and Kentish Plovers. p 44, **Pl 4**

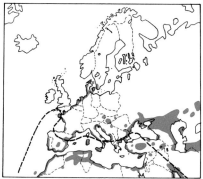

13. **Kentish Plover**. Migratory north of dotted line. Sandy beaches or flats along sea-coasts, also inland by lakes, sandy depressions and saline sites. Overall decline in north-west and much of central Europe. p 45, **Pl 4**

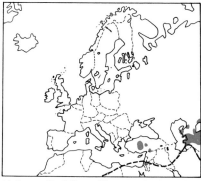

14. **Greater Sand Plover**. Migratory, wintering south of dotted line. Breeds on flat, arid, treeless areas. Winters on muddy coasts. p 48, **Pl 5**

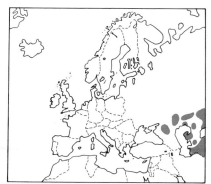

15. **Caspian Plover**. Migratory, wintering in East and South Africa. Breeds on dry steppes and semi-deserts. Winters on grassy plains, especially where recently burnt. p 49, **Pl 5**

16. **Dotterel**. Migratory. Breeds on stony heights and tundra, also on Dutch polders. Winters on stony steppes, semi-deserts and poorer farms, from N.-W. Africa (areas encircled) to Persian Gulf, a few also in Spain. p 51, **Pl 5**

212

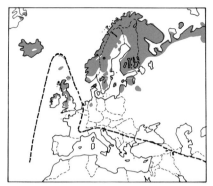

17. **Golden Plover**. Partial migrant. Breeds on hilly and lowland moors and in the arctic on coastal and riverine tundra. Winters on open farmland, also seashores/estuaries, but less on tidal flats than Grey Plover. p 55, **Pl 6**

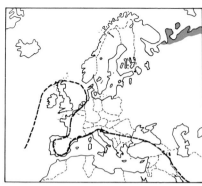

18. **Grey Plover**. Breeds on lowland tundra. Winters on sea coasts, broad mud-flats and sandy beaches. p 57, **Pl 6**

19. **Spur-winged Plover**. Migratory north of Lebanon. Breeds in marshy areas and other wetlands, also occurs along riversides, coastal marshes and deltas. p 59, **Pl 7**

20. **Red-wattled Plover**. Migratory in Russia, although resident or dispersive elsewhere. Mainly inland, near fresh or brackish water, also in cultivated land and on wasteland. p 62, **Pl 8**

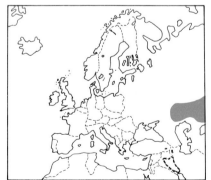

21. **Sociable Plover**. Migratory, breeding in steppes and wintering in Iraq, western India, Arabia (few) and East Africa – on grassy plains, wastelands near cultivation and in stubble fields. p 63, **Pl 8**

22. **White-tailed Plover**. Migratory in Russia, resident in the Middle East; breeds occasionally in central Turkey. Marshes, flooded fields and along swampy or grassy shores of brackish lakes and jheels. p 65, **Pl 8**

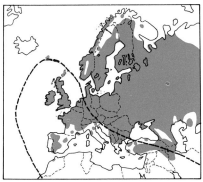

23. **Lapwing**. Mainly migratory. Predominantly a farm bird, favouring arable land, especially when newly ploughed or fallow. Also visits freshwater margins and marshes. In cold spells may resort to tidal flats. p 66, **Pl 7**

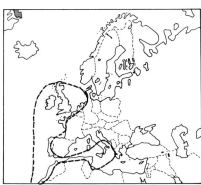

24. **Knot**. Passage migrant and winter visitor, non-breeders summer on western coasts of Europe. Breeds in Canadian arctic, Greenland and northern Siberia. Found in huge flocks on extensive mudlfats in winter. p 71, **Pl 9**

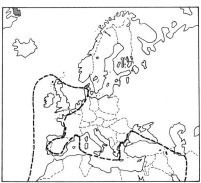

25. **Sanderling**. Passage migrant and winter visitor – mainly from two populations: Greenland and Siberia. Non-breeders summer on W. coasts. Frequents sandy beaches on migration and in winter quarters. p 73, **Pl 10**

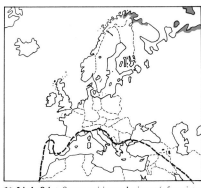

26. **Little Stint**. Summer visitor and migrant (a few winter in Britain). Quite scarce migrant on W. coasts in spring, more in autumn. Breeds on high arctic coastal mainland tundra. Winters on coasts, also inland. p 79, **Pl 10**

27. **Temminck's Stint**. Summer visitor and migrant – often moving cross-country, stopping on inland water margins. Breeds in wet sphagnum bogs, or willow scrub beside streams. Winters in sheltered coastal sites. p 81, **Pl 10**

28. **Purple Sandpiper**. Partial migrant, breeding on arctic tundra, heaths and moors, rocky coasts, also on higher inland fells or mountain tundra. Winters on rocky coasts, also attracted to breakwaters and piers. p 93, **Pl 9**

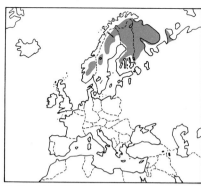

29. **Dunlin**. Migratory. Breeds on tussock tundra and hummocky grass moors with peaty pools, lowland mosses, or grassy saltmarshes. Winters on coastal mudflats and estuaries, also on inland marshes and lake-edges. p 95, **Pl 9**

30. **Broad-billed Sandpiper**. Summer visitor, migrating S. to S-E. in autumn. A few pass through W. Europe in spring. Breeds in wet bogs. Winters in Persian Gulf, Arabia, on muddy estuaries, salt marshes etc. p 145, **Pl 10**

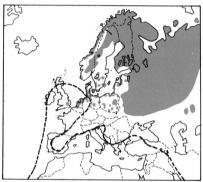

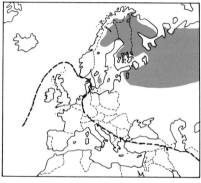

31. **Ruff (Reeve)**. Migratory. Breeds in low-lying grassy marshes, river meadows and locally in hayfields. Winters mostly in Africa on a variety of wetlands: saltmarshes, estuaries, muddy shores of inland lakes. p 149, **Pl 13**

32. **Jack Snipe**. Summer visitor. Breeds in wet swamps and bogs, often sharing same habitat as Broad-billed Sandpiper. Winters in similar habitat, avoiding more open, deep or saline waters. p 152, **Pl 14**

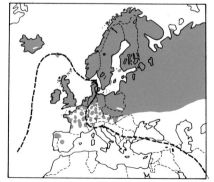

33. **Snipe**. Partial migrant, breeds in marshy bogs, moors, marshy shores of rivers and wetter patches of tundra. Winters in similar sites, but in frost may move to sea-shore. p 153, **Pl 14**

34. **Great Snipe**. Summer visitor, passage C. Europe. Communal display sites in subalpine wetland. Breeds on marshy and grassy ground. Winters in Africa S. of Sahara in swampy areas with good grass cover. p 156, **Pl 14**

35. **Pintail Snipe**. Summer visitor – just reaching eastern part of northern Urals. Breeds in grassy marshes along small river valleys and by pools. In Indian winter quarters resorts to marshy pool edges and paddyfields. p 158, **Pl 14**

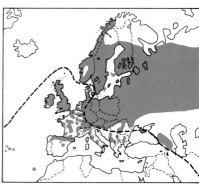

36. **Woodcock**. Mainly migratory, breeds in broadleaved, mixed or coniferous, moist woodland with rides and a good cover of bracken. Feeds on boggy ground and spongy places about ditches and streams. p 164, **Pl 14**

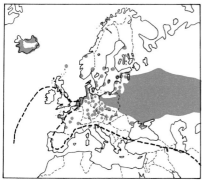

37. **Black-tailed Godwit**. Migratory. Breeds in water-meadows, rough pastures and marshes. On passages, more of an inland bird than Bar-tailed. Winters around sheltered coastal inlets and saltmarshes. p 166, **Pl 16**

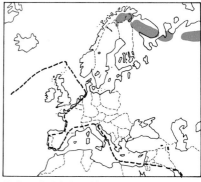

38. **Bar-tailed Godwit**. Migratory. Breeds in moss and shrub-tundra, swampy heathlands in willow/birch zone near tree-line. Winters on coasts and estuaries. Some non-breeders stay in winter quarters in summer. p 171, **Pl 16**

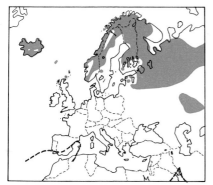

39. **Whimbrel**. Migratory. Breeds on N. and subarctic heaths, moorlands. Non-breeders summer on W. coasts. On passage – mudflats, rocky shores or adjacent fields. A few winter N. to Britain and Denmark. p 174, **Pl 17**

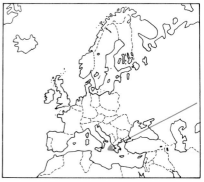

40. **Slender-billed Curlew**. Migratory (very rare and declining) breeding from N. fringe of the steppe zone over marshy regions of taiga. Probably winters mainly in Morocco and Tunisia, occasionally elsewhere. p 176, **Pl 17**

216

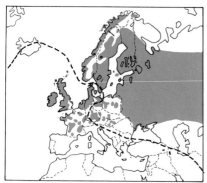

41. **Curlew**. Mostly migratory, some birds resident in west of range. Breeds on moist, poorly drained upland moors; also in rough grassy fields, damp pastures and farmland. Winters in marine coastal habitats. p 177, **Pl 17**

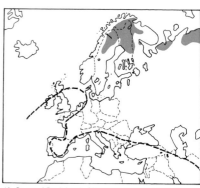

42. **Spotted Redshank**. Migratory. Breeds mainly in wooded tundra, also in overlapping open tundra and open or thinly wooded fringes of taiga. Winters in sheltered coastal sites – saltmarshes, pools, mudlfats. p 180, **Pl 18**

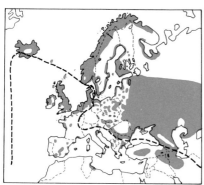

43. **Redshank**. Mainly migratory, though some resident on west coasts of Europe. Breeds in marshes, moors, watermeadows and coastal saltings. Winters on estuaries and mudlfats. p 182, **Pl 18**

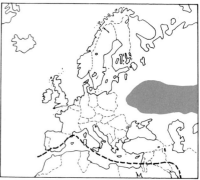

44. **Marsh Sandpiper**. Summer visitor. Breeds on grassy borders of lakes and rivers, freshwater marshes and flooded meadows. Winters around inland waters and marshes, seldom on sea-shore. p 184, **Pl 20**

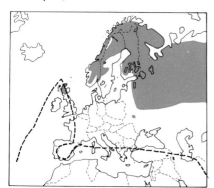

45. **Greenshank**. Summer visitor. Breeds on moors or in patches of grass or heath in pine forest, where lakes and shallow valley bogs are plentiful. Winters on saltmarshes, estuaries, lagoons, lakes and inland rivers. p 185, **Pl 18**

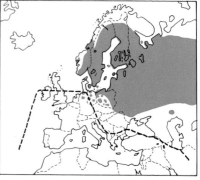

46. **Green Sandpiper**. Summer visitor. Breeds in swampy forest regions, often utilising old nests in trees. Winters along small streams, ditches, pools, marshes and sewage farms, rare on sea-shore. p 191, **Pl 19**

217

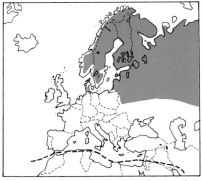
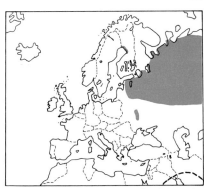

47. **Wood Sandpiper**. Summer visitor. Breeds in fairly open ground on edges of marshes in coniferous forest and swampy dwarf birch and willow scrub further N. Winters in inland wet habitats, avoiding seashore. p 193, **Pl 19**

48. **Terek Sandpiper**. Summer visitor. Breeds in marshes among willow scrub and marshy banks of small rivers. Winters on estuaries and exposed mud-banks, coral reefs and creeks of mangrove swamps. p 194, **Pl 20**

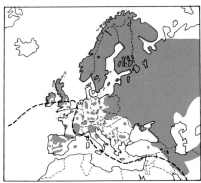

49. **Common Sandpiper**. Mainly summer visitor – some winter N. to Britain in mild seasons. Breeds on banks of streams and lakes. Winters in wet habitats, including mangroves, creeks and rocky headlands. p 196, **Pl 20**

50. **Turnstone**. Migratory. Breeds on exposed rocky ground on coastal islands and stony plains with only scattered low vegetation. Winters along rocky or pebbly coasts, some birds summer on winter range. p 201, **Pl 5**

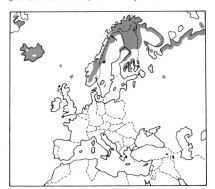

51. **Red-necked Phalarope**. Summer visitor. Breeds around small pools and shallow bays of lakes, usually with emergent vegetation. Winters mainly at sea, in warm low latitudes, ie Arabian Sea. p 205, **Pl 22**

52. **Grey Phalarope**. Summer visitor. Breeds in marshy tundra with scattered small pools, coastal lagoons, islets in fjords. Otherwise pelagic. Occasionally on passage along coasts and on inland waters after gales. p 207, **Pl 22**

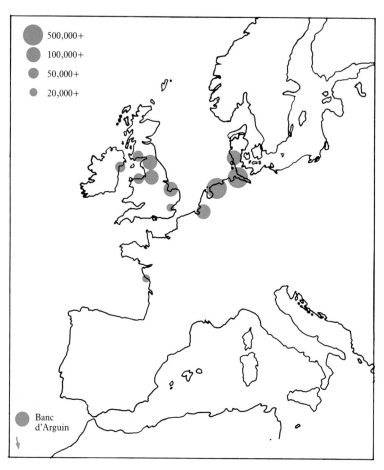

Main concentrations of moulting waders in the Western Palearctic

Reproduced by kind permission of A. J. Prater from his paper in: COOPER, J. (Ed.) *Proceedings of the Symposium on Birds of the Sea and Shore*, 1981. Cape Town: African Seabird Group.

The majority of the four million Palearctic waders which winter north of the Sahara moult between July and December, but mainly in August-September. During this period these waders are not distributed as evenly as they are in winter.

By far the most important moulting area is the Waddenzee area (Denmark/West Germany/Netherlands), which supports over two million waders. Even smaller sites, such as the Rhine Delta (Netherlands), Morecambe Bay, the Ribble and the Wash (Britain) and probably the Banc d'Arguin (Mauritania) each support over 100,000 moulting waders.

Index of Spanish Names

Index of French Names

Index of German Names

Index of English Names

The first figure, in normal type, refers to the bird's text description.
The second, in **bold** type, is its **Plate** number.
The third, in *italic* type, is its *Map* number.

Index of Scientific Names